continued . . .

"An inspirational guide to leadership . . . Dr. Sheila Murray Bethel has intricately and meticulously organized the new theory that is easy to read, adopt, and follow."
—Suhas Mehta, President, International Business Network (2008–09), Santa Clara University

"Leadership never goes out of style, but what it takes to succeed as a leader changes with the times. Sheila Murray Bethel zeroes in on the qualities required of twenty-first-century leaders . . . Her chapter on humility should be required reading for every CEO in America."
—Jeannine Drew, President, Drew Communications

"An inspiring read packed full of excellent illustrations of good leadership practices that are relevant to the private and public sector."
—Trevor Summerson, Senior Programme Manager, National College for School Leadership, Nottingham, England

"If you wonder whether you are the kind of leader needed in the twenty-first century, you're about to find out. Dr. Bethel identifies the attributes essential for today's leaders and illustrates them using real-life examples gathered directly from the people who set them."
—Jeffrey Riley, Executive Director, Structured Finance, GATX Corporation

"Sheila Murray Bethel has defined in a clear-minded analysis an obviousness rarely used in Real Life."
—Vilma Mansutti, Assistant of Direction, French High Council on Integration, Paris, France

"Whether tomorrow's leaders are born great, achieve greatness, or have it rudely thrust upon them, the golden rules championed in *A New Breed of Leader* will be part of their operating code."
—John Elkington, cofounder of SustainAbility, coauthor of *The Power of Unreasonable People*

"*A New Breed of Leader* redefines leadership concepts . . . Sheila Murray Bethel offers each of us the means for a formidable hope and the accomplishment for oneself."
—Alex Bouhr, Engineer, Intertek, Paris, France

A New Breed of
LEADER

8

LEADERSHIP QUALITIES
THAT MATTER MOST IN THE
REAL WORLD

What Works, What Doesn't, and Why

Sheila Murray Bethel, Ph.D.

BERKLEY BOOKS, NEW YORK

THE BERKLEY PUBLISHING GROUP
Published by the Penguin Group
Penguin Group (USA) Inc.
375 Hudson Street, New York, New York 10014, USA
Penguin Group (Canada), 90 Eglinton Avenue East, Suite 700, Toronto, Ontario M4P 2Y3, Canada
(a division of Pearson Penguin Canada Inc.)
Penguin Books Ltd., 80 Strand, London WC2R 0RL, England
Penguin Group Ireland, 25 St. Stephen's Green, Dublin 2, Ireland (a division of Penguin Books Ltd.)
Penguin Group (Australia), 250 Camberwell Road, Camberwell, Victoria 3124, Australia
(a division of Pearson Australia Group Pty. Ltd.)
Penguin Books India Pvt. Ltd., 11 Community Centre, Panchsheel Park, New Delhi—110 017, India
Penguin Group (NZ), 67 Apollo Drive, Rosedale, North Shore 0632, New Zealand
(a division of Pearson New Zealand Ltd.)
Penguin Books (South Africa) (Pty.) Ltd., 24 Sturdee Avenue, Rosebank, Johannesburg 2196,
South Africa

Penguin Books Ltd., Registered Offices: 80 Strand, London WC2R 0RL, England

This book is an original publication of The Berkley Publishing Group.

The publisher does not have any control over and does not assume responsibility for author or third-party websites or their content.

Copyright © 2009 by Sheila Murray Bethel, Ph.D.
Text design by Tiffany Estreicher.
Line art by Erin Dangar.
Please refer to page 387 for additional credit information.

PRINTING HISTORY
Berkley trade paperback edition / March 2009

Library of Congress Cataloging-in-Publication Data

Bethel, Sheila Murray.
   A new breed of leader : 8 leadership qualities that matter most in the real world : what works, what doesn't, and why / Sheila Murray Bethel.
      p. cm.
   ISBN 978-0-425-22590-5
   1. Leadership.   2. Leadership—Case studies.   I. Title.
HM1261.B48 2009
658.4'092—dc22
                                        2008048576

PRINTED IN THE UNITED STATES OF AMERICA

10   9   8   7   6   5   4   3   2   1

To the one and only Goldie,
best friend, adopted sister,
soul mate, and a true servant leader.
I miss her every single day.
May she rest in peace.

Acknowledgments

Since I believe that leadership is ever evolving, I want to acknowledge and thank all of the wonderful clients and extraordinary people I have worked with around the world. Each one has added to my personal view and worldview of what it means to be a leader and a follower in the twenty-first century.

During the writing of this book there were people who added their talents, skills, inspiration, and support through the stages from initial ideas to finished manuscript. Each in his own way made this book possible, for without these combined contributions, I would still have just an outline in some file on my computer.

To each I give my heartfelt thanks. In the beginning, Dale Fethering did a yeoman's job helping me craft the book proposal and the first two chapters into a saleable book. My colleague Chris Widener referred me to the DSM Literary Agency and Doris Michaels and Delia Berrigan Fakis, whose enthusiastic representation and support were and are invaluable.

The team at Penguin Group saw the possibilities when others did not: Leslie Gelbman, publisher; Susan Allison, editorial director; my editors Denise Silvestro, Adrienne Avila, and the indispensable Meredith Giordan, who made the back-and-forth smooth and fun. I'm indebted to text designer Tiffany Estreicher; copy editor Joan Matthews; Craig Burke, vice president of publicity; Liz Hanslik, director of advertising and promotion; and Rick Pascocello, vice president of marketing, and his team of sales representatives, who have had so many creative ideas.

Michelle Durant in Albuquerque provided critical transcription services for the interviews and was always there when I needed her. The artistic approach to the graphics was brought to life by Erin Dangar. I would run an idea by Erin and she would make it come alive, often with a better approach than I first envisioned. Quite literally, I would not have enjoyed writing the book without her. My friend and colleague Wally Nieburt provided the two cartoons; his humorous approach to serious matters always adds a touch of lightness that any book on leadership needs.

I am not an early morning person, so I could not have gone to print with this book without thanking the family of people at KDFC classical radio station here in San Francisco: Hoyt Smith, Betsy O'Conner, Dianne Nicolini, Rick Malone, John Evans, and program director Bill Lueth. Thanks for helping me to get into gear each morning and taking me through the day. I take them with me when I travel by listening online. The music was inspirational and their good humor gave me the smiles and the occasional laugh when I needed a break from the intensity of the writing.

Thanks to photographer Tom Tracy and web masters Barry Epstein and Pat Riley at Ovation Solutions, who gave my website a new look to match this new book, for all your patience and imagination. I have worked with Sean and Stacey Frame at Frame-by-Frame Productions for twenty years, and would like to thank them for their always super contributions.

I have gained immeasurable knowledge from the interviews with all the leaders you will meet in the chapters of this book. Their insights on leadership often took my thoughts and concepts to higher levels than I expected. I owe a debt of gratitude to each of them.

My greatest support came from my family and friends, who had faith that I could say something new on leadership. They helped me through the tough days of my husband Bill's heart attack and recovery. Stacy Evans's weekly calls were filled with love and prayers. Tom, David, and Pearl Bethel were constant lifelines, always full of encouragement. My new friend from Calgary, Sandy Gibson, was nearly a daily e-mail cheerleader, and Tony Alessandra always has wonderful ideas to share. Thanks to you both.

Ultimately the highest praise and deepest appreciation goes to my 24/7 partner, my best friend, a great researcher, editor, and critic: my husband, Bill Bethel. No one has made a bigger contribution to or difference in the outcome of this book. His nurturing and love smoothed the rough edges and soothed my sometimes frayed nerves from balancing a lecture schedule and a writing schedule. *A New Breed of Leader* is his book also.

Contents

A New Breed of Leader— Where to Begin?

It's not the strongest of the species that survives, nor the most intelligent, but the one most responsive to change.

—CHARLES DARWIN

WOULD YOU LIKE to be one of the new breed of leaders who inspires followers to look for creative and unique answers to our twenty-first-century challenges? If you could update your leadership qualities to build community, connectedness, and a shared sense of purpose, would you? If you had practical, real-world leadership concepts and actions that show you what works, what doesn't, and why, would you use them?

I'm sure the answer to these questions is yes! Together we'll explore what being A New Breed Leader means—at home, in your work, and in your community.

The Emergence of New Breed Leaders

Malcolm Gladwell wrote about *The Tipping Point*, where "ideas and products and messages and behaviors spread just like viruses do." In fact, there is a point where they hit a critical mass, and that is the tipping point. We are at just that point in the realm of leadership. It is no longer about hierarchy. Leadership lives and exists throughout organizations; it is distributed and shared leadership, especially in team-based entities. In Chapter Seven, "Power Matters," you'll read about the success of two very interesting women at Xerox: Anne Mulcahy, Chair, and Ursula Burns, CEO. They made a conscious and very purposeful decision to share leadership responsibilities based on their greatest personal leadership strengths.

Dr. Curtis R. Carlson, CEO and president of SRI International, supports Gladwell's tipping point theory. Carlson writes, "When it comes to understanding leadership, we have moved from heroic leadership and leadership by authority and power, to modern ideas about the interactive nature of leadership, and leadership by consent." Google recently took an interactive leadership role to solve some of our most urgent global issues. They sent out a worldwide public request for ideas about how to change the world and/or help others. They had 150,000 responses, from which they will choose the top 150 ideas and reward them with cash prizes.

To this new model of twenty-first-century leadership, add the ingredient that leadership expert Warren Bennis calls "crucibles," those "utterly transforming events or tests that individuals must pass through and make meaning from in order to learn, grow, and lead. The trouble for youthful leaders is that crucibles are rare and cannot be artificially reproduced." If you are a young leader or an aspiring leader, don't be afraid of the term "crucible." Events that you have overcome, such as a personal illness, or an extremely difficult event that you have experienced may indeed be life changing. You can gain strength as you work your way through it. Then, when you examine your actions and reactions, you will notice that you have gained valuable tools with which to build your leadership strengths.

Throughout this book, there are "crucible" stories and examples with which you can assess your own life and leadership. The important thing to know is that you will have, if you haven't already, moments and events that test the mettle of your personal and professional life and your core values.

In Chapter One, "Competence Matters," you will find an example of how a woman's swift leadership instincts brought her through a crucible event, and what she did as a result. In Chapter Two, "Accountability Matters," you will see how two crucible events—one personal, the other professional—shaped and defined two men and a global corporation.

Building a Better You

Learning you get from school. Education you get from life.
—MARK TWAIN

It is never too early or too late to become better educated, to consider a new type or style of leadership to help you be as effective as possible.

At age ninety-two, legendary Supreme Court Justice Oliver Wendell Holmes was ill and in the hospital. His friend President Roosevelt came to visit him. When Roosevelt entered the room, he saw Justice Holmes reading a Greek primer. "What are you doing, Mr. Justice?" asked the president. "Reading," answered Holmes. "I can see that," said the president. "But why a Greek primer?" Holmes answered, "Why, Mr. President, to improve my mind."

Regardless of your experience, you will be better able to fulfill your position as leader with the eight qualities that matter most.

As a *beginning leader*, you'll have a clear set of guideposts on which to base your growth.

If you are a *supervisor* or *midlevel manager*, you will be more adept at identifying your current strengths and weaknesses.

As an *upper-level manager* or *executive*, the benefit is the insight to reassess the leadership qualities that brought you to that position.

Now's the Time for Change

We are a nation built on hope, purpose, and a belief in better times, better ways of doing things, and a better life for our children. We are hungry for inspired leaders who will show us the way. The United States has gone through a transformational presidential election. Race, age, and gender barriers have been demolished. The reality of leadership has taken a quantum leap forward in empowering everyone to aspire to the stewardship of his or her organization.

The winds of change are blowing across the globe. We need bold new leaders at every level of society to solve our most pressing issues. It is time to view the tried-and-true concepts of leadership through a new filter and then update them. By combining the best leadership qualities of the past with a set of new

> **"Letting Go of the past"**
>
> Handling and accepting change comes about when you are willing to let go of old ideas, concepts, and attitudes. Then there is room for new leadership dreams and actions.

descriptors, measures, and actions, we will begin to change the huge disconnect that exists between our daily lives and our leaders in business, government, and other institutions.

William G. Dyer, author of *Strategies for Managing Change*, wrote: "The issue of change is surely the most important matter facing anyone who is responsible for a human organization—be it family, business, school, church, agency, club, or association." In a world that is changing as fast as ours, all nations are looking for change-master leaders who will take the risks and make the intellectual and emotional leaps into new ideas to find new answers.

The Twenty-First-Century Leadership Puzzle

We've all tinkered with jigsaw puzzles. It is rewarding to watch the finished picture emerge as we fit the pieces together. In an actual puzzle, you start with the picture on the outside of the box to give you an idea of the direction and form you're seeking. But when it comes to leadership excellence, there's no box and no picture. Instead, the puzzle develops as you do.

Each of the eight qualities discussed in this book is a piece of the New Breed Leadership Puzzle. The value of each piece lies in the tools it gives you to shape your personal leadership strength and to reinforce your ability to serve others. You'll be pleased to find that you already possess many of the leadership traits in the eight puzzle pieces. The possibility piece outside of the puzzle is one of the most exciting. It represents where you will grow and where you can maximize opportunities to expand on any of the eight qualities that you will need to be A New Breed Leader. Because leadership is a never-ending cycle of growth and change, possibilities are what will take you into the future. "Possibilities" are where you will need to go to remain effective, congruent, and relevant. As you read about and explore each puzzle piece, consider what potential you have to expand on them in your own leadership situations.

So what are the eight qualities that matter most when you are trying to build your own leadership skills? How can you recog-

1. Competence Matters

5. Values Matter

2. Accountability Matters

6. Perspective Matters

3. Openness Matters

7. Power Matters

4. Language Matters

8. Humility Matters

nize what legitimate leadership looks like, sounds like, acts like, and believes in?

Whether you are a community leader, a business leader, a union leader, a member of the school board, a volunteer advocate, or a leader in a religious setting, here are the pieces of the puzzle . . . here is what matters most for you to be a successful New Breed Leader.

The puzzle pieces give you something solid upon which to base your leadership growth. First, you develop these skills in yourself. Then, as you extend them to your families, jobs, and communities, you increase your personal commitment to new and better leadership with a passion for uniting us in our new century. With these eight qualities, you will become wiser and smarter; you will be the authentic leader we need so much.

Vision Built on Competence

You may ask, "Is having a vision still an important trait to attract and retain followers? Is having a vision still vital for me to be relevant as a leader?" The answer to both of these questions is yes. Vision and purpose are still your internal driving force. What is new is the type of in-depth personal analysis and preparation you need to bring that vision into reality and how you deal with the results. The leadership puzzle will give you that depth.

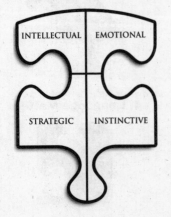

For example, the puzzle piece

in Chapter One, "Competence Matters," identifies four critical parts—intellectual, emotional, strategic, and instinctive competence—that give your vision its strength.

The component parts of competence are the major factors in fulfilling your vision. In recent years we have seen that all the good intentions and leadership vision mean nothing without a high degree of know-how and expertise. Vision without competence can turn into a disaster. But when your vision is backed by deep competence, you can create miracles.

In each of the other seven chapters, the puzzle piece is divided similarly to the competence piece to help you look deeper into that quality and confirm and reinforce its core value. Each quality will have critical questions that give you better direction and give meaning to your journey as a highly effective leader.

Here are four sample competence-vision-building questions:

- What new skills and attitudes do I need to acquire to make my vision come alive?

- Can I identify the parts of my vision that will motivate and inspire followers?

- How can I use these insights to guide me in my learning process so that I can measure success or failure?

- When I identify the critical parts of my vision, do I take into consideration the unintended consequences that may occur?

Hope Lives in New Beginnings

Look with favor upon a bold beginning.

—VIRGIL, Roman philosopher

As I crisscross our country and the globe, speaking and training on leadership, I see the concern in people's eyes and hear the longing in their words for reasons to be optimistic about our future. They are waiting for new leaders who have the competence, honesty, and communication skills to lead us out of our current quagmire. As individuals and as a country, we have the capacity and the intelligence to grow up and out of the hole into which we have dug ourselves.

> Our strength grows out of our weakness.
> —RALPH WALDO EMERSON

In past decades, we were bold and strong. We accepted great challenges and risks. And we can do it again.

As you assess your use of the qualities that matter most, you'll become a stronger leader and an example of the New Breed Leader.

The Age of Questions

One good question can be more explosive than a thousand answers.

—ANONYMOUS

We're living with the most complex issues since time began. There are no simple answers. It is critical to draw on well-thought-out questions to lay the groundwork for new solutions. Having all the answers is far less important to you than knowing what to ask. Both the questions and the answers will be invaluable guides for your new leadership effort and results.

> The person who knows how will always find a place in life. The person who knows why will inevitably be the leader.

Insightful questions open doors and throw light on unresolved problems. They give you an astute understanding of how to be a better leader. They free you from entrenched ideas and outdated procedures.

A four-year-old child may drive a parent crazy asking questions. But if you take a clue from the little ones and apply that same kind of inquisitiveness in your leadership quest, you will be greatly expanding as A New Breed Leader.

Use the "Five W's" we learned in school (who, what, when, where, and why) and add the question "how?" But of the six questions, "why" is most powerful. Many organizations and individuals have gone completely off course because they first asked *how* to do something instead of first asking *why* they should do it.

Truly successful leaders have the courage to pause and ask "why." They understand that "why" comes first because it's the foundation for making things happen.

They understand:

Why *competence*—intellectual, emotional, strategic, and instinctive—tops the list of effective leadership, giving birth to powerful visions and purpose.

Why being *accountable* for your actions and all that happens on your watch is the key to building credibility and trust.

Why *openness*, being direct and truthful, is the finest way to build leadership integrity.

Why *language* can tear down a person or an organization or build bridges as strong as steel between people and groups.

Why *values* bind us together in our shared purpose and common ideals.

Why *perspective*, the ability to help people keep life and business in balance in times of great change, is a critical leadership skill for moving into the future.

Why the *power* inherent in the charter between the leader and the led must be protected against all of our basest human instincts.

Why *humility* builds authenticity and why arrogance destroys it.

Asking *why* is one of the most significant contributions you can make to your organization.

The New Breed Leadership Pyramid

We're just getting started. We're just beginning
to meet what will be the future . . .
—GRACE MURRAY HOOPER, mathematician and first female U.S. Navy Admiral

Many leaders who qualify as role models of the New Breed Leader already exist. They are in responsible positions in every sector of business; in local, state, and federal government; and in every

SALESFORCE.COM

Marc Benioff smiles with pride when he talks about the fact that 85 percent of his employees are now active in some sort of philanthropic activity. "People are here to do more than just make money," he says. "They want to make the world a better place."

Asking penetrating, well-thought-out questions is a leadership quality Benioff used in 1977 when he was an executive with Oracle Corporation and began the company's first major philanthropic initiative. As successful as his work had been, he felt it could have made a much bigger impact. He began questioning what was done in the past, what the firm was currently doing, and what could be done better in the future.

As he found answers, he also began to develop his personal philosophy of what he calls "integrated philanthropy." To be most effective, he says, a firm's philanthropy must have the idea woven into its fabric from the very beginning, woven into the organization's DNA.

After leaving Oracle in 1999, he launched Salesforce.com and put his idea into action. He committed 1 percent of the company's stock, 1 percent of the company profits, and 1 percent of employee working hours to community service. He calls this his 1-1-1 model.

Building Salesforce.com and the Salesforce Foundation have been the most exciting and rewarding experiences of his life, Benioff says. And it all started when be began asking himself: How can we do better?

He is one of the New Breed Leaders who values the power of inquisitiveness to find bold, long-term solutions to help both the success of the company and the success of the community.

enterprise and part of the country. Some are working in quiet, unnoticed ways and not yet getting the recognition they deserve.

Others are the "new breed in training," preparing for positions of leadership. Some are young idealists just entering universities and the workforce.

Then there is the old breed of leaders who, if they have not already crashed and burned, soon will. Among them will be those who, like the mythical phoenix, will rise out of the dust of failure, having gained invaluable lessons and wisdom with which to continue their leadership.

Who will be our New Breed Leaders of the twenty-first century? Who will take the world to better places than we have ever been? Who will be the new stewards of civilization?

We don't know yet. Renaissance men and women are rare. But one thing is for sure: they are emerging.

We've always been blessed with rare people who have the gift of leading us in ways that solve our problems and change the world for the better. They fall into four categories:

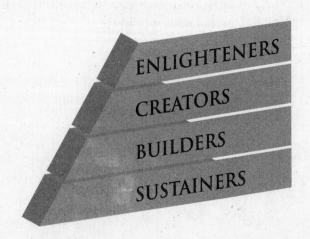

THE ENLIGHTENERS

The *Enlighteners* are the icons of humanity's greatest progress. Their personal commitment to a cause, to a movement, or to righting a social wrong has always been their greatest strength, their vision, and their goal. Their personal power gives them the inner strength to overcome adversity that would crush most people. That is why they have always stood above the other three categories of leaders.

In the twentieth century, Dr. Martin Luther King Jr., Moshe Dayan, Golda Meir, Nelson Mandela, Mahatma Gandhi, the Dalai Lama, and Mother Teresa embodied the very essence of leadership that can move mountains. FDR and Churchill inspired and led the world through World War II. All of their examples remind us of our need to truly be *"our brother's keeper."*

THE CREATORS

The *Creators* are inspired geniuses. They are the men and women who create the new industries and organizations, cultures, theories, lifestyles, and ways of thinking and living. They're the change masters who see opportunities others do not. They take action while others wait for a better or safer time.

Creators in science, medicine, and aeronautics gave us the visionaries who imagined what no one else could; Einstein, Hubble, and Edison moved accepted science into dramatic new dimensions. Doctors Denton Cooley and Michael DeBakey changed heart disease treatment forever with the first successful heart transplant. The Wright Brothers, Amelia Earhart, and Charles Lindbergh shaped a newer, smaller world and set the stage that launched our first astronauts, who helped us better understand our beautiful and fragile planet.

The writers who expanded our thinking and challenged our perceptions through literature comprise a huge list that includes Phillip Roth, Toni Morrison, Maya Angelou, J. K. Rowling, Tom Peters, Peter Drucker, Stephen Ambrose, and that powerful husband-and-wife team of historians, Will and Ariel Durant.

Classical music in the twentieth century gave us opera greats such as Luciano Pavarotti, José Carreras, and Placido Domingo, Maria Callas and Beverly Sills. The social-dance genius of Fred Astaire and Ginger Rogers, John Travolta and Karen Gorney, and Patrick Swayze and Jennifer Grey kept us glued to the movie screen. The innovative style of Bob Fosse startled us and opened a door of creativity still being expanded upon today. Russian ballet geniuses Rudolf Nureyev and Mikhail Baryshnikov hypnotized us with their innovation and power. George Gershwin, Cole Porter, Steven Sondheim, Andrew Lloyd Webber, Leonard Bernstein, the Beatles, Elvis Presley, Louis Armstrong, Barbra Streisand, and Ella Fitzgerald made the twentieth century a veritable wellspring of musical creativity.

Spiritual and religious leaders came in the form of Pope John Paul II, Billy Graham, Rick Warren, and Deepak Chopra.

The brilliance of *Creators* in business is embodied by Henry Ford, John D. Rockefeller Jr., Steve Wozniak, Meg Whitman, Bill Gates, and Andrew Carnegie, just to name a very small number of those who have made this country an economic giant.

THE BUILDERS

The *Builders* are the executives and CEOs who will take the work done by the *Enlighteners* and *Creators* and fashion existing organizations into long-term successful entities. They add new meaning to the old. Among the outstanding business executives in the last half of the twentieth century were Jack Welch, Ann Moore, Warren Buffett, Lee Iacocca, Andy Grove, Bill Marriott, Alfred Sloan, Andrea Jung, Indra Nooyi, and Steve Jobs.

When Dr. Jonas Salk invented the polio vaccine, he led the way by building on all the medical research that came before. Margaret Mead and Jane Goodall dramatically increased our understanding of anthropology. Explorers Sir Edmund Hillary, Sherpa mountaineer Tenzing Norgay, and Jacques Cousteau took us to new heights and depths of understanding of the symbiotic relationship between mountains, oceans, and human life.

We had athletic leaders who gave us a new view of our human capabilities. Champions Wilma Rudolph, Jessie Owens, and Jackie Robinson broke the race barriers, and Roger Bannister broke the four-minute mile. All of them drew on personal and collective past experiences to qualify as *Builder* leaders.

THE SUSTAINERS

Last but not least are the *Sustainers*. They're the team builders, consensus experts who have the special gift of making the organizational vision something in which everyone can take ownership. They lead by their skills of exceptional follow-through. Without them, nothing will hold up under the pressures and challenges of everyday life. They're the anchors who hold it all together so that the other three categories of leaders can continue their work. They are the long-haul–big-picture men and women.

In government, we can look to Senator Jim Sasser, former ambassador to China, Secretary of Health and Human Services

Donna Shalala, former Senator Bob Dole, former Secretary of the Navy Richard Danzig, Reagan Administration Chief of Staff James Baker, and journalist and former consultant to four presidents, David Gergen.

In business, insight comes from General Electric's CEO Jeff Immelt and Peter Ueberroth, chairman of the Contrarian Group and the U.S. Olympic Committee. In the nonprofit world, ACCIO, a lending and support organization for entrepreneurs, is being led by Maria Otero. Drew Gilpin Faust, the first female president of Harvard University, is another who is leading the way. The list is long, and I have left out so many who deserve mention. The ones I have included are simply to remind us that we have had great leaders do great things and we will have them again. We have not lost our genius for change, innovation, and creativity.

Chances are that you see yourself in one of the pyramid categories or you are aiming to enter a category. As you read about the eight qualities, think about role models who can help you clarify and define what you need to be in the pyramid. All of the questions throughout the book are designed to give you fodder for exploration and inspiration to identify whichever category you see for yourself and help you grow into it. Most of us agree the nation is headed in the wrong direction and collectively we have said, "That's enough." The exciting part is that we are on the move, and we are ready for the changes we need to make.

A Call to Action

If not you, who? If not now, when?

—THE TALMUD

Now is the time to redefine leadership, combining the best of the past with the best of a new model that fits the needs of our new century. Our new model needs to reflect the courage of our fore-fathers, who set the gold standard of leadership for our fledgling country and for nations everywhere. They created our democracy, our freedom, our promise, and our future. Let's revisit these pow-erful basics and enlarge them by taking risks, digging in, and get-ting to work asking the hard questions and doing the hard work of forging new beginnings.

One of our biggest leadership problems currently in the United States is the lack of knowledge, awareness, or even interest in life beyond our country's borders. It is a huge limitation of grow-ing importance as the global economy expands. Our boards of directors in all sectors include few members who are from other cultures. We must expand, not limit, our horizons, vistas, and visions.

Now is our opportunity to go boldly forward to remake our world. As Martin Luther King said, ". . . the fierce urgency of now" is upon us. We need smart, world-traveled, multilingual, geopolitically adept men and women who can see past borders and boundaries to prospects that can benefit everyone.

We have always been doers, innovators, and change masters who have the tenacity to commit to long-term actions. It's time to put aside personal gain, profits, allegiances, or party in order to serve the best interests of all the people while concentrating on what really *matters most* in all segments of our lives.

Let This Book Be Your Road Map

As you read, keep a highlighter and pen handy for those "a-ha!" moments or for a fresh insight. Write your own thoughts or ideas in the margins. Turn this book into your personal road map for growth and inspiration.

Keep some colored sticky notes handy to copy some of the ideas you like from the book. Or create your own to remind you of important thoughts. Visit my website www.anewbreedofleader .com, for free articles and the leadership action plans you will read about in the chapters.

Enjoy the quizzes, assessments, and questions in the chapters. I think you'll be inspired and encouraged by the stories and examples of our senior leaders who have so much wisdom to share, our current leaders who are showing us new ways to solve our problems, and our youngest leaders who are our future.

You'll gain insights and wisdom from leaders I interviewed:

- Arnold Palmer, golf legend

- General Colin Powell (U.S. Army, ret.), Former Secretary of State

- Bruce Gordon, former president, Retail Markets Group Verizon, former CEO, NAACP

- Dr. Donna Shalala, president, University of Miami

- Colonel Bill Smullen (U.S. Army, ret.), Army Hall of Fame and Chief of Staff to General Colin Powell in the White House and at the State Department

- Frank Keating, Former Governor of Oklahoma and current CEO of the American Council of Life Insurers

- Lieutenant Colonel Mary Lou Smullen (U.S. Army, ret.)

- Joe Driscoll, CEO of several highly successful health-care organizations

- Jim Sasser, former Ambassador to China and three-term senator from Tennessee

- Cathy Keating, Former First Lady of Oklahoma, member of the BOD, Express Professional Employment

- Graham Kerr, formerly the Galloping Gourmet, now a leader of the Healthy Eating Movement

- Susan RoAne, bestselling author

- Jeffrey Sheldon, Sheldon Consulting Group

Lifelong Learning

True leadership is not something you learn once; it is an ever-evolving pattern of skills, talents, and abilities that you craft and seek to perfect over a lifetime. Your leadership journey will never be finished. You are a wondrous work in progress as you become A New Breed Leader.

From today on, you will never be the same because you have

allowed new thoughts and ideas into your mind. When you stretch a rubber band, it will either go back to its former shape or break. You are different. When you stretch your mind and absorb new or different information, you never return to your former self and you certainly don't break . . . You grow, change, and become better and wiser.

A Ship to Guide You

The person without a purpose is like a ship without a rudder.
—THOMAS CARLYLE, Scottish essayist and historian

We live in new times that demand a new feeling of purpose, new actions, and yet-unseen solutions. Technology, globalization, fanaticism, immigration, environmental issues, energy concerns, emerging nations, new economic alliances, and political realignment all call for a new breed of authentic men and women who are physically strong, mentally quick, politically limber, emotionally stable, intellectually superior, and unselfish consensus builders to lead us.

A New Breed of Leader gives you a ship to sail on, a compass to guide by, and a rudder to steer your way through the stormy leadership seas and uncharted waters of the twenty-first century.

I wish you the best in your leadership development, for the benefit of your organization, your community, and your personal life. Because that is where it all begins . . . within you.

CHAPTER ONE

Competence Matters

BUILDING PURPOSE

If I were given six hours to chop down a tree,
I would spend four hours sharpening my axe.
—ABRAHAM LINCOLN

A S A NEW Breed Leader, *competence* will top your list of leadership qualities that *matter most*. When you know what you are doing, have the experience and knowledge to take risks and make wise decisions, and have a deep sense of purpose and a healthy dose of charisma, you can lead people through beneficial actions into positive results.

Vision and Purpose Backed by Competence

When I ask people what is the most important quality a leader must have, they most often answer, "A vision." I agree, there is no disputing the power of vision. It is essential to your effectiveness as a leader. However, without competence, your vision remains just wishful thinking.

Nobel laureate Toni Morrison said in a commencement address, "As you enter positions of trust and power, dream a little before you think." You need the dream—the vision—but then you need clear thinking to bring the dream to life. That's where competence comes in. Clear thinking leads to actions that add up to competence, which enables the dream. That is also a major difference between having a vision and being a visionary leader. A visionary lives in a constant innovation mode that gives him or her the competence to move the dream into reality. Haven't we all seen enthusiastic people fail because they didn't know how to turn their vision into action?

> Competence = Doing the right thing, the right way, at the right time.

While the dictionary defines competence as "properly or well qualified; capable," you need a more workable, action-oriented description to enhance your leadership. Try this: *Competence* means doing the right thing, the right way, at the right time.

With a workable definition in place, it is important to decide how to measure or judge competence. The best way to begin is by asking, *Were the results satisfactory?*

Review any recent task or project in which you led a group of people and ask:

- How and why was the result satisfactory or unsatisfactory?

- Can I clearly describe the competencies we needed to implement the project?

- What did I learn from the process about my leadership competence?

- What could I have done better or differently and why?

Judging competence is never a single event; it is a constant assessment of the way things are being done. One of the best and most public examples in the last century was in 1969 when *Apollo 11* blasted off for the moon. Every detail was relentlessly checked, rechecked, and checked again. The very survival of the crew and success of the mission depended on everyone involved knowing exactly how their part was functioning. The whole world was watching and judging the competence of our space leaders.

On September 11, 2001, America was again put under the world microscope. How well did we do in handling the attacks on the World Trade Center in New York City? Even though there were things that could have been done better, our performance was an amazing display of competence, caring, and commitment to work together. The world saw us come from all across the country to lend our know-how to those in need.

In his seminal book on leadership, Robert Greenleaf, the father of the modern servant-leadership philosophy, said leaders must be challenged to keep their organizations alive and well:

> Most institutions that survive over a period of time do so because they have a survival pattern, a dogma that gives a general direction of rightness. Those who administer and staff the institution become highly competent in operating within that pattern. Yet unless they are periodically challenged on the adequacy of that pattern, eventually they lose survival ability.

Long before that happens, they probably cease to function at their best.

While you may not live in a fishbowl as NASA did, or be leading a historic or life-or-death project, the survival and success of your organization will depend on your ability to ask the tough questions that check and recheck your competence and strengthen your purpose. Fostering your commitment to grow and expanding your competence on a daily basis are fundamental to everything you hope to achieve.

Two Leaders . . . Two Views

One of the most interesting parts of writing this chapter occurred when I received a different view of vision building from two highly respected leaders, one from the military and government and the other from academia and government: Former Secretary of State General Colin Powell (U.S. Army, ret.) and Dr. Donna Shalala, president of the University of Miami and former Secretary of Health and Human Services in the Clinton Administration.

I asked Dr. Shalala how vision building in the twenty-first century differed from the past. She said, "It's more collaborative. It is fundamentally different than having a hierarchical kind of approach. In the twenty-first century, no one should ask, 'What's your vision for this organization?'"

She surprised me with this answer. I asked her what they should ask.

"They shouldn't ask the question at all," she replied. "They should be part of a process in which you work through where you want to go."

I know that she is very strong on the subject of strategic competence, so I delved further. "If there's no particular stated vision, how do you get the buy-in from all of those involved?"

She replied, "By participation. You develop a strategy and metrics for determining whether you are on track, but you do it collaboratively. That's the difference."

When I asked General Powell about leadership in the new century, he gave me a contrasting view:

Leadership will be no different in the future than in the past. Leaders need to have a vision, [and] communicate that vision with passion so followers are inspired. Then, "take care of the troops." Train, equip, reward, and prune the followers. Leaders execute and supervise aggressively. Works in every organization I've been in. I learned it all as a young lieutenant and all the books and lists I've read and courses I've attended have merely refined my beliefs.

Now that you have read their differing responses, ask yourself:

- What do I think about their different responses?

- Is one opinion better than the other for my people?

- How can I utilize the expertise of these leaders to build my people and my organization?

Remember, there is no right or wrong answer. Your style of leadership, the circumstances you work within, and various events will determine how you view vision building.

Leadership Is Earned, Not Claimed

One of the most important insights in your leadership toolbox is the understanding that leadership is earned, not claimed. We make some real leaps of faith when we assume that people in positions of power or celebrity are competent leaders, but . . .

Just because you have money doesn't make you a leader.

Just because you have celebrity doesn't make you a leader.

Just because you have written a bestselling book doesn't make you a leader.

Just because you have the ability to get publicity, yell the loudest, be the most abrasive, or get the most attention doesn't make you a leader.

Just because you are head of a company or organization or department doesn't always make you a leader.

Just because you are a sports, media, television, or radio star doesn't make you a leader.

Just because you can get into the movies, on the TV screen, or create a presence on the Internet doesn't make you a leader.

Leadership is earned, not claimed!

Just because you represent a religious group doesn't make you a leader . . . and

Just because you can get elected doesn't automatically make you a leader.

Instead, leadership is *earned* by understanding and developing the qualities that *matter most*.

Where Vision and Competence Can Change the World

For an example of the power that could ensue when vision and competency come together, let's look at the issue of oil dependency. When leaders in every sector of business, government, education, research, and religion make oil independence the top national priority, we'll change the world and the life of every person on this planet. We can't tell China and other big oil users not to use so much energy, given what energy gluttons Americans are. We can only lead by example with a vision or a purpose so commanding it will attract followers from around the globe.

Doing so will change the balance of power with rogue nations. It will put millions upon millions of people to work in businesses not yet imagined. It will create economic engines that will far outweigh the oil industry and its associated enterprises. It will improve the living standards of all societies, to say nothing of the fact that it will all but eliminate hydrocarbons from the atmosphere and slow down global warming.

Thomas Friedman, the *New York Times* foreign-affairs columnist and author of *The World Is Flat*, wrote that ". . . a country that can double the speed of microchips every eighteen months ought to be able to innovate its way to energy independence. Focusing the nation on great energy efficiency and conservation is the most tough-minded, geo-strategic, pro-growth, and patriotic thing we can do."

Clearly, a nation that was able to put a man on the moon is competent enough to make us oil independent if we put the national mind, heart, creativity, and energy behind the cause. Will you be among our new breed of leaders with the combined vision and competence to begin? Tremendous courage—and leaders of heroic proportions—will be required to change our lives so dramatically.

A Glimpse of Competent, Vision-Driven New Breed Leaders

David Gergen, journalist and adviser to four U.S. presidents, wrote in *Eyewitness to Power: The Essence of Leadership*, "The vision thing is a sense of purpose with competence. It's not intended to be a statement of who we are, but of what we dream of becoming, realizing that the journey never ends. It's our communal vision." He was referring to our country, but the reference applies to any organization, large or small. When everyone involved feels a sense of ownership, the vision takes on a life of its own.

Look closely and you can see our new breed of leaders emerging. In 1999, for instance, Bill Gates was describing his vision for Microsoft: "To empower people through great software anytime and place and on any device." Just three years later, he added, *"To enable people and business throughout the world to realize their full potential."* His vision had grown along with his competence. Further, in describing why he and his wife, Melinda, created the Gates Foundation, they wrote, ". . . from those to whom much is given, much is expected. We benefited from great schools, great health care, and a vibrant economic system. That's why we feel a tremendous responsibility to give back to society." That's the kind of purpose to expect from a new breed of leader.

Or take Oprah Winfrey, who is watched by viewers in 118 countries. When asked about her purpose, she said, ". . . I can talk to anybody about anything with a sense of respect and integrity." Whether she's promoting a book on television or encouraging literacy or other causes in South Africa, this charismatic woman clearly understands that she has built an empire on her ability to connect with her audiences. Her leadership is fueled by her people-competence, or, as she puts it, "I relate to the core of everyone's pain and promise."

Starbucks chairman Howard Schultz once said, "We are not in the coffee business. We are in the people business." Of his leadership philosophy, he says, "There is no long-term shareholder value if it isn't linked to building long-term value for your people." His New Breed Leadership stands out when you hear him talk about his vision—not just to be the biggest coffee seller in the world, but to share the Starbucks experience of connecting to people in every nation in which it operates.

All of these leaders have had grand visions. However, it's their high degree of competence and nearly fanatical thirst for learning that brought their visions to fruition. They've fired the imagination of generations to come by passing on a sense of contribution and pride in building a new and better world.

I often work in Washington, D.C., and each time I'm there, I visit the Lincoln Memorial late at night when I can be alone to think. As I stand at the bottom of the steps and look up at the floodlit memorial, I think about the courageous men and women who trekked across the continent to start a new life on the frontier. I think about all the small and large visions and competencies that gave us the states whose names are carved around the top of the monument.

As I walk up the steps in the silence, I'm overwhelmed by Lincoln, looking down with those benevolent eyes that seem so real. As I read the words of the Gettysburg Address inscribed in the marble, I—like others—am deeply moved and feel the power of Lincoln's vision. (In fact, it's said that since the memorial was built, every sitting president has visited Mr. Lincoln in the wee hours of the morning seeking inspiration or solutions for critical problems.)

Lincoln's vision was to maintain "one nation, indivisible, with liberty and justice for all." The Emancipation Proclamation was framed by a statesman, not just a politician. He gave us powerful examples to live by and to lead by. Though it was far too slow in coming, the fight for racial equality was sparked and driven by the brilliance, clarity, and power of Lincoln's vision.

Can You Make Something Better?

Seeing how people, places, and things can be better than they are is the first step toward improving anything.

Where will your competence lead you? Do you have the passion of an *Enlightener* to change the world, or to right a societal wrong that will take us all to a new place in history? Are you a *Creator* of a new industry or inventor of a tool to help us solve the problems we face in this new century? Do your skills and abilities fall into the *Builder* or *Sustainer* category? One is not better than the other. We need men and women from every part of society to fill all the levels of the New Breed Leader.

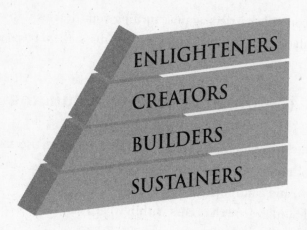

When your vision is backed by competence, it is exciting, contagious, and can achieve wondrous results. How can you check the power of your vision? Ask yourself:

- Do I have a vision of a better world that others do not yet see?

- Am I able to imagine people performing better than they can see themselves?

- What am I doing to build both my vision and my competence?

When the times get tough, the passion of your purpose gives you the courage and tenacity to push on. When times are good, your purpose can explode your potential and you fire the enthusiasm of everyone around you.

People and organizations are eager to have an authentic leader guide them to better places and better times. It's never too early or too late to become a visionary leader. There's no age limit and no socioeconomic barriers against turning your dreams into visions. The only obstacle is your competence to make them come alive.

Continual Competence Building

As your leadership takes you to new levels of expertise and positions of importance, be sure you continually appraise your competence, and continue to grow.

All human growth occurs within what I call the:

Competence-Confidence Cycle

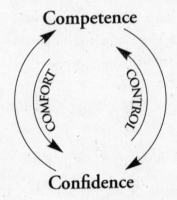

When your competence grows, you will feel more control over your environment, which increases your self-confidence. As your confidence grows, you relax and feel more comfortable to continue your competence building, which results in the ability to give life to your vision.

One of your major challenges as A New Breed Leader is to work with your teams to support their growth with the same cycle. When one of your organization's common goals is continual development, everyone benefits, in both their work and their personal lives.

Nontransferable Competence

Nontransferable competence has become an issue in recent years. Corporate boards of directors have lured high-performing executives from one company or industry and inserted them as CEOs into a different kind of organization. Sometimes it works, sometimes it doesn't.

It can be a major mistake to assume that a person's specialized competence is always transferable. Boards need to ask: Does this person's previous success work in the context of the prospective position? Both Carly Fiorina and Gary C. Wendt are examples of the transferable competence challenge.

Fiorina's success and star executive status at AT&T and Lucent brought her to Hewlett-Packard, where the association seemed doomed from the beginning of the fiery relationship. The big question remains: Why did the board of directors bring a sales executive into an engineering-based company, a straight-talking leader into a conflict-avoidance culture, and why did she accept?

Shares of Conseco did leap in 2000 when Gary C. Wendt, former head of GE Capital, became its new chief. However, he was unable to continue the company turnaround, and two years later he relinquished the chief executive slot. Conseco soon filed for bankruptcy protection. "GE people are good at getting structure, system, and strategy right, but they don't always understand the soft issues like culture," said Boris Groysberg, an assistant professor at the Harvard Business School, who recently studied twenty star GE managers who went on to run other companies.

If we could do an in-depth survey of every short-term CEO for the last dozen years, we would probably find a large number

A MIDWEST COMPANY
CASE STUDY

Two years ago I was invited to give the keynote address at a leadership conference of top management in a specific business sector. In the audience was a CEO of a Midwest company with offices in nine locations around the state. He invited me to lunch after my presentation and asked if I could help him with his company.

He had just been installed as the new chief executive and was excited about the vision he had to move the company forward. The company was an established organization with a good track record and good reputation in all nine locations. After several meetings with him, his executive staff, and with key individuals in the company, we agreed on the major issues that needed addressing that were within my expertise.

The problems

■ The company had a stodgy, risk-averse comfort zone, *"that is how we have always done it"* attitude.

■ It was stuck in a rut of the 1990s.

■ It was losing market share and its competitive edge.

■ It was not attracting new talent or generating innovative ideas, processes, and services.

The strategy

Here is the strategy we used to move the company into a learning/competence mode, while increasing esprit de corps with an innovative attitude.

■ We immediately instigated some serious training in people skills such as risk taking, decision making, conflict resolution, negotiation, communication skills of both listening and speaking, customer service, and effective change.

■ We brought in outside industry experts to lay the groundwork to jump-start the process of building new products and services that would give the firm a twenty-first-century competitive edge.

■ Simultaneously, we went after the creativity and innovation issues with seminars, games, and nonthreatening team challenges.

■ Then we took it to the personal level and gave everyone the opportunity to learn something fun, new, interesting, or different. We asked everyone to try something they had always wanted to try. Do things that had nothing to do with work, but were of a personal interest.

Results

Igniting the competence of the company was a two-year, multilevel project. None of the strategies worked overnight. The CEO was very aware that to make a serious culture change without disrupting the entire organization and having a mass exodus of staff, he and the executive team would need to get behind all four steps in the plan. Everyone from executives to the newest employees went on a learning/competence spree.

Here are two of the most fun stories about personal growth and learning that occurred:

One woman always wanted to learn to tap-dance. But she was twenty pounds overweight and felt that she didn't have the energy to take on such a strenuous task. After a little encouragement, she decided to give it a try. In six months she lost so much weight, she went down two dress sizes and had so much fun tapping her way through two evenings a week, she and her husband are now taking ballroom dancing.

A man said that as a teenager he had always wanted to build exotic model cars but just never got around to it. Now that his children were in college, he thought he would get into the spirit of the learning challenge and look into it.

I have a friend in Paris, France, who is the same age and has a collection of exotic model cars that he has built, many of which are not available in this country. I asked both men if they would be interested in communicating with each other. To make a long story short, they began with e-mail and are now planning on reciprocal visits to each other's homes.

There were some people who refused to take part, afraid to take a risk, deriding the idea of any training or learning. That will always happen, so we just ignored them and focused on those who were enthusiastic about the programs. The peer pressure was interesting to watch as some of the resistant folks got on board.

At the end of the first year, they began to see distinguishable changes in the culture. During the two years the firm did increase market share, and innovation became welcomed, not feared. That is not to say it was all easygoing; it was not. There were potholes, resistance, and the status quo to overcome.

The company now has a full training department using all the tools possible to continue the pattern of learning. It rewards and recognizes those who are at the forefront of new competence.

Early on, the CEO was able to move into other vital issues that will ensure the success of the company and his employees.

who were unable at best, and incompetent at worst, to carry out their duties at the new company. Their capabilities just weren't transferable. For a variety of reasons they may not have thought they needed to question their own competence. Or, if they did, they may have been under such pressure to perform quickly that there was little, if any, time to build new competencies.

When you as A New Breed Leader have a persistent desire and willingness to hone your skills, talents, and abilities, you will rarely fall into those two kinds of traps.

To earn the respect of all your stakeholders, it takes a deep commitment to learn all you can, in as short a time as you can, in order to be the best leader you can.

The Competence Puzzle Piece

The leadership competence puzzle piece has four core traits: *intellectual*, *emotional*, *strategic*, and *instinctive*. You can't take away one of the pieces without affecting the whole. Each is inevitably linked to the other.

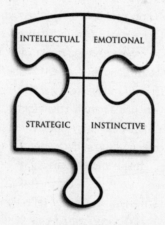

Intellectual Competence

Permanent success cannot be achieved except by incessant intellectual labor, always inspired by the ideal.
—SARAH BERNHARDT, actress

You'll never have enough time to learn everything you need. So you need to surround yourself with the brightest and the best

MOO

What do you get when you combine two different competencies in one company? Add to that a passion for a purpose and a vision to change the way the world views organic food. Stir in a unique yogurt culture and recipe—and you get Stonyfield Farm, the world's largest manufacturer of organic yogurt.

The combined expertise of Samuel Kaymen and Gary Hirshberg has enabled this firm to fly right by its biggest competitor, and by 2007, sales exceed $300 million. That's a long way from its start twenty-three years earlier when Kaymen milked his seven cows and produced the first batches of yogurt in a little room off the barn.

Gary Hirshberg is now president (and as he says, "CE-Yo") of Stonyfield. "Samuel and I were ideal partners because we had a real healthy respect for what each other knew and didn't know. He was the yogurt guy. He created the culture and the recipe. I had the financing, accounting, people-management, and marketing skills."

Kaymen adds, "Gary had a natural talent for business, and we were on the same page of values." They both attribute their success to the fact that they couldn't just produce yogurt. They had to create a unique company, one that blended focus on business with a focus on the environment.

Stonyfield Farm's mission is a direct reflection of Kaymen's and Hirshberg's personal belief systems: *to educate consumers and producers about the value of protecting the environment and to serve as a model that environmentally and socially responsible business can also be profitable.*

colleagues, plus ramp up your own learning to attain the highest level of intellectual competence.

Intellectual competence includes recognizing other people's abilities and skills as well as questioning your assumptions about yourself and the current situation. In fact, erroneous assumptions and invalid expectations are at the root of most bad decisions, difficult relationships, or poorly functioning groups. Checking your assumptions tells you where you are and where you should be going. This checking isn't always easy because our assumptions are usually familiar and comfortable. However, if you are going to tap your creativity and advance your competence, you need to be willing to let go of outdated assumptions.

> Evaluate your assumptions, and let go of outdated ones.

Play the "what-if" game when facing a challenge. Begin by listing your assumptions about the situation. Then ask yourself: What if this happened? What if I did this instead? How would it work if I did this first and then this?

Next, make a statement you believe to be true about each of the following areas of your leadership competence:

My credentials . . .

My vision . . .

My job description . . .

My areas of responsibility . . .

My decision-making skills . . .

My ability to communicate . . .

My priority management . . .

My ability to deal with conflict . . .

My ability to motivate others . . .

Then test the validity of the above statements, your assumptions, by playing devil's advocate.

Study each of your assumption statements and ask yourself:

- To what degree is my statement true or not true?

- What evidence do I have that I am operating at my highest level?

- Is there something I am overlooking?

- What am I taking for granted?

- What actions do I need to take?

- What are my expectations for the future?

Some of your answers will identify areas in which you need to reevaluate your assumptions. Too many leaders spend their time fighting skirmishes because they don't take the time to clarify the present and prepare for the future.

The next step requires you to take a risk and put your courage to work: Ask a trusted colleague to evaluate your statements. You'll probably have to endure some criticism. It's never pleasant to hear that you are not as effective as you imagine. On the other hand, your colleague may give you a better evaluation than you gave yourself.

Examining your assumptions helps you avoid being trapped in a bog of false concepts about yourself and sheds light on how your followers view your leadership. Don't be afraid that your assumptions will not stand up to scrutiny. If they don't, you're strong enough to reframe them or replace them with better ones.

Emotional Competence

No guts, no glory. It's my motto. I will have
it engraved on my tombstone.

—BETTE DAVIS, actress

The second component of the competence puzzle piece is emotional competence. It's the most difficult of the four competencies. While mental prowess—good old brainpower—is critical, the highest level of leadership won't be reached without emotional capability. It takes personal courage—"guts," as Bette Davis said—to tackle this capability because it forces us to turn inward and learn about ourselves. Work done in recent years by Daniel Goleman, author of *Emotional Intelligence*, and other behavioral researchers make persuasive arguments that emotional maturity is crucial in terms of how well we do in our own life and in leading others.

The emotional intelligence of a highly competent leader reflects, as Goleman outlines, inner competencies that enable you to manage yourself. These inner competencies include self-awareness, personal motivation, self-discipline, empathy, and essential social skills such as conflict management, mastering influence, and team building.

The emotional self-confidence of a legendary sports leader was revealed in the final seconds of an especially tense Boston Celtics game. The coach called a time-out and began to quickly diagram a play, only to have star forward Larry Bird say, "Get the ball to me and get everyone out of my way."

The coach shot back, "I'm the coach, and *I'll* call the plays."

Then the coach turned to the other players, saying, "Get the ball to Larry and get out of his way." That's the kind of influence you're seeking. You want to become known as a "can-do" person with the emotional competence to take charge in critical times. When you speak, people listen, regardless of your title or position.

When a highly intelligent but emotionally immature person is placed in leadership positions, disaster can result. They are often unable to build teams or partnerships or even handle the ups and downs of daily business and life. Such "leaders" often abuse their power and destroy the cohesion of an organization by, for example, having unreal expectations of others even though they can't meet their own high expectations. They often punish risk-taking because they're afraid to make a mistake themselves. Frequently using their position to fill their emotional voids, they often discount competent followers.

EMOTIONAL MATURITY

Part of being emotionally intelligent is being able to do things such as identify and label your feelings, be empathetic, delay gratification, and read and interpret (often unspoken) social clues.

Maturity Gap

INTELLECTUAL RESPONSE

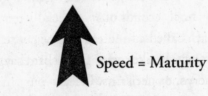

Speed = Maturity

EMOTIONAL REACTION

This is emotional maturity. When these emotional skills are well developed and partnered with intellectual competence, it's an unbeatable duo for good leadership.

Maturity is emotion tempered by intellect. We have an emotional reaction to almost everything. The most effective leaders can temper their emotions and use their intellectual response system. The shorter the time between the emotional reaction and the intellectual response, the more emotionally mature the individual is. A leader must have emotional maturity in order to effectively handle conflict. When you are dealing with conflict, you are usually dealing with emotions first. When you approach upset people, be aware they're probably responding emotionally and you may need to give them time to get to their own intellectual responses. As the leader, you must control your emotions and manage the emotions of your followers.

COMPETENT COLLEAGUES

Another sign of emotional intelligence is to have the self-confidence and inner strength to surround yourself with the best people available, not just those who most resemble you or agree with you. It's natural, of course, to be attracted to those who are like you. That's how friendships and relationships are built. But if you only consult with like-minded colleagues, you run the risk of cutting off vital information and expertise. As a leader, you want to avoid cronyism, which almost always produces bad results. The best way to do that is to find and retain the best and brightest people you can attract. It takes courage to hear things that challenge your beliefs, ideas, or decisions. Check your current ability with the following:

- Where can I find "the best and brightest" to help me?

- Am I willing to let others' knowledge and experience help me make the best decisions possible?

- Do I read and study great leaders from the past, gleaning ways to inspire and guide others into the future?

- Have I analyzed and discussed why so many leaders don't learn from past experiences?

- Am I open to all ideas no matter how they sound at first?

These are tough questions, and no one can answer them for you. By asking them, you find a more authentic view of yourself and your leadership capacity. The answers give you some surprising insights to make a quantum leap into being an emotionally competent leader.

It is exciting and highly contagious when followers know that you, their leader, have the self-esteem to embrace competent counselors, advisers, and guides to move the entire organization in a positive direction.

CRITICAL THINKING QUESTIONS

Being skillful at asking critical questions adds a significant element to your competence. Having all the answers is far less important than asking penetrating questions. But as you do find the answers, you'll greatly enhance your value and your ability to influence others, because of the quality of the inquiries. It is vital to ask yourself: *Do I really care about examining my capabili-*

ties? *What is my personal definition of competence? What am I doing to improve both personally and as a leader?*

The emotionally competent leader has the courage to ask "why" in order to challenge tradition, to seek new and innovative ideas, to set the example of welcoming change and to think in a tactical fashion, which leads us to the third part of our puzzle.

Strategic Competence

Each age is a dream that's dying. And one that's coming to birth.
—W. B. YEATS

Strategic intelligence is the proactive way in which people think about and create the future for themselves and their followers. It's both a daily and a long-term way of thinking. It always involves change for you personally and the organization as a whole.

While a good manager can maintain direction, you as a leader must be able to *change* direction by doing three things: looking at what has happened in your past experience, having a plan for today, and constantly searching for future opportunities to improve your organization.

"No Monday morning quarterbacking" is a common expression. But you can bet every professional sports team plays and replays past games to find ways to improve. When they stop questioning, they lose their edge. We can see businesses that are losing their competitiveness because of a lack of introspection.

Indra Nooyi has several rules to which she attributes her remarkable success as CEO of PepsiCo. Her strategic competence has at its core her rule of "never stop learning regardless of one's age, and such learning should not be restricted to academic knowledge, but be supplemented with 'street smarts' and being aware of matters and issues in the real world. Keep that natural curiosity." She goes on "market tours" and walks around grocery stores to understand the competition. She adds, "Keep an open mind. It is a multicultural world out there and we all have to interact with people who are different . . . success comes with reaching out and integrating with the community . . . and giving back to the communities and neighborhoods, more than what you took out of them."

BRINGING OTHERS ON BOARD WITH YOUR GAME PLAN

All talk about strategies is moot unless you can nudge your superiors and subordinates along the road to innovation.

Colin Powell wrote: "You have achieved excellence as a leader when people will follow you everywhere, if only out of curiosity." Are you able to bring your team along for the ride? Will your people follow you, even just out of curiosity?

> People change when they either feel the heat or see the light!

One of the most dangerous elements an organization faces is members stuck in their comfort zones. They're reluctant to move forward with new ideas. They certainly won't come up with any ideas of their own. And without the ability to evolve or improve, the organization will lose relevance and eventually die.

As the old story goes, one frog is put into a pot of hot water and immediately jumps out. A second frog is placed in a pot with cool water and is quite comfortable. Gradually the water is heated and the frog adapts as the temperature rises. Regardless of how hot the water becomes, the frog never becomes uncomfortable enough to jump out of the pan. In fact, the frog stays there and becomes dinner.

So another important question to ask is: "Am I as leader—are we as an organization—in a comfort zone? Am I—are we—missing opportunities and new realities?"

If you feel boxed in by less strategic thinkers at any level of your organization, try to learn what's keeping them in their comfort zones. Are you, or your organization, a contributing factor? If so, how and why? Have freethinking, creativity, and risk taking been penalized? If so, see what you can do to change that. How can you improve a risk-averse culture and support strategic thinking? Here are three ideas:

- Be a good listener who spurs imaginative thinking, pull out and piece together ideas from followers at all levels, and then have the courage to take those ideas "upstairs." Be sure to give credit to those who contributed.

- Praise against-the-grain thinking. Seek to become known as someone who doesn't fear boldness. Be a leader who will sometimes ignore the organization's rule book for the sake of a greater good, all the while praising the new thinking.

- Expect and accept errors. Then be fully committed to learning from them. Don't dwell on mistakes. Constantly test your courage by keeping your eye on future opportunities.

Play the "if the world were perfect" game to improve an environment of creative-strategic thinking:

1. If we didn't care what it cost, how would we solve this problem?

2. If we were starting from scratch, how would we handle this?

3. If we didn't need anyone's authorization, what would we do?

4. If we didn't care what anyone else thought, how would we act?

5. If this were a perfect world, what would our next step be?

6. If we'd be respected no matter what we proposed, what would we propose?

When you become a champion of bold ideas, whether yours or others', you become a magnet that attracts followers. Previously reticent colleagues will shower you not only with more ideas but also with loyalty that will be an enduring testament to your leadership.

STRATEGIC COMPETENCE QUIZ

- What methods do I use to remove barriers of resistance so I can create new visions and objectives?

- How well do I describe results before selecting the ways and means to get to the new objectives?

- What methods do I use to define the gaps in our plans and goals?

- What are the high payoff results in this new model?

- What am I doing to identify the "what and how" to move us from our present model to a future one?

- How does our new model add value to our organization?

- What permanent, pervasive, and profound shifts will influence our future?

- What plans and actions do I have prepared for these changes?

- How will I measure our success along the way to the ultimate goals?

- Have I very clearly defined what our goals are?

- What steps do I have prepared to adjust course along the way?

This quiz is one that you can return to often to be sure you are on track in the tactical areas of your competence.

The strategically competent leader knows that seeing things others can't see is not only a quality of leadership, it's a responsibility. It means being part pragmatist and part mystic. This talent—as much an attitude as an aptitude—is not as rare as you might think. Reinhold Niebuhr said, "Nothing worth doing is completed in our lifetime." But A New Breed Leader knows it *must* begin in our lifetime. We must have high expectations, projecting others and ourselves into a positive future scenario.

Instinctive Competence

Good instincts usually tell you what to do long
before your head has figured it out.

–MICHAEL BURKE, organizational behavioralist

Instinctive competence is the most mysterious ingredient of the puzzle pieces. How do you explain or define this elusive power? It's a gut feeling, an impulse, that little voice inside your head that tells you when it is time to "GO!"

I once asked participants in a seminar to give the simplest example they could of leadership instinct. One gave a perfect answer: "When the building is on fire, don't call a meeting to see who will leave first, never mind trying to figure out what started the fire or how much damage it'll cause—just get everyone out right now!"

A good sense of gut instinct almost always grows out of a deep and thorough knowledge of the subject. And one important way we gain knowledge is by making mistakes.

Growing and learning from your mistakes is a building block of instincts. The more experience you have, the more mistakes you make, the more success you have. In the process of this learning cycle, you make judgments, some good and some bad. Either way, you increase your awareness of what works, what doesn't, and why. Every decision is a judgment—a choice between alternatives. One of the payoffs is that each decision helps to develop good judgment and your gut reaction.

As your leadership instincts increase and you become more confident in them, you will find that when you go against those gut reactions, you'll usually be wrong. Instead, try to read them and honor them as signposts. But it takes courage to "go with your gut" because people and exterior forces can present compelling reasons not to listen to your inner voice.

You can't be overly strategic in your thinking and planning or try to learn everything there is to know about a subject. You can't afford the "paralysis of analysis." Sometimes you will be compelled to act solely on instinct. Even though the other elements of competence are critical, your instinct must be sharpened to a razor's edge.

HEALING INSTINCTS AT THE PERFECT TIME

Cathy Keating was born and raised in Tulsa, Oklahoma. She graduated from the University of Oklahoma with a B.S. in education and a minor in special education. Although they had both lived in Tulsa, she did not meet her future husband, Frank, until after she had graduated from the university. They met on a blind date and were married seven months later.

> Cultivate and trust your instincts . . . then follow them!

You may recognize them by their formal positions: Governor Frank Keating and First Lady Cathy Keating, of Oklahoma, 1994–2003, during the time of the Oklahoma City bombing.

I've had the pleasure of knowing Frank and Cathy since the late 1980s. I recently spoke with them about being A New Breed Leader. You will hear from both of them again in other chapters. Here is part of the conversation between Cathy and me about instincts and what a leader must do in a time of crisis.

Being a leader is about seizing the moment and then rising to the occasion. Sometimes in life, your opportunity to make a difference is unplanned. When Frank was elected governor, I inherited the wonderful job of First Lady. It doesn't come with a job description, you make your own, and then you decide your level of involvement.

My philosophy in life has always been not to let any grass grow under my feet. Make a difference. Leave a legacy. I saw this as one of life's opportunities to really make a difference in the lives of others where government can't or shouldn't be involved and where the private sector should and would love to be involved. So the first lesson I learned was to seize every opportunity to lead as it presents itself.

The memorial service for the victims of the bombing of the Federal Building in Oklahoma City was the first attempt to do that.

I said to Cathy, "When the bombing occurred, I remember watching television, and the first face I saw on the screen was yours. I knew Frank was doing what a governor needed to do in a horrific instance like that, and there you were. How did you decide what to say on camera and what was your philosophy about your message?"

Truthfully, I just followed my heart. I knew it was important to be honest about the unbelievable devastation, not to sugarcoat anything but to share the experience because it wasn't something that just happened to us. It was a loss for America, and people all over the world were sharing our emotions, our outrage. We were grieving and the world grieved with us. Even though Frank and I both had determined that we would do everything in our power to be strong in public, make no mistake about it, we were grieving deeply, and I think that came across. Man's inhumanity to man was staggering when the bomb went off and we saw the devastation. But we never lost hope. We never lost our faith in people.

Help came in droves and we wanted the rest of the world to know about it and share the experience. There was such an unending generosity of spirit, love, and countless sacrifices of the rescue workers, volunteers, and the whole community came together instantly. Businesses were opening up their pocketbooks and saying, "What do you need, how much do you need," not wanting anything in return, other than to help everyone get off our knees and back on our feet.

The day of the bombing people started calling me to ask how they might help. Since Frank had only been in office three-plus months, I had not yet put my "First Lady systems" into place. With the help of a dear friend, I determined that my first role was to help not only Oklahomans but Americans heal. What better way to begin than with a prayer . . . or a memorial . . . service, a vigil, if you will.

At nine-thirty that first night, I called and asked five of my new Oklahoma City friends to come over to the Governor's Mansion to begin the planning process. I felt that it was important to include the Reverend Billy Graham, as he had the greatest moral authority to address why this wrong had happened, and of course President and Mrs. Clinton and all the cabinet officers who had offices in the Federal Building.

Also, sometimes leadership just seems to spring into action. Brenda Edgar, who was then the First Lady of Illinois, called me and said, "Cathy, I'd like to send teddy bears. I have a program where we give teddy bears to abused children. We partner with Marshall Field's and I'd like to send teddy bears to the families of children who were killed in the bombing." I said, "Brenda, it's really nice of you to offer to do that, but I don't think we can give teddy bears to just the children of the families who lost little children because there are lots of children who have lost parents and many parents who have lost grown children. And if we're going to do it for one, I really think we need to do it for all." She said, "Well, how many people do you think we're talking about?"

Now this had not even been twenty-four hours at this point and I had no idea. I said, "We just don't have a clue." "Give me a guesstimate," she said. I told her, "Two hundred and fifty people have been affected." Her immediate answer was, "Okay. It's a done deal." I asked, "How quickly can you get them here?" She said, "I'll get them to you as quickly as possible." On Saturday, the day before the memorial service, we determined that we actually needed 650 bears. I called her back and asked her if she could get them, and she said, "It's Saturday. Marshall Field's is closed." I said, "Well, if you can get them to open, I'll find a plane to get them here." Herb Kelleher, CEO of Southwest Airlines, was kind enough to send one of his planes to pick up the bears.

Federal Express trucks drove up with boxes and boxes and boxes, a garage full of teddy bears. I decided that we were going to give the bears out at the memorial service, to every family who had lost loved ones, who were missing loved ones, or whose loved ones had been injured. Brenda, Marshall

Field's, and Southwest Airlines took the lead and we were able to hand them out that morning.

At the memorial service on Sunday, April twenty-third, they all came, Billy Graham, President and Mrs. Clinton, and the cabinet members who were affected.

As people entered, we gave a teddy bear as well as a yellow rose. Several Oklahoma City florists had organized a call for help, and florists from all over America responded by sending the beautiful yellow roses.

During the prayer service, one of the photographers snapped a picture of Dan McKinney, whose wife was killed in the bombing. He had his arms crossed over his chest hugging a teddy bear, his head was back, and he was sobbing. That picture popped up on the front page of newspapers all over the country and in magazines. (It later won a Pulitzer Prize.) Teddy bears began appearing at the fence surrounding the bombing site.

I told Cathy how much I admired her strong leadership instincts and responses to the tragedy. Her reply: Well, it was the right thing to do. I can't be absolutely certain, but I believe that on that day a teddy bear became an international symbol of hope. They appeared again after the shooting in the schoolyard in Scotland and again after the Columbine school shooting. Now it seems that when there is some sort of major tragedy, teddy bears appear because Brenda Edgar had the instincts of a leader and she picked up the telephone and offered a way to help. So leadership is sometimes unplanned and it continues to live on and on long after the deed is done.

The Hunt for Red October

One of the best examples of superior leadership "gut" instinct is in the film *The Hunt for Red October*, based on the bestselling novel by Tom Clancy.

Red October, the Soviet Union's newest secret weapon, is a stealth submarine as big as a World War II aircraft carrier with enough atomic weapons on board to destroy most of the major cities on the eastern U.S. seaboard. It is commanded by Russia's most experienced submarine captain, steely-eyed Marko Ramius (Sean Connery).

Ramius has stolen the sub and is going to defect to America and take the sub with him. Every ship in the Russian fleet sets out to find and destroy *Red October* before it can get into the hands of the Americans. Meanwhile, the United States thinks Ramius is coming to launch the missiles. CIA analyst Jack Ryan (Alec Baldwin), who has made a personal study of Ramius and his career, convinces the military that Ramius is going to defect, not attack. Ryan is sent out to the U.S. sub that has located *Red October*. They are in hot pursuit.

Ramius orders the navigator to head for Thor's Twins, deep-water canyons near Iceland, where they may be able to hide. As they enter the underwater canyons, they're navigating blind, using speed and time and Ramius's instincts to guide them. A Soviet torpedo is right on their tail and, in front of them is a huge underwater mountain, the Neptune Massif. Ramius must reach into his gut and use his instinct as to exactly when to turn past the massif to avoid both it and the torpedo.

The navigator is counting the seconds to turn. You see the extreme tension on the crew's faces and hear the countdown.

"Thirty seconds and counting," says the navigator. "Three, two, one, turn, Captain!" The camera stays on Ramius's face as we see his lips moving, counting. "Captain, the turn?" Ramius ignores the navigator and goes deep into his intuition and begins his own silent count. His lips move. "Ten, nine, eight, seven, six, five, four, three, two . . ." Ramius's instinct kicks in, his steady voice orders, "Right full rudder, reverse starboard engines." The crewmen are certain they're all going to die. The huge ship shudders and slips past the massif with only inches to spare. The torpedo slams into the massif. Ramius calmly gives the next order.

As we watched Ryan through the movie, it is clear that he is an expert on Ramius. However, he underestimated Ramius's deep instincts that gave him the edge over the Americans and the Soviets.

BUILDING INSTINCT

Intuition is not contrary to reason, but outside the province of reason.

—CARL JUNG, psychologist

As a leader, you can increase the effectiveness of your instincts by being open to, and searching out, new experiences. If you accept new challenges and take new risks, you learn from both success and failure. But when we are successful, we don't normally say, "Wow, that was great. Now let's see what I did well to achieve this success." We usually just move on.

In contrast, we seem to learn more from failures. If we have the emotional maturity to step back from a failure and examine our thoughts and processes, we learn volumes about ourselves, our organizations, and what we can do better next time. Intelligence, combined with a good dose of emotional maturity and strategic competence, is the petri dish in which instincts can grow and multiply.

In author Rex Stout's detective novels, supersleuth Nero Wolfe tells Archie Goodwin, his sidekick and partner in crime solving, "Use your judgment [intuition] tempered by experience." That's instinct!

As you take the time and effort to build the other three competencies, your intuition will develop. When the opportunity arises, you can then use your instinct guided by intuition to make wise decisions and act with immediacy.

Mentors and Coaches for Competence

Very early in my career I met and had the privilege of having Bill Weise, vice chairman of Motorola, as my business mentor/coach. We agreed that he would never hold back or soften his opinions. He would give it to me straight, and my job was to listen to his views, grow where I needed, and question him where I felt I should. For fifteen years I had access to his superb business acumen. As I developed new material, he would review it for its real-world applications. He played devil's advocate and questioned my logic, assumptions, and desired outcomes. An invaluable source of expertise and insights, he made one of the most important contributions to my growth and my understanding of corporate America. He was one of the twentieth century's most significant strategic leaders, both in the United States and globally.

Do you have a strategic competence coach or mentor? Whom

do you know who could give your leadership development the kind of wisdom and expertise that Bill Weise shared with me?

It is intriguing to ask specific questions of highly successful leaders. They have strong and diverse opinions.

Dr. Donna Shalala had a different approach to mentors and how they helped her succeed. I asked her how she saw her rise to power in relation to mentors. She said, "The real insight into my career is that I always overreached. I was never in a job in which the consensus was that I was qualified. I always had to maneuver within each of those positions to learn about the job, to find people that would help me be successful." I asked specifically if she had mentors. "Not particularly," she replied, "but I counted on many people. I observed very talented people throughout my career, but I would not describe myself as having a mentor in the traditional sense of a mentor." "But do you think developing leaders should find mentors?" I asked. "Yes," she said. "However, being a mentor is interesting; either it fits or it doesn't fit. I help lots of people, but it doesn't necessarily mean I'm there for every nuance of a career."

I agree with her. However, when it does fit, there are ways you can manage the mentor-protégé relationship that will be of great benefit to you and respect the time and position of your mentor.

Here are some tips on making the most of the mentor-protégé relationship:

- Two kinds of mentor relationships exist—formal and informal. An informal relationship can be as powerful as a formal one. A casual get-together in the hall, on the Internet, or by telephone can work very well. However, if you and your mentor would like to have a more formal arrangement, don't hesitate.

- Be very careful of your mentor's time. The quickest way to alienate a mentor is to seek repeated information and unimportant details. On the other hand, don't be afraid to ask what you may think is a dumb question. There are no dumb questions, only uninformed, unprepared people. If you have already covered the issue but you still have questions or need further clarification and help, then certainly contact your mentor.

- Take careful notes so you don't have to go back for repeated information. This will help you prepare intelligent, meaningful questions and retain the jewels of wisdom the mentor will share.

- If you ask the advice of a mentor, take it! Protégés, in their enthusiasm, often ask advice and then argue the point. Don't reinvent the wheel.

- Report back on the results or actions taken. Your mentor may see that you need a slight adjustment or correction. Small action-plan refinements can be extremely helpful. If you are proceeding correctly and all is well, you need to know that also. Reporting to your mentor will give you this knowledge.

- Finally, once you have had a mentor or coach, pass on the legacy—becoming one yourself is a wonderful and rewarding endeavor.

The power of OPE (Other People's Experience) is the basis of the mentor-protégé relationship. None of us succeeds alone, and most who are successful in life and/or business will be proud to share their knowledge and experience. If you find someone who can act as your mentor or coach, it will be a wonderful process for both of you. He or she will be a source of inspiration and information.

My Mentor and Action Plan

One of the most powerful traits great leaders have in common is *action*. And that's the next step for your personal leadership journey—taking action to maximize all your leadership potential.

To grow in this area, take a good look at how your followers are acting and what they are doing. Are they working well as a team? Do they seem to have a common goal? Have you empowered them to take risks and make decisions? The answers to these questions will tell you whether your vision is clear and whether your competencies bring people together. Having a clear, strong, value-based mission is the secret of building charisma and long-range leadership.

Turn the page for an action plan to help you make the best and most respectful use of a coach or mentor.

MY ACTION PLAN FOR: QUALITY #1
COMPETENCE MATTERS — *BUILDING PURPOSE/VISION*

People I will ask to act as my mentor or coach:

| | *Name* | *Email Address* | *Telephone Number* |

1. _____

2. _____

3. _____

The three most important questions I will ask about the quality of Competence:

1. _____

2. _____

3. _____

What leadership situations or experiences would I like to discuss with my mentor, in order to gain insights into my role as a leader using this quality?

_____

_____

_____

MY LEADERSHIP
CHALLENGE 1:
Competence

My three most critical leadership challenge questions for this quality are:

Do I focus on the competence I need to build my vision each morning to help keep me on track? _____

Do I continually clarify both my competence and my vision? _____

Is my vision setting a positive example for others? _____

Here are the three steps I will take to clarify and strengthen my leadership readiness and effectiveness in the arena of Competence:

1. _____

2. _____

3. _____

Today's Date: _____

© 2009 Sheila Murray Bethel, PhD.

If you would like a free copy of this Action Plan simply go to my website, www.anewbreedofleader.com, and click on the "Resources" tab. There will be an Action Plan for all eight New Breed Leader qualities.

Humility Strengthens Purpose

When you recognize that competence begets competence and that knowledge shared is knowledge multiplied, you're saying, in effect, to your followers, "We can learn and grow together." You build a sense of connectedness and a community of growth.

While your competence develops and your purpose and vision emerge, a truly competent leader also has the powerful quality of humility. "Knowledge is proud that he has learn'd so much. Wisdom is humble that he knows no more," wrote poet and hymn writer William Cowper.

When we study the Enlightener leaders of the last century—Martin Luther King Jr., Moshe Dayan, Golda Meir, Nelson Mandela, Mahatma Gandhi, the Dalai Lama, and Mother Teresa—it is clear that, as strong, committed, and decisive as they were, they also had an enormous degree of humility that drew followers to them, changed the world, and set an example for leaders everywhere to follow.

No matter where your competence takes you, no matter what your leadership accomplishes, it's exciting to know that you are in the process of "becoming." You are a constantly changing composite of the things you say, the books you read, the thoughts you think, the company you keep, and the dreams you dream. Openness, humility, accountability, language, values, perspective, and the wise use of power are each ingredients of a truly competent New Breed Leader.

CHAPTER TWO

Accountability Matters

FOSTERING TRUST

Am I my brother's keeper?

—GENESIS 4:9

OCTOBER 2, 1982. All the evening news programs carried the shocking story. Seven people in Chicago had died from taking cyanide-tainted Tylenol capsules. It was a catastrophe. But the response from Tylenol's maker, Johnson & Johnson, was swift, responsible, and courageous.

James C. Burke, J & J's CEO, stood before the television cameras. His comforting words told a frightened nation there'd been a terrible tragedy of individual terrorism and that he, as CEO, was acting immediately. He asked everyone not to take any Extra Strength Tylenol capsules until further notice. Even though there might not be a drop of cyanide in any capsules consumers had, Burke urged that all Tylenol pills be destroyed. Each household was asked to go to its medicine cabinet and return for exchange or credit all its capsules. Further, every retail store in the nation was to immediately return any capsules from its shelves and stock.

That was no small task: More than 22 million bottles of Tylenol were believed to be in the hands of consumers or on pharmacy shelves. At retail prices, that was almost $800 million worth of the drug. But there was no buck passing, denial, or any hint of lack of care for any of J & J's customers. The recall cost the firm tens of millions of dollars.

No one who saw the announcement that evening would ever doubt Burke's sincerity and concern. He and J & J went beyond just doing what was contractually required or what was needed to meet legal guidelines; they took a moral and ethical stand that set the gold standard of corporate accountability for decades to come. It was James Burke's "crucible" leadership test, and he passed with flying colors.

The Power of Accountability

Very little in the realm of leadership is more important than the trust that accountability generates. Leading is primarily about the relationship between the leader and the led, and trust is at its core. It's the contract you make with your followers by holding yourself to account and then following up with strong ethical actions. Your accountability includes the faith others have in your reliability. You are judged on a daily basis by your example and every decision you make is part of your actions.

You earn trust when you . . .

. . . *look* people straight in the eye and say, "You have my word, count on me." That statement of honor puts your reputation on the line.

. . . *set* high standards and then live up to them. That gives you the authority to lead.

. . . *clearly* communicate that you expect followers to do the same. That's a steel fiber woven through the fabric of your organization.

. . . *are* trustworthy so your followers will follow you almost anywhere. That means they'll stretch beyond their comfort zones and be more open to new ideas.

. . . *consistently* prove that you can be trusted.

The trust that J & J built with its customers was shown by the quick rebound of the Tylenol brand. Within fifteen months, it recovered 90 percent of its market share. In addition to saving lives and creating the tamperproof bottles common today, J & J's accountability greatly enhanced its reputation.

Accountability is about doing what's right. It's the backbone of any successful organization and continually speaks to the integrity and ethics of your organization and you as a leader.

Leading by Example

The time is always right to do what is right.

—MARTIN LUTHER KING JR.

Leaders live under a microscope. Nothing you say or do escapes the scrutiny and examination of your followers. That's one of the most important tenets of leadership: *Followers mirror the example set for them.* Whether it's accountability, or any of the other seven qualities, be sure to continually ask yourself:

- "What example am I setting?"

- "What message am I sending?"

- "Am I walking my talk? Do my actions match my words?"

- "What environment am I creating?"

- "If my followers are not being held accountable, do I have the courage to look in the mirror and hold myself accountable first?"

- "Have I remembered today that as a leader I am never *not* modeling?"

Whether you're leading at home, in the community, or at work, even one example of accountability can set others on the road to a deeper commitment, no matter what the cause.

> I lead first by example. Everything I say or do sets a tone, sends a message, and teaches people what to do or what not to do.

Fostering Trust

To build a bond of mutual trust with your followers, remember that it's an everyday effort built person by person, moment by moment, and issue by issue.

> Trust is built person by person, moment by moment, issue by issue.

For example, Ryan Cooper, a

trainer and coach from Halifax, Canada, has written in his blog this clear and simple description of how trust benefits a team:

> Trust is a wonderful thing. When the team has a high level of trust, they don't waste time with political maneuvering. They don't hold back suggestions that can help the team improve. Team members aren't afraid to ask for help and are willing to help each other. They spend time collaborating to create solutions rather than arguing over details. When a team has a high level of trust, goals of individuals are aligned with goals of the team. There are no distractions. Productivity can soar. When a team doesn't have trust, it's not a team at all. It's a group of individuals each with separate and often conflicting goals. This wastes time and reduces productivity.

Ryan is right, and I'd add that people can only trust each other when they're not worried about whether someone is going to try to shift blame to them and whether they, in turn, can pass it on to someone else. A culture of blame destroys people, teamwork, creative thinking, and the willingness to try new ideas. Blaming undermines morale, positive actions, and attitudes while sending a message that there's low self-esteem in the leadership ranks.

Three important questions to ask in order to stay on top of this destructive force are:

- Do I allow the blame game in our organization?

- Are we losing productivity or profits from lack of accountability?

- If either of these is true, what can I do immediately to begin reversing them?

AN EXAMPLE OF TRUST, BALANCE, AND PERSPECTIVE

When Gerald Grinstein moved from Seattle to Atlanta in 2005, he was coming out of retirement to take on the monumental task of piloting Delta Airlines through bankruptcy. He was well aware of the critical problems the airline faced because he'd been a director since 1987. A bloated firm, it was low on cash, faced soaring costs, and had inefficient planes and routes. Its pilots were threatening a strike, and Wall Street was predicting doom as months, or even years, of litigation and infighting loomed.

Grinstein and his management team took full responsibility and devised a very human approach to getting through the crisis. They committed to respond to issues within days, not months. When dealing with creditors, their chief outside attorney Marshall Huebner said, "We want anybody with an issue to call. Don't file papers; don't launch missiles, just call." It was hard for many people to accept such a responsible and open attitude. But this approach achieved results with a speed rarely seen before in a corporate bankruptcy.

In addition, Grinstein did the unthinkable: He cut his own CEO salary by 25 percent to $338,000 a year and gave up millions in potential bonuses. "There has to be restraint on the part of management," Grinstein said. "Everybody has made sacrifices, and incentives for management can't sound excessive."

(By contrast, when United emerged from its three-year, contentious bankruptcy in 2006, CEO Glenn Tilton's $39.7 million compensation package was greater than the firm's entire profit that year. The same year Northwest Airlines management disclosed a plan to exit bankruptcy that rewarded its 400 executives with an average $1 million each, with nothing back to flight attendants, whose wages, benefits, and working conditions had been reduced in bankruptcy. US Airways flight attendants endured massive pay cuts over several years while executives rewarded themselves multiple millions in stock bonuses and double-digit pay increases.)

While many of the airlines are still on thin ice, Delta, at least for now, seems to have a leg up in the game of airline survival and sustainability. More important, where are the signs of personal accountability, balance, perspective, and trustworthiness in these other examples? The distrust and disconnect this lack of accountability creates with the airlines' stakeholders likely will be a problem for years to come. How can employees, unions, and suppliers be inspired to work together in mutual trust and accountability when compensation is so distorted?

INSIGHTS FROM FUTURE LEADERS

When you search the Internet for the word "accountability," millions of entries appear. One that stands out is a survey Yale University posted on its website. It asked recent alumni and their friends to define responsibility and accountability. The wonderful responses inspire hope and faith in those who will be our future leaders. Here are two of the best:

Lynn Chang, class of 2006, wrote:
To be accountable is to consistently demonstrate the dedication to stand up and support an individual, group, or community, and to have the courage to do so even if you stand alone. It is a devotion that is only truly evident during the toughest of times.

Vipan Nikore, class of 2006, answered:
It is at the heart of your efforts to fulfill your vision, build a sense of community, increase follower morale, create a risk-taking

environment, foster creativity, and nurture trust between all. Accountability means being a rock that my family and friends can count on, providing a product or service that truly adds value to my customers, producing results and actually earning my paycheck for my employer, giving 100 percent effort during a game for my teammates, and using whatever talent and power I've been blessed with to help those less fortunate. Trust is ultimately built through accountability, and the ability to garner trust is the common thread of all true leaders; thus, accountability is the essence of leadership.

Lynn used the word *dedication*. Vipan said that his accountability *was about being a rock people could count on*. Both add value in more ways than just the bottom line. They described how accountability can inspire and bring people together around a shared purpose and a common set of values. Imagine the examples these future leaders will set when they reach positions of power.

The Ripple Effect

It's vitally important to communicate to all your followers that the smallest success, or failure, of accountability can create a ripple effect that goes far beyond the current issue or event.

The Hilton Hotel family ran an advertising campaign recently entitled "Be Hospitable." The heading reads, "Business is about more than just making money; it's about making a difference." And the ad copy reads:

Today, companies are not only looking for ways to improve the bottom line, they're looking for ways to improve our environment, community, and the overall social climate. Whether you're part of a large corporation or an individual wanting to give back, here are a few tips that can help make our community a better place.*

The ad has little clip-art pictures of ways to make a difference, with a paragraph describing what each person can do. For example, it shows the green recycle icon and describes how we can each help the environment. Other examples include: "Get involved," "Donate clothes," "Plant a garden," "Share a ride," and "Giving money." The message is that the Hilton family has one philosophy: *Be hospitable*.

This is a sensitive and caring way to attract customers. It also promotes personal responsibility. The ripple effect of a major corporation asking people to be accountable by "making a difference" is commendable and is a strong example of corporate citizenship and of New Breed Leadership.

When everyone on your team knows that accountability matters no matter who the person, or what his or her position, you'll have gone a long way in truly building accountability into your organization's culture.

An important question: Why is the current crisis of accountability so significant? Because accountability and trust say so much about our personal and national ethics and integrity. When one of us loses credibility because of distrust, we all suffer.

> If once you forfeit the confidence of your fellow-citizens, you can never regain their respect and esteem.
> —ABRAHAM LINCOLN

Our recent business scandals of executive fraud, disloyalty, disregard, and irresponsibility have dishonored the image of American

---

* Copyright and Permission Courtesy of Hilton Hospitality, Inc.

executives and how they conduct business. Each time a new scandal is revealed, it's as if we are in a race to the bottom of our moral imperatives of truth and honesty.

Each scandal also creates a backlash. Followers see the lack of accountability. While they may use a boss's disloyalty to further their own ends, they'll also consider that leader a risk and limit their trust in him or her.

The consequence comes in many forms. An untrustworthy leader may suffer from a lack of power, an inability to achieve goals, relationship problems, low self-esteem, negative emotions, and unhappiness. Since cause and effect come into play so strongly in accountability, it always reflects the way team members make ethical decisions, take initiative, or act proactively and creatively. A denial of responsibility impairs all of these important behaviors.

In short, if left unimpeded, unethical behavior creates havoc. When there's no penalty for doing something wrong or when improper or bad actions are condoned, when lack of accountability goes unchecked, the leader has broken the sacred promise of implied trustworthiness. As Lincoln once noted, when trust and loyalty are lost, it rarely returns.

A STARK CONTRAST: RUMSFELD VERSUS GATES

During the Iraqi war there was a stunning contrast between Defense Secretary Donald Rumsfeld's lack of accountability over the torture and military misconduct at the Abu Ghraib and Guantanamo prisons and that of his successor, Robert Gates, who handled the Walter Reed Army Medical Center outpatient controversy.

Neither Rumsfeld nor any other high-ranking official in the administration or any high-ranking military officer was ever held accountable for the torture at Abu Ghraib, the acts of rendition (kidnapping prisoners and taking them to foreign countries where torture is condoned), or the lack of justice for inmates at Guantanamo. No top officials apparently were concerned about the long-lasting consequences to our national reputation and world standing.

As the Center for Constitutional Rights wrote, "They pushed it all down on the lowest members of the military. Here in the U.S. they may not have been held accountable for what they did in the Iraqi war, but the rest of the world does. It's one thing when small countries in the world [conduct torture] and get yelled at. But when the U.S. does it, who's going to hold them accountable?"

The Abu Ghraib examples were illegal acts of torture. And the world court of public opinion found the United States guilty on charges of inhumane conduct established in the Geneva convention at the end of World War II. Imagine what a difference it would have made if our military and government had taken immediate and sincere action, as J & J did in the Tylenol crisis. That would have gone a long way toward defending our moral authority.

Accountability at the Highest Level

Later, when it was revealed in the press that returning Iraqi veterans were being neglected at the Walter Reed Army Hospital, the public could hardly believe it. Seeking to avoid responsibility, the military seemed to brush off the controversy until Defense Secretary Robert Gates, who succeeded Rumsfeld, went into action. Heads rolled and changes were made as those involved were held accountable in real terms through demotions, retirements, and reassignments.

Gates didn't allow Veterans Affairs head Robert Nicholson to get away with his excuses and backpedaling. Even before Congress held hearings, Gates's sincere anger and immediate action made clear his view that "Support Our Troops" should be more than just a popular slogan. In fact, Gates's strong leadership and instant acceptance of accountability were such a stark comparison to Rumsfeld's that the whole affair even reignited the earlier controversy over the incompetence and lack of caring and accountability following Hurricane Katrina.

Unfortunately, the media does not give any attention to the hundreds of thousands of managers, executives, and leaders who *are* accountable and who would never knowingly hurt their stakeholders. As you direct your teams, take an accountability lesson from the contrasts between the actions of Gates and Rumsfeld. And keep in mind the words of Anna Sewell, the nineteenth-century author of *Black Beauty*, who wrote: "My doctrine is this, that if we see cruelty or wrong that we have the power to stop, and do nothing, we make ourselves sharers in the guilt."

When Will We Learn the Lesson?

Why do we need to keep relearning the moral code of personal responsibility on the world stage? Reflecting on the values of a free nation, it's critical to ask: "Is it possible to sustain our democracy without accountability?"

At the end of World War II, when the full extent of the Nazi holocaust became known, this powerful and stirring poem was recited by Protestant pastor and social activist Martin Niemoller:

> It is time to speak your truth, create your community, be good to each other, and do not look outside yourself for the leader.
> —HOPI Indian advice

First they came for the Jews, and I did not speak out—
> *because I was not a Jew;*
Then they came for the communists, and I did not speak out—
> *because I was not a communist;*
Then they came for the socialists, and I did not speak out—
> *because I was not a socialist;*
Then they came for the trade unionists, and I did not speak out—
> *because I was not a trade unionist;*
Then they came for me—
> *and there was no one left to speak out for me.*

The Accountability Puzzle Piece

Few things help an individual more than to place responsibility
upon him, and to let him know you trust him.

—BOOKER T. WASHINGTON, American political leader, educator, and author

Your authenticity and personal accountability as a leader go hand in hand. Living the values of conscientiousness and trustworthiness

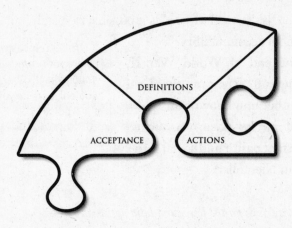

will make or break your effectiveness. As A New Breed Leader, you can be an integral part of fixing one of the most serious problems we face: helping people understand the importance of accountability.

The puzzle piece of accountability fits into the competence puzzle piece to continue expanding and clarifying A New Breed Leader. Just as in the competence model, the accountability puzzle piece is made up of different components—in this case, definitions, acceptance, and actions—and each builds upon and enhances the other parts. As definitions become clear, acceptance comes more easily and appropriate actions follow. Those support and validate further definitions in an ever-ascending pattern.

As each person does his or her part, he feels more connected to the other members of the team. All work together, defining, monitoring, and enjoying the benefits of accountability. Followers' self-respect is enhanced; their feeling of being a person of worth is increased.

When all the components are present, you greatly increase the opportunities to help people fulfill their potential by learning to become voluntarily accountable.

Being Proactive and Reactive

Two central aspects come into play when defining accountability. One is building a foundation that helps prevent problems from occurring—being *proactive*; anticipating problems and preparing in advance. The second is being *reactive*—dealing with problems quickly and effectively, then learning from them and taking immediate steps to prevent more in the future.

No matter how proactive you are or how well you prepare, you'll never be able to predict or prevent all the problems you'll face. Even with that reality, how you react in a crisis—and how your

DENNY'S RESTAURANTS TOOK IMMEDIATE ACTION

Denny's restaurants used both aspects of accountability—reactive and proactive—to avoid permanent damage when its discriminatory practices were revealed in the early 1990s. First, it reacted well and demonstrated a true willingness to overcome these practices. Company leaders immediately and directly apologized to Denny's customers and pledged not to tolerate discrimination in the future.

Then, they settled a class-action lawsuit, compensating the injured parties to the tune of $54 million. They accepted blame immediately and began to work with the NAACP to find appropriate ways to remedy their behavior. They diversified their contracting and franchising practices and trained all employees on nondiscriminatory practices.

Such swift and appropriate action not only saved the chain's reputation, it also built proactive attitudes and procedures into the corporation's foundation to head off such problems in the future.

followers think about and act on issues of accountability in critical times—will affect the overall success of your organization.

When you recognize, admit, and correct your mistakes as fast as possible, you set an example of maturity and strength and let people know what your leadership is about. Doing so quickly makes handling any crisis easier and helps minimize the damage.

THE *EXXON VALDEZ* OIL SPILL

In 1989, the Exxon Corporation was responsible for one of the worst environmental disasters in history. On March 24, the *Exxon Valdez* oil tanker ran aground, spilling approximately 257,000 barrels—more than 10 million gallons of oil—into Alaska's Prince William Sound. Efforts to contain the spill were slow, and Exxon's response was even slower. While pictures were flashed worldwide of birds and otters dying in a river of thick black oil, Exxon was silent. People everywhere were shocked and then outraged by Exxon's unwillingness to take immediate action or to come forward and take responsibility.

The biggest criticism of the company stemmed from the fact that CEO Lawrence Rawl waited six days to make a statement to the media and that he didn't visit the scene until nearly three weeks after the spill. Combined, these actions left the public with the strong impression that Exxon didn't take this accident seriously.

Exxon's name became synonymous with environmental catastrophe. The incident would go down in crisis management history as a textbook case of how *not* to respond and, in so doing, how to alienate the public and damage your reputation. Exxon's image was permanently tarnished. Angered customers cut up their Exxon credit cards and mailed them to Rawl, while others boycotted Exxon products. According to a study by the Porter Novelli public relations firm several years after the accident, 54 percent of those surveyed said they were still less likely to buy Exxon products.

You'll never go wrong by continually assessing your accountability, preparedness, and responses to emergencies.

Look at the hard-learned lessons of Hurricane Katrina. Apparently, no one assessed the factors of accountability, preparedness, and resources in time to avert the tragedy. We can also learn what not to do by looking at one of the worst examples of accountability in the twentieth century involving a corporation, the *Exxon Valdez* incident.

James Burke and the J & J executives (the makers of Tylenol) knew exactly where the buck stopped and gave us a terrific example of corporate responsibility. Denny's gives us a case study of discriminatory practices and proactive repairs. As for Exxon, its leaders didn't have a clue about how the public felt or how to act as a responsible corporate citizen. It was a corporate crucible event and they failed miserably.

Most every example of failed crisis management comes down to either denial and/or lack of willingness to take responsibility, or slow response to the problem. As A New Breed Leader, you should try to be as proactive as possible, seeking to learn from your mistakes. Then turn them into lessons of good management and wise leadership. Build them into the nature of your organization with clear definitions of what accountability means. Let accountability, responsibility, dependability, trust, and confidence between you and your followers be the starting point for everything that happens, not just a response to problems or crises.

My Accountability Inventory

- How do I define my leadership accountability?

- To whom am I accountable (responsible)?

- What risks will I personally take to speak out and be accountable?

- What standards do I use to measure my accountability?

- What actions do I take to show I mean it?

- Do my followers see it as I do?

- Do I really know how and what they feel and think about my level of accountability?

- How do I react in an emergency?

- How do my fellow leaders show accountability in a time of crisis?

As you grow and deal with critical problems, your skills at being both proactive and reactive will send an important message to your followers.

The Crucial Role of Definitions

*Treat people as if they were what they ought to be, and you'll
help them to become what they are capable of becoming.*
—JOHANN WOLFGANG VON GOETHE

As a leader, you must define what accountability means to your organization. Responsibility, clear measurements, standards, and most of all, the expectations of accountability must be defined and clearly presented to all members of the organization. When these are clearly defined, followers can respond deliberately with self-control and make sound choices.

Just as trust is the foundation for your effectiveness as a leader, *definitions* are the foundation of accountability. The other seven qualities that matter most—Competence, Openness, Language, Values, Perspective, Power, and Humility—must have an underpinning of accountability to give them credibility, humanity, and authority.

But accountability can be open to wide personal interpretation—and even misuse—because of all our differences. All the values that we grapple with in a diverse society come into play. And our personal filters alter in small, but important ways, our perceptions of accountability or the lack of it.

Definitions become even more significant when you add to this mix the fact that the world has become so complex and fast-changing that people often feel confused or even threatened. Amid such flux, constant vigilance is needed to keep accountability definitions clear. That's one of your primary tasks as A New Breed Leader.

Becoming an Enabler

When you're accountable, you become an enabler, helping followers define and accept accountability, and act responsibly. Accountability begins by doing one thing reliably, conscientiously, and with a sense of duty. No matter how small or large that issue, when your leadership is responsible for doing something that has long-term benefits, it's a powerful human motivator.

So, regularly you should gather your teams and encourage them to define and reexamine the meaning and value of accountability. People take much more ownership for that which they create, and that sense of ownership builds pride. When viewed as a shared value, accountability changes the entire approach to being a reliable, dependable, and trustworthy person.

Delegation and Accountability

To build your leadership vision, you need followers to whom you can delegate. And effective delegation always involves followers taking responsibility, beginning with clear definitions of jobs, tasks, and actions. Part of your role as a leader is to let people know that they must try to find their own solutions to problems before handing them up to you. But they also need to know that if they refer problems upward, they will not be punished.

> Accountability: Accepting the consequences, good or bad, for the outcome of a situation for which you are responsible.
> —U.S. Coast Guard

It's said that Napoleon Bonaparte didn't like to answer letters and would often wait thirty days before replying. His philosophy was that if the response was still needed at the end of a month, then he would reply. While that's not an effective twenty-first-century attitude, it does speak to the idea of letting your followers be responsible for solving their own problems.

There's never a time when responsibility can be taken for granted or considered to be permanently established. Constant work is needed to update your standards for accountability. Gather a team of managers, or executives with whom you work, and take an in-depth look at the processes and attitudes you are currently using to define accountability. Ask:

- Have we had a discussion with our followers about how they personally view accountability? What did we discover?

- What are the core standards and best practices people should use to make accountability a permanent part of our organization?

- What are the skill subsets, checklists, and strategic plans that ensure clarity of the descriptions?

- What methods of operation do we use to judge accountability and responsibility?

- What form of checks and balances do we use?

- Have we set up a feedback process to help establish clear definitions free of retaliation for new and different thinking?

- How often do we explain and demonstrate the results of having and not having accountability?

- Have we engaged our followers in the process of continually maintaining a high and current understanding of both accountability and responsibility?

As you define accountability, be careful not to confuse being accountable with being "culpable." Culpability (being blameworthy) is often about criminal or illegal and unethical acts. Just because someone is acting nonaccountably doesn't necessarily mean they're breaking a law. On the other hand, be vigilant for illegal actions that can bring down an entire organization. Look at what happened at Enron; the culpability of Chairman Ken Lay, CEO Jeffrey Skilling, and CFO Andrew Fastow destroyed thousands of lives and cost society tens of millions of dollars while seriously damaging the business community's reputation.

When you feel you have a good handle on accountability definitions, the next step is to move on to part two of the puzzle piece, *acceptance*.

The Importance of Acceptance

Responsibility is a unique concept. It can only reside in a single individual. You may share it with others, but your portion is not diminished. You may delegate it, but it is still with you. You may disclaim it, but you cannot divest yourself of it.
—ADMIRAL HYMAN RICKOVER

Accepting responsibility is a make-or-break point in your life as a leader as well as for the organization you lead. Ask:

- Are you a *"Creator"* in the leadership pyramid? If you include acceptance of responsibility into the core of your endeavor, you have the power to change almost anything.

- Are you a *"Builder"* leader? While definitions are the concrete in your foundation, acceptance is the steel core giving it staying power and strength.

- Are you the *"Sustainer"* leader? If so, recognize that nothing will survive for long without all three pieces of the accountability puzzle—definitions, acceptance, and actions. Your challenge is to be sure that your personal and organizational leadership includes each of them.

ACCEPTANCE QUIZ FOR YOUR ORGANIZATION

- As leaders, how do we feel about our source of authority, accountability, and responsibility?

- How do our organizational core values pertain to accepting responsibility?

- What's the driving force for accepting responsibility in our organization?

- How is accountability most evident in our organization?

- Who inspires accountability acceptance in our people?

- Do we reward and recognize people who take responsibility and are accountable?

We're all motivated by self-interest. We want to know why something is important, why it's beneficial, why we should care, and what it will do for us. We make decisions based on what we feel is beneficial not only to our work, but to ourselves. We often have internal accountability dialogues that may go something like this:

- "Once I'm given clear definitions of the accountability, I'll have to take ownership for the results. Do I really want the responsibility?"

- "Will anyone recognize or honor my efforts?"

- "Will I be rewarded or acknowledged for being accountable?"

One of your jobs is to help followers find answers to these very human questions. When people know their efforts will be acknowledged and even rewarded, positive and empowering feelings result.

MEET BRUCE GORDON

I first met Bruce Gordon at a Bell Atlantic conference where I gave a keynote address to a large audience made up of his team managers. He kicked off the meeting, and his high-level communication and leadership skills were evident immediately. He was very connected to his people. He was very approachable and open. He was also very curious and interested in people.

In 2002, *Fortune* magazine named him sixth on a list of the "50 Most Powerful African Americans in Business."

Through a series of mergers, Bell Atlantic became Verizon, and when Bruce retired in 2003, his last role there was president of Retail Market Groups, which was the group of companies in Verizon which served the consumer and small business markets. Since then, he has been the CEO of the NAACP and currently sits on the boards of various corporations and not-for-profit organizations.

When I began to outline this book, I knew Bruce would have much to say that is important to you as A New Breed Leader. I asked him about accountability:

> I believe there are people who feel like victims, who say that everything that is wrong in their lives is somebody else's fault but not their own. I believe that the greatest source of power is accountability, and that's the belief that whatever the situa-

tion is, it's yours to handle. If something is going wrong, don't look to somebody else to fix it. Don't blame somebody else for it. Don't conclude that you can't do it. Be accountable. Assume that you're powerful. Acknowledge your realities. Build your own solutions. Own them, and make them happen.

I found that probably one of life's most important lessons to me was learning to be accountable. I can't tell you that it was an easy lesson for me to learn, and I don't even take credit for having discovered it all by myself because I didn't.

We were at a stage at Bell Atlantic where we had been formed as a company for a couple of years but we had moved from being a monopoly to being a fully competitive enterprise. And our CEO at the time was Ray Smith.

As CEO he was trying to figure out how to change the monopoly culture to a competitive culture. He developed what we called the *Bell Atlantic Way*, which was our new value system, our new culture. Included was accountability. Of all the principles in the *Bell Atlantic Way*, what seemed to affect him most was accountability. It became his centerpiece.

For many months, those of us who reported to Ray just despised how frequently he called us "victims," a very offensive term. We felt insulted and belittled. Here we were, men and women in these big jobs, big titles, major responsibilities, and our boss was berating us and calling us victims. We didn't like it, but basically he was telling us that we weren't being accountable. One day I had an experience that made me understand that he was right, that I was not being accountable, that I was being a victim. Once I figured that out and changed my approach to being accountable, I thought that it was actually a life-changing experience.

Ray had said to me at the beginning of a particular year, as we were dealing with competition in the consumer market in particular, that I should develop a loyalty program, you know, like a frequent-flier program. So we got toward the end of the year, and we were actually doing the planning for the next year. I was presenting my plans to Ray and my colleagues. He said, "Bruce, by the way, what happened to the loyalty program? Where does that stand?" and I answered, "I didn't get it done." He asked, "Why not?" I said, "I couldn't afford it. I just couldn't fit it in my budget." He paused, and said, "Really? Well, how much would the loyalty program have cost?" I said, "I don't know. Maybe a million dollars, possibly two." And he said, "And how large was your budget this year?" I said, "Four billion." "So let me get this right," he said. "I asked you to create a loyalty program, and you're telling me you didn't do it. And the reason you didn't do it was because you couldn't afford it. It would have cost at most two million dollars and you've got a four-billion-dollar budget. Is that right?"

I knew I sounded stupid. Now if I had said to him (and this, by the way, was the truth, but I just did not present it right), "Ray, I know that you said to me that you wanted the loyalty program in place, but as I looked at the year and I looked at the things that needed to be done, I decided, in the overall scheme of things, that a loyalty program was not high enough priority for me to spend my resources on. So I chose not to do it." If I said that, he would have been fine.

I would have been accountable. I would have said I looked at my reality, and my reality said that a loyalty program did not fit. I chose to take that one or two million dollars that I could have spent on a loyalty program and put this particular initiative in place, which I believe was the better use of my funds at this stage of the game, and by the way, here's what happened with that two million dollars and here's why at year's end it was the right choice. If I had said that, I would have been fine.

But that's not what I said. Instead, I sounded like a victim, blaming the lack of budget. At that moment the light went on. And once that light went on, I understood accountability differently.

While I may have been accountable in the past, I realized that I did not always *recognize* when I wasn't being accountable. I think that's important. There are people who think they are accountable who are not.

In the overall scheme of things, one could argue it was a relatively small incident, but we all have these moments, these a-ha! moments when the light comes on. It was actually life changing. I am a huge, huge evangelist when it comes to promoting accountability.

When I took on the opportunity as CEO at the NAACP, at my very first meeting, the second day on the job, with the staff in headquarters in Baltimore, I took them through an abbreviated list of Gordon's principles and had a very clear discussion of what was in the *Bell Atlantic Way* called the Accountability Ladder. It means that much to me. By the end of my tenure at the NAACP, I had come up with something I called E-squared, A-squared. It's education and employment. It's accountability and activism. That's the focus on what I'm about. Accountability has become a centerpiece in my life.

As A New Breed Leader, can you be as candid, open, and focused as Bruce Gordon is, while taking full responsibility for yourself? If you can, you will rise to the top of whatever profession you choose. P. J. O'Rourke, American political satirist and writer, wrote, "One of the annoying things about believing in free choice and individual responsibility is the difficulty of finding somebody to blame your problems on. And when you do find somebody, it's remarkable how often his picture turns up on your driver's license."

The Legacy of Actions

*If your actions create a legacy that inspires others
to dream more, learn more, do more, and become
more, then you are an excellent leader.*

—DOLLY PARTON

The day before a national election I was flying home from Dallas and I chatted with my seat partner, general manager of a company with offices in the United States and Costa Rica. At one point we got to discussing the next day's election. He told me he was coming home to vote. I asked him why he didn't use an absentee ballot. "I want to vote in person," he said. "I feel more accountable when I do." His answer told me a lot about his feelings toward personal responsibility. That he gave up something of himself to perform his duty shows how important he felt about taking an active part in our democracy.

That conversation inspired me to mention him in my speeches and put him in this book. I came away from the flight encouraged about the quiet leadership that is going on in places and in ways that we often don't see on the front page of the newspaper or hear on the talk shows. At first glance he seems to me to be A New Breed Leader, quietly exemplifying accountability by his actions.

Actions Count Most

What you do speaks so loud I can not hear what you say.
—RALPH WALDO EMERSON

To simply say "I am responsible," and not back it up with open, honest, and appropriate action, is just rhetoric. It's a neglect that shows followers they, too, can avoid being responsible. As a result, the entire organization is endangered: Followers drift, unable to chart their way through the challenges of their daily work and lives. When that happens, the whole system—be it a family, an organization, or a nation—quickly begins to break down.

In ancient Rome, when engineers built an arch, the head engineer would stand under it as the capstone was put into place. That's a rather dramatic way of taking responsibility for your work! But it certainly brings home the message of accountability and leading by example.

Your personal actions produce a powerful cumulative effect. Each time you display leadership responsibility, it's like a pebble thrown into a still pond, causing concentric circles to expand in an ever-widening ring of influence. Every person you touch, directly or indirectly, is affected by your sensible, reliable, mature actions of standing up and being accountable. Great leadership is often based on this simple premise. As Winston Churchill wrote, "The price of greatness is responsibility."

No Assumptions

When a problem occurs, don't automatically assume it is coming from the outside. First, look internally at your systems, your policies, and your people.

I recently went into a store to buy a pair of walking shoes. It was near closing time, and as I asked a few questions, it became clear the young clerk's interest was about going home, not helping me find the right pair of shoes.

It was also clear she didn't connect her salary to the profitability and reputation of the store. She didn't understand that fulfilling my needs would result in important word of mouth. However, I can't put all the responsibility on her. She obviously found no personal benefit in being accountable. Clearly, the store didn't have accountability on its training agenda.

> As a leader, you can never assume that followers have been taught the value of accountability and the trust it brings.

You probably have a dozen similar stories. If we multiply this a thousand times across thousands of businesses, it becomes clear that, as A New Breed Leader, you'll need to reintroduce the concept and benefits of accountability at every level of your organization and courageously examine accountability from the ground up. Bessie Rowland James, author of *Adlai's Almanac 1859*, counseled readers, "No matter how lofty you are in your department, the responsibility for what your lowliest assistant is doing is yours." Some 150 years later, that's still good advice.

JetBlue reexamined its internal operation for ways to better handle weather emergencies. It hired and trained additional staff

2007 . . . THE WINTER FROM HELL

Ice storms shut down air travel, schedules went out the window, travelers were stranded, and nerves and patience were frayed. Every U.S. airline had major problems, and JetBlue was no exception. What was different, though, was how JetBlue CEO David Neeleman handled the response to a much-publicized delay that kept passengers trapped for many hours in a plane sitting on a runway.

He immediately took responsibility for not handling the situation better. An apologetic e-mail went out to all who fly JetBlue: "You deserved better—a lot better—from us last week, and we let you down. Nothing is more important than regaining your trust, and all of us here hope you will give us the opportunity to once again welcome you on board and provide you the positive JetBlue Experience you have come to expect from us."

Neeleman and his team also created what they call a Customer Bill of Rights, clearly outlining what customers can expect.

and honed procedures to improve the flow of information so the problems of the 2007 weather crisis wouldn't recur. Its officials understood the importance of timely actions to keep their customers informed and updated. Even though Neeleman may not have been personally responsible for the delays and reaction, he took responsibility for his employees' actions.

MEET JEFFREY SHELDON

Jeffrey Sheldon is president of Sheldon Consulting Group in Burlingame, California. He graduated from UC San Diego in 2005 with a bachelor of arts in political science. He is one of our young upcoming leaders. He says, "Most of my education has come from trial by experience in business." His focus is developing, branding, and viral marketing for the arts. He is a young New Breed Leader. Jeff and I talked about what kind of qualities he looks for in a role model.

There are two qualities that, to me, define a true leader: they must be a visionary and they must be someone who is accountable. Leadership is about movement. It's about taking a group of people, no matter how big or small, and helping them to accomplish something. In order to move, there has to be a direction and this starts with the vision of the leader. They have to know where they're going and why. In addition, I think most people feel this from those that they admire and are willing to follow. I can always hear this quality in a leader's voice. I can see it in their stature, and feel it in their presence.

And because the leader is the one with the vision and the responsibility for creating movement, they must also be completely accountable for every outcome. I've seen this in my mentors, college coaches, admired bosses, and the many successful people around me. When they succeed, they credit only their constituents, not themselves. And when they fail, it was nobody's fault, but their own. There's no outward glory. There's no true glamour as a leader, it's always internal. They understand the accomplishment and they understand the need for humility. They understand it's about something bigger than themselves.

I am most inspired by the genuine leadership of individuals who commit their lives to youth education. Whether it is through Big Brothers or Big Sisters, or as an administrator, teacher, or coach. But a title doesn't make a true leader. It takes somebody who is willing to open up kids' minds to the world and inspire them to think about their personal place in history. They are the foundation to movement. If we give them a positive vision and powerful tools, this world will be a better place, I guarantee it.

As a leader, I have to ask myself: If I make a statement that is bold and in your face, will I inspire any action? Will my words even mean anything? But what if I pose a question that you have to reach deep down to answer? And what if that question hits you very personally? That can create a fire inside. If my question challenges you to think and it starts to burn, then that creates energy, and you need energy to create movement.

Psicanica, a self-help philosophy, has an interesting way of simplifying responsibility:

In any situation, if you have any possibility of action, then you are responsible—you do not need to be the initial cause of the situation. For example: you are not responsible for it raining. However, you are responsible for standing outside in it and getting wet as long as you have any possibility of action such as going inside or opening an umbrella. If you have no possibility of action—for example, you are chained to a post—then you have no responsibility for getting wet. Any possibility of action establishes responsibility.

Competence, you'll recall, is described as doing the right thing, at the right time, the right way. It's judged by asking if the result was satisfactory. But how do you measure and judge accountability? Points to focus on are:

- Which methods need to be updated to respond to our current situation?

- What specific actions do our managers and executives take to model accountability?

- Have we set accountability target dates and clear end results?

- What kind of team feedback do we have as we reach for goals?

- What criteria are we using to determine proper actions?

> What gets rewarded gets done.

- Do we empower the team to come back together and make adjustments?

- How do we reward and recognize follower effort as well as results?

Accountability, Consequences, and Discipline = Wisdom

In reading the lives of great men, I found that the
first victory they won was over themselves . . .
self-discipline with all of them came first.

—PRESIDENT HARRY S. TRUMAN

One of your goals should be to grow wiser about building trust with all followers. That wisdom increases when the gears of *accountability*, an understanding of the *consequences* of action, and *discipline* all work in harmony. These three are at the top of the list of critical leadership skills.

Accountability is a great teacher of discipline. It's a continual process that must be guarded ferociously with a passion for truth, honesty, humility, and openness. George

> Discipline . . . the ability to do what you should do, when you should do it, to the best of your ability, whether you want to, or like to, or not.

Washington was passionate about accountability, and during the War for Independence, he stated, "Discipline is the soul of an army. It makes small numbers formidable, procures success to the weak, and esteem to all."

If you look at the internal workings of a beautiful Swiss watch, you'll see the gears turn silently and precisely, resulting in accurate time and dependability. When an organization has the same kind of internal workings, the results are teams who work smoothly together and can weather the storms of change and adversity while still producing good products and services.

As a young man, my neighbor Herman was a fine jeweler, an expert at repairing and caring for Swiss watches. When I showed him the graphic of the three gears, he painted this clear picture:

The smallest gear is the workhorse, rotating more than the other gears. It keeps everything going. The largest gear is the strongest, and it drives the whole mechanism; without it a watch is just a collection of expensive metal and jewels. The large gear is more apt to wear out because it is driven by the main power source, with tremendous pressure being constantly put on it. It must be kept clean and the bearings must be lubricated or they wear out and the watch will eventually stop.

It's easy to see the same is true in any organization. While discipline keeps moving everyone and everything toward good decisions and outcomes, the leaders have tremendous ongoing pressure to set an example that's the centerpiece of keeping the organization running and viable. When you use your influence to make sure that everyone in the organization has clear accountability definitions from which to work and accepts the consequences of their words and actions, it releases their energy, potential, and creativity.

In a Swiss watch, the gears form a community of accuracy. In life and business, accountability creates a sense of purpose and builds a community of trusting and trustworthy people. From there, you can establish grounds for a common cause, or a common goal.

Both in business and personal life, discipline creates a productive tension between what you want to become and what you turn out to be, what the organization's mission is and what it becomes. It's not the work that's hard, it's the discipline. "If we don't discipline ourselves," author William Feather says, "the world will do it for us." Ouch!

As you work to find your authenticity and uniqueness as A New Breed Leader, you'll be demonstrating the self-discipline to be held accountable. And you'll be leading the way for others to bring out their own personal best.

Your Accountability Legacy

One of the biggest why's of accountability is: Our
children see this, and learn to imitate it.
—THOMAS JEFFERSON

Movies have always been about entertainment. However, at times they are precursors of our future and act as teachers to break through our personal protective barriers.

A Few Good Men

Master storytellers Rob Reiner (director) and Aaron Sorkin (author/screenwriter) take a rather predictable plot and make a drama about accountability.

The plot builds around Nathan Jessep (Jack Nicholson), the base commander and a powerful senior Marine Corps officer, as the fanatical CO at Guantanamo Bay, Cuba. He orders his hard-nosed young officer Kiefer Sutherland to bring a platoon trouble-maker, PFC William "Willie" Santiago, into line using a severe and unsanctioned form of hazing known as a "Code Red."

When Santiago dies during the incident, the two young Marines who administered the Code Red are charged with his murder and flown to Washington to stand trial. Lieutenant Daniel Kaffee (Tom Cruise), a usually lazy attorney, is brought face-to-face with his personal challenge of responsibility not to plea-bargain, but to properly defend the two Marines. His fellow defense lawyers (Demi Moore and Kevin Pollak) work with him and give him the moral support he needs to do his best.

As the trial proceeds, we see the accused, Lance Corporal

Dawson (Wolfgang Bodison) and PFC Downey (James Marshall), stoically refuse to talk about the Code Red. They cling to the Marine Corps philosophy of "Unit, Corp, God, and Country." They believe they did nothing wrong, that they were only following orders.

Jessep is finally forced to testify. He's so angry he can hardly contain himself. His body language, voice, and facial expression let everyone in the courtroom know that he thinks he is above accountability. Kaffee's job is to turn Jessep's arrogance and anger against him and admit that he did order a "Code Red." Kaffee hammers Jessep with question after question, and the judge forces Jessep to answer.

The camera keeps going to the faces of Dawson and Downey and back to Jessep and Kaffee. The tension builds as Kaffee keeps pounding him about honesty, accountability, and truth. Finally, Jessep breaks and yells back, "You want the truth? You can't *handle* the truth." He tries desperately to justify the Code Red until he realizes that what he has just said has hung him. He jumps up and starts to walk out of the courtroom, thinking he is beyond reproach. The judge orders the sergeants at arms to take him into custody. The courtroom crackles as he gives Kaffee a look that could kill.

In the final scenes, the jury returns to the courtroom and quietly renders a not-guilty verdict for murder. But Dawson and Downey are found guilty of conduct unbecoming a Marine and are to be dishonorably discharged. Their faces show utter shock as they move from disbelief to the emotions of pleading for help. "What does that mean?" Downey asks Dawson. "I don't understand. Colonel Jessep ordered the Code Red. What did we do wrong? We did nothing wrong."

All pretense is gone from Dawson; he has hit the truth in the moral obligation of personal accountability.

"Yah, we did," he replies. "We were supposed to fight for people who couldn't fight for themselves. We were supposed to fight for Willie."

Bam! The whole movie comes to rest on two sentences. The message is loud and clear: We are our brother's keeper. There's a moral accountability code that takes precedent over a military code.

Your Action Plan Questions for Quality 2
ACCOUNTABILITY

1. In what ways do I give my followers reason to trust me?

2. When something goes wrong, am I forthright in accepting responsibility and in taking remedial actions?

3. In reacting to a crisis, do I also take proactive steps to prevent a recurrence of the problem?

Remember: A free download of the Mentor Action Plan is available at my website, www.anewbreedofleader.com. Click on the "Resources" tab, and you'll find it there.

The Time Is Now

Barbara Jordan, the first African American woman elected to the U.S. House of Representatives, was addressing the national Democratic convention, the first African American woman to do so. She was eloquent and moving when she addressed our national accountability to care for one another.

And now—now we must look to the future. Let us heed the voice of the people and recognize their common sense. If we do not, we not only blaspheme our political heritage, we ignore the common ties that bind all Americans. Many fear the future. Many are distrustful of their leaders, and believe that their voices are never heard. Many seek only to satisfy their private work—wants; to satisfy their private interests. But this is the great danger America faces—that we will cease to be one nation and become instead a collection of interest groups: city against suburb, region against region, individual against individual; each seeking to satisfy private wants. If that happens, who then will speak for America? Who then will speak for the common good?

She spoke these words in 1976, and we are still struggling with the same challenges today.

We have no time for the luxury of irresponsibility; we need strong leadership accountability now. As a people, as organizations, and as a nation, we can do much better!

I once read that "accountability is who you are when no one's looking." This quote should be engraved above the entrance of every government office and be displayed in every business, every school, and every home. Indeed, it allows us to move from our current accountability malaise, and interestingly ties so closely to a quote by John F. Kennedy.

> *Our privileges can be no greater than our obligations.*
> *The protection of our rights can endure no longer*
> *than the performance of our responsibilities.*
> —JOHN F. KENNEDY

CHAPTER THREE

Openness Matters

GENERATING INTEGRITY

*I consider it my job to nurture the creativity of the people I
work with because at Sony we know that a terrific idea is more
likely to happen in an open, free and trusting atmosphere than
when everything is calculated, every action analyzed and
every responsibility assigned by an organization chart.*

—AKIO MORITA, Cofounder, Sony Corporation

COMPETENCE AND ACCOUNTABILITY are more easily "quantifiable" than openness. It is a soft "skill" that is harder to measure. Nonetheless, openness and its associated values of honesty and truth are bedrock qualities in your leadership and of equal importance in your leadership tool bag.

Openness involves candor and frankness that a leader lives by and demonstrates. Its most important by-product, integrity, is at the heart of earning the right to be called a leader. A true leader cultivates this in others and within the whole environment in which they are leading. Integrity reveals your true intentions and greatly affects your followers and your entire organization because it reflects on everyone who is associated with you.

The actions of James Burke and Johnson & Johnson in the Tylenol-tampering tragedy (described in the last chapter) were an example of not only great accountability but also of openness. Burke held nothing back, his emotions were clear and honest, and he gave the nation the unvarnished truth. The quick, transparent actions of the company earned it such integrity that the incident is still being used in case studies by many business schools.

The Truth Factor

One of the most interesting human attributes is our built-in "sonar" that tells us when someone is not open, not authentic. Our senses warn us that a person has a personal agenda that doesn't serve us or others well. It's as though they have a blinking red light on their forehead announcing, "Beware, don't trust me!" You've met leaders you instinctively don't trust. The feeling can be hard to put into words, but people "get it" when a leader is closed and secretive.

On the other hand, followers also have a positive gut reaction to the "truth factor" in openness. Candid speech is a trademark of an open leader, and transparent actions and policies are the currency by which a leader earns loyalty, commitment, and willingness of followers. The combination—candid speech and transparent actions—unleashes creativity and innovation and sets the stage to bring out the best in people.

> Congruent words and actions earn trust.

The ability to match words and actions is at the core of sincerity. You can't teach sincerity or authenticity; however, you can learn to value both the truth and being truthful.

A Heads-Up

[I have a] preference for criticism that is open-ended, capable of surprise, and subversive of traditional standards and forms.
—BLANCHE H. GELFANT, Dartmouth professor

Being open and striving to retain integrity in all your dealings are not without pitfalls. You may get push-back. You may even be attacked or ridiculed by those who fear openness. When you're open, you can be seen as a threat to closed minds, to the power-and-control people. An open leader rattles the cages of convention, questions everything, and constantly looks for opportunities, innovation, and creativity, both personally and organizationally.

There's no such thing as a little bit open. It's like being pregnant: you either are or you aren't. However, it's hard work to be open, stay open, and live an open life. Being truly open may even conflict with things in which you have a great investment such as your belief systems and values. It takes courage to go through the mental gymnastics of questioning why you do what you do or why you think as you do. But the strength gained from openness far outstrips the supposed safety that secrecy provides.

To feel more secure about being open, ask a mentor what experiences he or she has had in this area. Did the mentor need to defend himself from those who wished to keep secrets?

To assess your ability and willingness to be a leader who values honesty and truth, gather your peers for a frank discussion of openness and its by-products, honesty and integrity. The very fact that you're doing this signals your openness. To get you started on the path to being more open, ask yourself the following:

- How do I define openness?

- What's the relationship between integrity and openness?

- On a scale of 1 to 5 (5 being the highest), how do you rank openness as a quality of A New Breed Leader? And why?

As a leader who has the self-confidence and self-esteem to be open, you'll always be in high demand.

The Wisdom of Honesty and Truth

Honesty is the first chapter in the book of wisdom.

—THOMAS JEFFERSON

The more power you have and the higher your leadership skills take you, the more critical it becomes to maintain openness and have access to the truth. As former U.S. Senator Sam Ervin of South Carolina said, "It is impossible to overmagnify the importance of seeking truth. This is so because truth alone can make us free." That's true in government, business, communities, and our personal lives. Only when we know and understand the truth can we make wise decisions and take sensible actions.

In reflecting on the damage he caused during the Watergate break-in and cover-up, President Richard Nixon said, "I can see clearly now . . . that I was wrong in not acting more decisively and more forthrightly in dealing with Watergate." His belated, but welcome, frankness should be a lesson to twenty-first-century leaders. When openness is lacking, the ambiguity it creates can stop a family, a company, or a country in its tracks. When people get lost in the shadowland of secrecy, they don't know how to operate. Initiative and

> We swallow greedily any lie that flatters us, but we sip only little by little at a truth we find bitter.
> —DENIS DIDEROT, 1762

potential are destroyed because everyone is trying to figure out what the true situation is, where they fit in, and how to operate amid the hazy actions and double messages. "Sunshine is the greatest disinfectant against secrecy," Supreme Court Justice Louis Brandeis famously wrote in *Harper's Weekly*, December 1913.

One of the most significant insights for A New Breed Leader is that rampant and excessive secrecy is a critical danger to democracy and any free enterprise.

When truth is absent, we're robbed of our ability to make good decisions, chart the proper course, and establish a moral compass. When the leader begins with truth, right actions follow. The actions may not be easy, but they always end up being easier to live with than deceit, lying, corruption, or fraudulence. Humorist Stephen Colbert wasn't being totally funny when he said, "You don't look up truthfulness in a book, you look it up in your gut."

Truth and integrity are Siamese twins in the leader's arsenal of superior qualities. But getting to the truth isn't always easy for a leader. As an old story has it, when a new president of a large firm was named, one of the older directors warned him, "You have heard the truth for the last time." As A New Breed Leader, you'll need renewed courage to maintain a high level of integrity by searching for truth at every level of your organization and within yourself. Let's move on to reestablish openness as the rudder that guides our ship of leadership. Maybe it's even time to add a position of CTO, Chief Truth Officer, to the array of executive positions we now have in our organizations.

Meet Joe Driscoll

Joe Driscoll is such an authentic leader, so comfortable in his own skin and with such a passion to succeed, that I will be quoting him at length throughout this chapter in the hope that his wisdom, clear thinking, and successful use of openness will inspire you to be an open leader.

In 1990, Joe Driscoll left Blue Cross Blue Shield of Massachusetts, where he had a twenty-year career and rose to the level of Senior Vice President of External Affairs to form his own consulting practice. He is currently President & CEO of two companies in Puerto Rico: Socios Mayores en Salud, a TPA, and American Health Medicare, a Medicare Advantage HMO. In 1998, he became COO of Private Healthcare Systems (PHCS). Within a year he became CEO of PHCS, which was losing $1 million a month and faced a huge turnaround challenge. By 2006, when PCHS was acquired by MultiPlan, Joe and his team were able to deliver a tenfold growth in the value of the company. It was during this acquisition period that Joe hired me to design and conduct a program for his management team entitled "Leading Effectively During a Time of Great Change." I was struck by Joe's openness and how he made it a part of the DNA of his firm.

The first time I met Joe was during a telephone meeting in

which we discussed his ideas about my participation. He was an excellent listener, which made me feel that he really cared about what I had to say. He asked in-depth questions and follow-up questions. He put all of his key points in perspective by telling me about the company's history and the challenges he was facing in the acquisition. He did not hold back; I knew I was getting the unvarnished truth.

When I finally met him in person, his demeanor, his voice, his handshake, and his smile made a strong statement about his open personality. I watched how openly he interacted with his people. He is a humble man who does not need the trappings of a high position. The truth factor is in full boom in Joe Driscoll. I asked Joe about openness and integrity.

If you're going to be open, then you've got to have integrity. They are inextricably connected. You can't be open and be misleading people, and they know that. When they know that there's integrity in management involved, it reinforces credibility and leads to real commitment to the corporate objectives.

One of the first things I said when I got to Private Health Care Systems was to tell everyone that this is going to be an open group of people. We're going to work together. We're going to respect each other, have full and complete discussions, be honest with each other, and then move forward to get the job done. I said that from day one. I knew it was the right thing, and I knew it because I had seen so many other companies not do as well as they could have because they were not open. I believe it absolutely has to begin at the top. And it didn't in the examples that I saw previously in my career. A big part of it is seeing others and maturing and knowing I had made mistakes along the way by what I'd call perhaps a brash openness and learning to lead in an open way, by example and not by challenge.

It's a lot like coaching. I've been involved with my kids in youth athletics, and I played a lot of ball myself. I always believed that as a coach or a player, people respond much better to *"Way to go, good job, keep it up,"* as opposed to the negative approach that many coaches take, like a Bobby Knight, let's say. It's not my style.

Positive reinforcement works better if you approach it in a fashion that says you want the people who work for you and work with you to really do well, to grow, to achieve, to be happy, it'll work. Thomas Aquinas defined love as a wishing well. If you think about it, that really is a pretty good definition.

The Openness Puzzle Piece

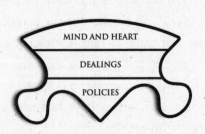

Little is gained in a lifetime if what you believe at age seven is still how you feel at age thirty-seven. . . . New things cannot come where there is no room.

—MARLO MORGAN, author and retired health care professional

The openness puzzle piece has three components. The mind and heart lead to open dealings, which support open policies. The policies give vent to the mind and heart again and the cycle perpetuates.

Open Mind and Heart

Now that you've seen examples of how not being open can lead to sabotage and that adopting a sense of openness can lead to effective leadership, let's look at what's involved/what comprises this trait. Openness of heart and mind go hand in hand. They are the elements of using your head in a logical way and using your heart in sensitive ways. I have not yet found a leader with an open mind but a closed heart, or vice versa, or an organization with open policies but not open dealings. They are all interlocked. Change and adaptability are inherent in their openness. You cannot be averse to change or to being adaptable if you intend to embrace openness and use it to its highest and best application. Everything you do depends on how you accept, handle, and proceed with change.

When you examine the concepts of and differences between philosophy and ideology, you'll quickly see the power of openness and willingness and ability to change.

Philosophy: You have a belief system, possibly even a very strong one, but you're willing to listen to the other point of view and perhaps adapt or change. It's the door to openness and the future.

Ideology: Your mind is made up; you don't listen or even consider the evidence or another way of thinking. You have cataracts of the mind and heart and can't see what's possible. It's a dead end and involves living in the past.

As a twenty-first-century leader, you'll need to get past ideology so your followers, regardless of their own philosophy, can be inspired to follow your example of openness.

One key skill for this is curiosity. It is such a big part of being open. As children, we are so curious about how things work. Little children are an open book. They just say it like it is and deal with people and situations in honest terms. They don't learn guile, slyness, and deviousness except by the example of others. When they are taught to be open in their thinking, they develop an open philosophy toward life.

Curiosity also means bold thinking and innovation. These are vital traits of an open leader who creates open environments where followers flourish.

Andrea Jung, CEO of Avon, and Joe Driscoll exhibit a philosophy of open mind and heart, dealings, and policies.

I first met Andrea Jung when she was president of Avon America, and it's been fascinating to watch her career. She is now chairman and CEO of Avon and on the board of directors of General Electric and Apple and is a member of the boards of New York Presbyterian Hospital and Catalyst.

Once, when I was the keynote speaker at one of Avon's national meetings, I watched Andrea and two of her senior executives on stage taking questions. It was a courageous, no-holds-barred session. Their open, candid responses and sense of partnership with the group were exceptional. On one particularly delicate issue, Andrea said, "I don't know the answer to that. What is your name? Okay, I'll find out and get back to you." She was known for her dependability, so when she said that, it defused the whole issue because the audience knew from past experience that she'd keep her word to respond.

I found out later that she did follow up, and it was easy to see why she's earned enormous credibility with her followers.

In 2007, Andrea was ranked Number 9 on *Fortune* magazine's "50 Most Powerful Women in Business" list, which she's been on since its inception. She's also been one of the *Wall Street Journal*'s "50 Women to Watch" since 2004, and she was one of only eighteen executives included in *U.S News & World Report*'s "America's Best Leaders 2007."

Ground Rules for Followers

Be sure to lay out the ground rules. Let your followers know that, good or bad, easy or hard, truth and openness will be the standards by which your organization will live. When everyone knows the rules about openness, it releases creativity by freeing them from the need to build silos in which they protect themselves.

You owe it to your followers to give them clear guidelines about openness, as Joe Driscoll did at PHCS.

It absolutely begins with top management, and that takes a certain amount of strength and confidence in yourself because you're not always going to be right. When you're really open, sometimes you're going to have to come back and say, "Okay, we're going to make an adjustment here." People will accept that when they trust you.

When we were going through the sale, they understood I could not tell them everything about the process. They knew that I would tell them what I could, when I could. There were some things that I simply could not talk about because of confidentiality issues. They knew as soon as we could tell them, I would. I had been operating this way long enough that they trusted me.

Openness has to permeate the organization. It begins with the senior group. The way we conduct ourselves is certainly observed by the next level and two levels down and perhaps everybody. We worked very, very hard at that, because that was part of succession planning, too. That was part of what I felt was very important in the personal growth and the management growth of the next level down. It was important that people not feel threatened if they said something wrong or incorrect. I constantly communicated the importance of giving reinforcement for all contributions.

Joe went on to talk about the benefits of openness.

Openness has so many benefits to the organization. There are so many uncertainties in personal life and business life, I used to say to people, "We're here working together most of our waking hours, and we should really work together as friends and family. If you're walking down the corridor, smile at the person you're passing. Say hello. We're not in different camps or in separate groups. We're *all* PHCS. I think you'll find that nothing is better than a smile to generate a smile. And being open with one another is critically important.

Sparking Creativity and Innovation

Creative experiences can be produced regularly, consistently, almost daily in people's lives. It requires enormous personal security and openness and a spirit of adventure.

—STEPHEN COVEY

Allowing others to be open in mind and heart while encouraging them to be honest and candid allows for a good exchange of ideas. Creating an environment where thoughts flow freely and naturally breeds originality and innovation.

As you build creativity among your followers, it raises the bar for everyone. It's like a contest between two champions— each brings out the best in the other. When both competence and openness are present, almost no limits exist to what you can accomplish.

In 1976, for example, years before personal computers were common, Steve Jobs and Steve Wozniak were twentysomethings with little but a radical dream: "Computers are going to be the bicycle of the mind. Low-cost computers are for everyone." They sold a van and two calculators to raise $1,300 and opened Apple Computer, Inc., in Job's garage. They not only had the technical knowledge to build a computer, but they had the creativity and boldness to stick to their dream. Six years later, they were selling 650,000 computers a year, validating their dream of changing people's lives. Surprising progress often results from an open, honest, creative, and inventive atmosphere in which everyone is contributing.

Take a few minutes to delve into your ability surrounding

imagination and creativity. Ask: *How can I grow in these areas? What can I do to enhance or bring these powerful tools to my followers? How would my organization benefit from an infusion of new thoughts and ideas, and inventive and resourceful ways of operating?*

"Thinking outside the box" with what are often called blue-sky questions is an idea from the twentieth century that's still valid. It prods you to see things differently, to be innovative, to nudge your followers out of their comfort zones. Try your version of these three challenges:

- What would you do if your R & D budget were tripled and you could develop any product you wanted?

- What would you do first if you were made CEO of this organization?

- What would you do tomorrow if you won the lottery and did not have to work for money anymore?

Wilfred A. Peterson, philosopher and author, wrote that you use imagination to "look at everything with fresh eyes, as though you had just come forth from a dark tunnel into the light of day."

Here are five creativity builders to give you "fresh eyes" and help move others, both above and below you, into a more open and innovative environment:

1. Use your experiences
Learning from your experiences helps you build the kind of skills you need to attract and maintain good followers. In fact, you already have many such insights of which you are probably unaware. There's gold in the hills and rivers that you've traversed

to get to where you are today. The nuggets of wisdom are just waiting for you to find them. Let's take a backward journey with some insightful questions and pan for some riches.

Hit your mental replay button and think of a boss or company for whom you worked that was closed to new ideas and lacking in creativity. Then ask:

- What impact did this have on my attitude about my job?

- What impact did it have on my team's ability to solve problems?

- What impact did it have on the quality of service I gave to customers?

- What do I like least about our boss or the company?

- What did I learn about open creative people versus closed people?

- What's the most difficult thing about dealing with a closed person?

- By contrast, what's the best part of dealing with an open person?

Take some time to examine how you can use these insights to be more open and creative. And how you can foster openness and creativity among your followers.

2. Nurture your curiosity

Reignite and nurture curiosity in yourself and others. Use the habit of looking at things backward, upside down, and inside out, to rekindle your childlike curiosity. Thomas Huxley, a British biologist, wrote, "Sit down before facts like a child, and be prepared to give up every preconceived notion, follow humbly wherever and to whatever abysses Nature leads, or you shall learn nothing."

A teacher asked her kindergarten student what she was drawing. "I'm drawing a picture of God," the child said.

"But, sweetheart," said the teacher, "no one knows what God looks like."

"They will in a minute!" the child replied.

Are you that imaginative? Nudge yourself to do at least one offbeat thing each day—take a different route to and from work; what do you see? Strike up a conversation with a stranger and see if he or she adds to your perspective. Play the "What if . . .?" game when next faced with a knotty problem. Venture beyond your normal way of looking at solutions. Research other companies in your field and seek to glean ideas from their problem-solving skills and processes. Read a magazine you know nothing about, or as Bill Gates wrote in *Business @ the Speed of Thought*, "Read books on topics that don't pertain strictly to your business or industry. It's the best way to maintain a broad perspective."

Ponder what you would do if you had to get by with only half your staff—how creative would you need to be? Change your environment by taking a walk in the middle of the workday to clear your head and boost your physical energy. Take a course at a local college about something in which you have absolutely no interest because cross-training opens your options. For instance, the invention of Velcro, the modern theory of electrons, and other advances were made possible because their creators had training in diverse fields.

> The person who won't read isn't any better off than a person who can't read.
> —ANONYMOUS

Find people of other cultures and expertise and begin a dialogue about both of your interests. Be willing to be open and withhold judgment as they talk. Prejudices and preconceived ideas and processes will get in the way, so learn to shut them down. Talk to others about what you're doing, too, and encourage them to do the same. Once again, your example plays a strong role in moving others along the road to increased inquisitiveness.

> The more narrow you are, the fewer options you have.

Prod your curiosity and that of your followers by asking questions like:

- If we didn't care what it cost, how would we solve this?

- If we were starting from scratch, how would we handle this?

- If we didn't need anyone's authorization, what would we do?

- If we didn't care what anyone else thought, how would we act?

- If this were a perfect world, what would our next step be?

- If we'd be respected no matter what we proposed, what would we propose?

Make asking such questions a deeply imbedded part of your organization's culture. Encourage the insight gained from this Chinese proverb: "One who asks a question is a fool for five minutes; one who does not ask a question remains a fool forever."

3. Feast on a creativity "sandwich"

Before he can create, man must have a deep
awareness of the world about him.

—HAROLD A. ROTHBART, author

John Cleese, the English comedic actor best known for being among the founders of Monty Python, has legendary creativity. He says, "We all operate in two contrasting modes, which might be called 'open' and 'closed.' The open mode is more relaxed, more receptive, more exploratory, more democratic, more playful, and more humorous. The closed mode is the tighter, more rigid, more hierarchical, more tunnel-visioned. Most people, unfortunately, spend most of their time in the closed mode."

Your creativity is waiting to be expanded by a childlike state of exploration in which everything is possible. To tap into that creativity, use the method of analysis (the bread), then brainstorming (the meat), and then more analysis (the bread) to make your creativity "sandwich." For instance, start out with a left-brain-like dissection of a problem (for example, how to boost soda sales). You might think about ways to improve the product, energize the sales force, or increase advertising. Then practice switching into more of a free-form, right-brain process. ("Why do people buy sodas? What's the function of advertising? Is it to increase the demand for sodas in general or only to increase public desire for ours?") Finally, return to logical thinking to see how you can apply the fruits of your imagination.

Most of us tend to stay in our comfort zones, resisting change of strong habits built to deal with problems. We may not even realize we've closed our minds to possibilities. The sad part is that a closed mind isn't only closed to outside thoughts, it's often closed to itself as well, closed to anything that threatens the status quo.

To break the bonds of old thinking, it helps to have a sense of humor. I smiled when I read what British author Terry Pritchett said about openness: "The trouble with having an open mind, of course, is that people will insist on coming along and trying to put things in it."

> Keep an open mind; something good may just fall in.
> —SCOTT FRIEDMAN, humorist

That's your goal: to have teams of people putting new ideas into each other's minds. So try to nudge others out of the comfortable. If you can open the doors, maybe just a crack at first, ideas that have been patiently waiting at the gates will flood in.

4. Reject perfectionism

Albert Einstein, whose imagination was legendary, wrote, "I think and think for months, for years. Ninety-nine times the conclusion is false. The hundredth time, I am right." Perfection was not his MO, and neither should it be for creative leaders or followers. Instead, finding the kernel of a great new idea is what an open mind is all about. Thus, the old adage "Anything worth doing is worth doing well" might be rewritten to say, "Anything worth doing is worth doing poorly at first."

It's good to remember that the best baseball player only gets a hit once every three or four times at bat. Encourage your followers to take plenty of swings at the ball before expecting to get a hit. Leave room for exploration and curiosity in a punishment-free environment.

In a course nicknamed "Failure 101" at the University of Houston, students were asked to build the tallest structure possible out of ice pop sticks, then to look for what they could learn from each failure. Those who ended up with the highest structures inevitably experimented the most and suffered the most collapses along the way, while, it was said, those who got stuck following a fixed idea from the outset never finished first.

Your followers should know that you expect and accept error and failure along the way and are committed to learning from mistakes. That eliminates the need for perfection and opens the door to innovation. The most successful people and organizations have a high degree of accepting failure and mistakes. Communicating the message that everyone is encouraged to keep their eye on future opportunities is one of your strongest leadership examples.

5. Encourage and praise against-the-grain thinking

One of your most challenging tasks as a leader is to provide new information to expand your followers' thinking, new ideas to spark their creativity and broaden their horizons, and new experiences to build a belief in the value of change. If you did a survey about openness, you'd find that most of us are imprisoned by our habits and by organizational culture. We're probably more timid in our thoughts than we need to be. As business guru Tom Peters says, "Every organization needs at least one weirdo on the staff." Maybe "weirdo" isn't a term to aspire to. Perhaps "bold thinker" or an "independent mind" is better. Whatever the term, seek to become known as someone who doesn't fear boldness, who will encourage and praise against-the-grain thinking.

> One of the most rewarding experiences a leader can have is watching followers blossom and grow from new ideas, information, and experiences.

Be a leader who will sometimes ignore the organization's rule book for the sake of a greater good. As a leader, you need to reduce or get rid of the barriers of inhibition and self-criticism in your organization. Start encouraging provocative, even outlandish ideas. It takes courage to get used to the inherent messiness of the idea-generating process.

Ask: *"What am I doing to lead others to think in bold fresh ideas? Do I praise people when they do?"* Bold thinkers all seem to have faith in their own talents and skills. More important, they have faith in the desire of others to do well. It's vital that you use this faith as a motiva-

> Rejecting ideas too soon is like opening a package of flower seeds and then throwing them away because they're not pretty.
> —ARTHUR VAN GUNDY, Ph.D.

tional tool to point your followers in a positive, productive direction. Ask yourself, *"Am I giving them the time and encouragement they need to think creatively?"*

At the 3M Company, employees are encouraged to spend 15 percent of their work time on non-task-related creative thinking. Performing this "skunkworks" duty, as it's called, has paid big dividends: Post-it Notes, three-dimensional magnetic recording tape, and disposable medical masks are just a few of the products spawned as a result. In fact, nearly 70 percent of this Fortune 500 firm's annual sales come from creative ideas originating within its own workforce.

What can you do to spur creativity in your followers? One of the best ways to both get results *and* encourage a new style of thinking is to be open to "brainstorming." That's a group problem-solving methodology in which people bounce ideas off each other. No idea is excluded or criticized, no matter how ridiculous.

KEYS TO SUCCESSFUL BRAINSTORMING

1. Create the right climate. Brainstorming works best when these conditions are met: (a) the group contains a lot of diverse expertise; (b) you clearly explain that you want its members to take "ownership" of an idea or solution; (c) you're prepared to be creative, really let your hair down, and listen to some "out of the box" ideas and (d) you want them to have fun and enjoy the game.

2. Seek maximum contribution with minimum inhibition. Maintain control without blunting the enthusiasm. You should write on a blackboard or flip chart every idea, or even a shard of an idea, that pops up. And give constant recognition: Praise not the content but the offering of each idea. Don't allow criticism of the idea, no matter how bizarre.

3. Ask outrageous questions. Taking on challenges that have no solution can jump-start creativity and open-mindedness in followers. Here are three to begin with.

- You have twenty-four hours to bring about world peace. How do you do it?

- You have one year to clean all pollution on Earth and make sure it doesn't return. What is your plan?

- Aging is not for sissies. How do you eliminate it?

4. Coalesce the ideas. When the group runs out of ideas, take the lead in scouring the list for those that have promise. Stand ready to entertain new ideas at any time. Keep recording the main points the group makes. Distill the semifinalists, and then focus the discussion on these until there's a group consensus about the preferred solution, idea, or concept.

5. Praise—and pick. As the leader, it's your responsibility to decide whether to adopt the consensus decision in whole or part. But whatever you decide, make sure participants feel their contribution was an important one, that their role in the process was valued. Openly acknowledge their participation and contribution.

6. Ask yourself a final question: Is the idea one that you would've thought of on your own? It probably won't be. If so, you will have proof positive of the value of future brainstorming sessions.

Encouraging Bold Thinkers

Encouraging your followers to feel free to participate supports open dealings which involve both the head and the heart (logic and sensitivity).

Joe Driscoll gives a good example:

A story I told often was about walking out of a meeting with a guy who immediately started complaining that they didn't cover this and they didn't cover that. So I said to him, "We were just in the meeting. Why didn't you bring it up?"

I told my employees all the time, "We need you, we need your input in the meetings. That's why you're invited to the meeting. You have a wonderful background, skill, and talents that we need, and it means more than sitting there and observing. It means participating and not being afraid to participate."

So the openness goes down, and then people grow. I saw

wonderful growth in our leadership group. It was a very significant objective of mine to bring them along, and I took an honest joy in seeing them grow in and beyond their jobs. They were encouraged to ask questions and so they learned to make comments beyond their areas of expertise.

Try to mold an organization that is free of criticism when bold thinking and actions occur. Encourage a bias for risk taking, and use failure as a springboard to future success.

When you become a champion of bold ideas, whether your own or others, that's a magnet that attracts followers. It's part of your authenticity and integrity. It shows them that it is about the team and not about "me."

Open Dealings

Relationships are all there is. Everything in the universe
only exists because it is in relationship to everything
else. Nothing exists in isolation. We have to stop
pretending we are individuals that can go it alone.

—MARGARET WHEATLEY, writer and management consultant

The transparency, the openness, of your interactions speaks volumes about your approach to leading others. The servant leader uses every opportunity to build open relationships in transactions with all stakeholders. Transparency does not mean giving away your organization's proprietary products, services, or ideas. It means adapting the old GE tenet of making the work seamless where everyone knows what everyone else is doing so that the process runs smoothly. Transparency also means avoiding the silo mentality where people horde information to enhance their position.

We're all interdependent. We need the open minds who think differently, those geniuses who make up the Enlightener and Creator groups in the pyramid of New Breed Leaders. But while they set the stage for change, it takes teams of individuals willing to work together to make their visions a reality. The relationship between the leader and the led must create a sense of membership in a community of common values and goals. Once again, let's ask some pointed questions:

- What kind of relationship do I want my openness to create with both my followers and other leaders?

- How can I use open dealings to build these relationships so that together we can translate our vision into specific objectives and strategies?

- How can I use openness as an anchor of stability in the midst of the constant change we're experiencing?

While the twenty-first century has some unique challenges, there is no exception to the rule that your dealings with others must be grounded in fairness and integrity. And that you expect the same from others. Both of these are an open head and heart issue. Your authenticity and credibility depend on your open dealings.

Followers need to be able to trust that you will support them and stand by them. They must also know that if someone in the organization acts unethically, improperly, or tries to stab anyone in the back, you as leader will not tolerate it. You will take action immediately and appropriately.

Joe Driscoll gives an example of this:

> I fired a very old friend who was in a very senior executive position because he very badly managed a sexual harassment issue that I knew nothing about until it was a mess. He is a very good guy, great guy, but he did not want to be supervised. I had several people in the organization come to me to say, "Thank you." They said that I was being watched to see what I was going to do because they knew he was an old buddy.

Your people must have confidence that there's enough integrity in the organization that they are not going to get stabbed in the back, or if they are, that the boss isn't going to let it stand.

As a leader, you must be able to make hard decisions. You need unpolluted information; otherwise you end up with GIGO (garbage in, garbage out). When dealing with others, a leader must search for answers and ask probing questions, such as: *What's their bias? What have they left out? What else should I be looking for? What's the full story?*

Respect and sensitivity to people and situations are the keys and require using both an open mind and heart. You want answers, of course, but you want to ask questions in a way that builds relationships, not destroys them. Putting people on the witness stand and interrogating them never works. You don't get the information you need, and people resent being grilled. Instead, try to:

- Question without being paranoid and cynical
- Probe without being disrespectful
- Insist without being aggressive
- Search without being biased

Astronomer Vera Rubin writes about the importance and power of "dark matter" in the universe. She tells us that in space, what is *between* particles is equal or even more important than the particles, no matter how minute. We're just beginning to learn about dark matter and its effect on our entire universe.

Let's look at leadership in a similar way. In leadership, what you don't see can be more telling than what you see. For example, a beautiful annual report filled with feel-good numbers and facts can be quite misleading. You'd have to read between the lines to find the truth, and even then may not find it all. If authorities and investors could have seen the truth in the annual reports of companies like Enron, WorldCom, Adelphia, or Tyco—which not only inflated profits but lied about the actual strength of the firms—we might have been spared a lot of human pain and corporate disgrace.

As a leader, you must strive to be open in all your dealings: with your employees, your supervisors, your customers, your shareholders, and even your board of directors. Joe Driscoll also exemplifies this:

> I was on the board of PHCS as well, but as far as all the management dealings with the board, I applied the same principle I wanted from my employees. Whenever the opportunity presented itself, I would say, "I want to hear the bad news." And I dealt with the board with absolutely full disclosure. That was the only way to deal with them, that's how they got everything. There was never anything nuanced, let alone held back. I was straightforward and gave them all the facts they needed. Whether it was good news or bad news, they had it all so that there could be a full discussion and full understanding of what was happening with the company.

Joe talked about openness in dealing with customers:

> I was always as honest and straightforward as I could be with customers. It's the old expression, "underpromise and overdeliver." I tried to instill that in people. Our customers would go out of their way to comment on how straightforward we were and how they could believe what our people said to them. They could "take it to the bank."

COMMUNICATIONS AND HONESTY

Very little is more ethereal than trust. You come by it from many avenues and especially from all forms of your communications—how you talk, how you walk, what you do with, to, and for others. Honesty and directness—especially in speech with forthright, frank, and straightforward language—will keep communication lines open.

When PHCS was in the process of being sold, it was a very stressful time for employees. They had many questions, fears, and concerns. Although there were some things Joe could not discuss because of confidentiality issues, he took steps to make sure his employees knew he was being as open as he could be.

> I would have meetings with employees in person when they could ask questions, but I knew it was intimidating for many people to get up in a group and ask a question. In recognition of that we established an e-mail box entitled "Ask the President." This was done in the context of the transaction (acquisition) because I knew there would be a lot of rumors.

The employees could ask anything they wanted. In fact, when I told them about this, I said, "You're going to have all sorts of questions. They will be treated anonymously, and I anticipate that many of the questions are going to be what-about-me questions. That's the most natural thing in the world, so don't hesitate to ask them."

I had a discipline that I'd respond within twenty-four hours to all questions and that we would publish all the questions and answers. We set up a place on our website, our Intranet, where people could go to "Ask the President" and see all the questions that had been asked historically over months so that they could look at all the questions and what my answers to them were. So it really did an awful lot to put away their fears. Two days before we completed the sale, I received about 125 e-mails from employees. Many of them talked about the openness. It touched me deeply.

Even if your message as leader is not positive or welcome, candor will empower everyone. This also applies to your superiors. Talking truth to power is not easy. Your followers may hesitate to tell you the unvarnished truth. (We'll talk more about this in Chapter Seven, "Power Matters.") Bad leaders will kill the messenger because they don't like the message. The good leader welcomes the news as a means of keeping in touch with all stakeholders and to keep his or her power in balance.

Philosopher Wilfred Peterson wrote, "Out of crises flow new ideas, new approaches, new patterns, new inventions, new discoveries, new leadership. . . . A crisis is a test and those who meet it and overcome it become stronger in the process."

BUILDING OPENNESS BRINGS VALUE

Minds are like parachutes—they only function when open.
—THOMAS DEWAR

The best way for you to build a culture of openness involves using team participation to create a common plan for autonomy and self-expression. When followers define openness with the emphasis on results and outcomes, using the *who, what, where, when, why,* and *how* methods we discussed in the introduction, they discover the formula for achieving the outcomes. The more your team creates its own definitions, the more realistic it becomes, and its sense of ownership encourages people to want to be more open. The benefit is that input from everyone creates a commonality of goals and a community atmosphere. Peer pressure can be a very positive tool, especially when it comes to being an open person.

At times, it will take great courage to take the long-term steps that instill transparency as the standard way of operating. You'll meet resistance. It's imperative that you watch for the dangerous signs of "covering your back," sabotaging learning, avoiding responsibility, and resisting change. A strong hand (yours) at the helm will steer your organization through the rough waters of either changing a closed culture to an open one or creating an open one from the beginning.

A culture of openness has many benefits. It brings stability to the organization, helping you retain good people. It creates value for all shareholders and it adds value to the company. Joe Driscoll shared with me how a culture of openness improved PHCS:

The value of the company improved. The focus on the customer improved. The focus on absolute quality was in all that we did, and we would talk about that a lot. Quality was operational quality. It certainly was clinical quality. It was quality in the responsiveness to the customer. We would talk about quality all the time, and we were able to deliver it better and better because we had a team that was really growing and maturing in their jobs. We had a wonderful situation with a group of people who knew that politics was anathema, that if they had a problem, they should be open about it. They should be articulate in expressing their opinions, but then once a decision is made, they should make sure that we're all rowing in the same direction.

I worked at companies in the past where that didn't occur. There would be discussion, one person or two or however many wouldn't get their way, if you will, and they wouldn't revolt but they would be passive-aggressive. They'd leave the room, and they simply wouldn't be on board with what was good for the company or the customer or other stakeholders. At PHCS we didn't allow that. It was always clear what our direction was once we had a full discussion.

I think that when you have an open culture and an open environment, it covers more than just the boss being open and telling the truth. People like predictability. People like to have confidence that when they come to work, things aren't going to be different today than they were yesterday and that they understand where the company is going; they understand what the goals and objectives are, and they understand what their job is to get us to those goals and objectives. Openness establishes integrity within the organization.

> Belief in the integrity of the leadership team creates tremendous trust among all the employees. That *trust* will bring most employees to *believe* in the goals and objectives of the organization and then to *commitment* to the achievement of those goals.

Open Policies

Now there's a man with an open mind—
you can feel the breeze from here!
—GROUCHO MARX

While Groucho was joking about an empty mind, he really did hit upon something important. Creativity, innovation, and excitement about possibilities die in closed environments with hidden agendas. When we encounter open policies, it's like a cool breeze that refreshes us.

Be sure you approach all of your stakeholders with the idea of *"Doing right is what works"* versus *"Doing whatever works is right."* There's a huge difference, and your and your organization's reputation could hinge on that difference.

In this new century, it will take leaders at all levels, in all sectors, and across the globe to move to new ideas and processes. Transforming visions and strategies in outmoded systems or organizations will not be easy. As A New Breed Leader, you have a powerful tool to help you begin, and that is the quality of openness. It is the fuel of your commitment to transform your organization, whether it is a small shift or a major overhaul.

The cycle of continual transformation begins with your commitment, which inspires followers to create the vision, and fires the creativity, enthusiasm, and imagination of teams across all functions. When their ideas and actions are valued, it attracts even more energetic and committed followers, which reinforces your commitment to be open to all possibilities.

The Power of a Transformational Leader

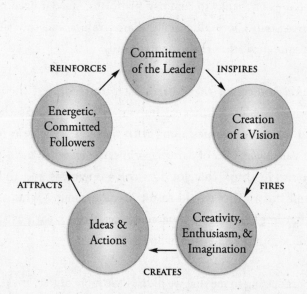

The people who lead the way in finding answers and solutions to our local, national, and global problems will be the transformational leaders of the twenty-first century.

Rosabeth Moss Kanter, the Harvard professor and bestselling author, wrote in the *Harvard Business Review* (January 2008) about companies—such as IBM, Proctor and Gamble, OMRON, Cisco, and Banco Real—that produce meaningful innovations quickly and globally:

A decisive shift is occurring in what might be called the guidance systems of these global giants. Employees once acted mainly according to roles and decisions handed down to them, but they now draw heavily on their shared understanding of mission and on a set of tools available everywhere at once. They more readily think about the meaning of what they do in terms of the wider world and include external partners in the extended family. Authority is still exercised and activities are still coordinated—but thanks to common platforms, standardized procedures, and, above all, widely shared values and standards, coherence now arises more spontaneously.

As Kanter indicated, these firms have transformed themselves from impersonal machines to human entities, and as they do, they pull other companies along with them. They appear to have in their values the idea of *doing right is what works best*.

One might think that Joe Driscoll's openness and the value he brought to PHCS would result in subordinates who grew so much they left for what were perceived as better positions at other companies. But, he says, that's not the case:

It was amazing to me that we didn't have more of that level person moving on. They enjoyed what they were doing. They loved their job. What happened in allowing them to speak more, to grow more, to realize more that they're a part of a team was that they stayed. Work was very enjoyable to them. In fact, I would comment at meetings and say, "Look around the room. Remember where we were five or six years ago? A lot of you have been in the jobs you're in, more or less, for five or six years now. You are really subject matter experts." I would point that out to them that this team was one that was very, very good at what it did and they were really experts at what they did.

Your Openness Legacy

No pessimist ever discovered the secrets of the stars, or sailed to an uncharted land, or opened a new heaven to the human spirit.

—HELEN KELLER

When you look at leaders who've left a positive and long-lasting legacy, you'll find at their core an attitude, a spirit, of openness. As Helen Keller alluded to, they're optimists. They have the gift of hope in the future. They're willing to put in the hard work of discovering new ideas, taking bold actions, and creating positive expectations. They're able to lift everyone and everything to a better place because of the integrity their openness generates.

How can you begin a legacy in your organization? For starters, try to get a good reading on your perceived openness by asking your followers to rate you. Of course, it's not easy to open yourself to criticism. However, there's much to gain by discovering what your followers think and feel about your openness.

Give them the short assessment form that follows, and ask them to respond anonymously. Provide them with a deadline and make it easy for them to give it back to you privately. (That may mean giving them a hard copy instead of e-mailing it.) This assessment is also posted on my website so you can download it at no cost. Simply go to www.anewbreedofleader.com. You will find the assessment in a PDF format that you may print and distribute.

This evaluation will help you discover how your followers rate your openness. Here's a rough guide to judging the results. If you score:

- 35 or less . . . start working diligently on the fundamentals outlined in this chapter.

- 36–50 . . . pick one or more dimensions where you need work and focus on improving them.

- 51–75 . . . you're well on your way to becoming a paragon of leadership openness.

- 76 or more . . . pat yourself on the back—and buy your company's stock.

As you read the results, understand that . . .

- Some people will say what they think you want to hear.

- Some people will use this opportunity to take a personal shot at you.

- Some people will respond with their true feelings.

For best results, eliminate perfect or near-perfect scores and the lowest or worst results. That doesn't mean you don't need to improve. Instead, the idea is to produce a bell curve to see how *most* followers rate your openness.

OPENNESS ASSESSMENT

On a scale of 1 to 10 (with 10 being highest) how would you rate

_____ (leader's name) on his/her

openness to you and others in your company or organization?

1	2	3	4	5	6	7	8	9	10
Poor		so-so		fair		good			excellent

_____ He/she is always as candid as circumstances will allow.

_____ He/she speaks plainly; one doesn't need to "interpret" his/her meaning.

_____ He/she works to create a culture of openness throughout the organization.

_____ He/she shows personal respect and sensitivity in a way that builds relationships.

_____ He/she tolerates a reasonable amount of error and mistakes if they lead to eventual improvement.

_____ He/she is open to new ideas, even if they're offbeat.

_____ He/she encourages the asking of questions.

_____ He/she in times of crisis works openly and calmly with the team.

_____ He/she discusses with followers the need to be open.

_____ He/she accepts bad news without the need for "sugarcoating" it.

_____ TOTAL

With those results in hand, you can chart a course for your development in leadership legacy.

A History of Openness

Space travel seems so ordinary today. Flights to and from the space station are ten-second sound bites on the evening news. That's sad to me because humans need a grand vision, such as looking at all the mystery and wonder of the universe. Opponents of space exploration are the same sort of folks who would have urged Christopher Columbus to stay home, told Einstein to quit fooling around with crazy equations, and chided Amelia Earhart for her daring.

Apollo 13

The film takes place in 1970. It gives us a perfect example of open leadership.

Just a year before, Neil Armstrong took his first steps on the moon. Following that historic flight people became rather casual about space travel. It was a "Been there, done that" feeling.

But now it's April 1970, and it's Jim Lovell (Tom Hanks), Fred Haise (Bill Paxton), and Jack Swigert's (Kevin Bacon) turn to return to the moon for in-depth scientific research.

Earth: April 11. The sunrise is spectacular. The three astronauts say good-bye, blow kisses, and assure their families that "I'll see you soon" and "I'll be back." Lovell gives his wife a thumbs-up. They take the elevator to the top of the huge Saturn rocket and slide into their seats in the small capsule as the portal is slammed shut.

The huge rockets shake the earth and propel the small capsule and landing module into space right on time. The center engine cuts off just after release of the capsule from the booster engine. They are in outer space.

Earth: Day 3, April 13. Gene Kranz (Ed Harris) says to Lovell, "Jim, it's time to stir the oxygen tanks."

Space: "Copy," answers Lovell. Pilot Jack Swigert performs the common "housekeeping procedure." He hits the oxygen-stir button. Flash! We see deep in the guts of the engine a catastrophic explosion. Sparks fly, and we hear the horrible sounds of wires and tubes breaking. The startled crew looks out the window to see the trail of leaking oxygen. Pieces are falling off the command module hitting the lunar module. Lovell's voice is both calm and anxious as he says, "Houston, we have a problem. Repeat, we have a problem."

Earth: The late-night TV show host Dick Cavett says, "Ladies and gentlemen, I have to interrupt our show. *Apollo 13* has lost all power; their oxygen supply is in danger."

The entire drama in now laid wide open as the world press watches, listens, and analyzes the tiniest bits of information.

Space: *Apollo 13* is in the moon's orbit, and as the spaceship prepares to go around the dark side of the moon, the three astronauts move from the command module into the lunar module to conserve power and try to stay warm. They haven't slept. They're very cold. The stress is clearly taking its toll. Lovell says to Kranz, "See you on the bright side." They fly out of communication range. The minutes drag by like an eternity.

Earth: Famed news anchor Walter Cronkite and Mercury astronaut Wally Schirra are discussing the worst-case scenario—too much carbon dioxide, no heat, and no electricity to run the computers to get back to Earth. The press is now in high-crisis mode repeatedly covering all the worst possibilities. Thousands of people amass in Times Square to watch huge television screens and listen to every word from Cronkite. Pope Paul leads 50,000 people in prayer in Saint Peter's. We see people praying at the Wailing Wall in Jerusalem. The whole earth is holding its breath, waiting.

Gene Kranz, clearly controlling his anxiety, says to the whole team, "We will not lose those guys. Failure is not an option, people. Work the problem, guys, work the problem." Everyone at the command center is working frantically to figure out how to recover a few tiny amps of power so that the capsule computer will function. Another team is making a filter out of plastic and duct tape (items available on the spaceship) so that the astronauts can make a filter to clean the oxygen and remove the carbon dioxide, giving them the lifesaving oxygen they need to return to earth.

Earth: Astronaut Ken Mattingly speaks to Lovell. You can see the reassuring affect his voice has. Lovell asks, "Are you in charge, Ken?" Mattingly says, "Yes, let's bring you guys home."

Space: The three astronauts follow the instructions and build a crazy plastic filter and move out of the landing module into the capsule. They reenter the earth's atmosphere and the heat shield becomes so hot that rain falls inside the module. The g-forces press the three suffering astronauts back in their seats. The capsule is a fireball. The silence begins as the capsule hurtles through the atmosphere to crash into the South Pacific. TV stations broadcast every minute detail of what's happening and depict all the disasters that could occur.

Finally, the parachutes open and the capsule splashes into the ocean. The astronauts are brought aboard the aircraft carrier. The tragedy was avoided.

An important lesson learned from this film is that confident, trained, courageous, humble leaders and teams are not afraid to let others see what they're doing.

The Orbits of Leadership Openness

- Would the strength of your leadership bring the calm and strength needed to save lives?

- Could you lead a major project and let the entire world watch?

- How would you and your team perform under that kind of scrutiny?

Charles F. Kettering was an inventor and creative genius who would have admired the *Apollo 13* teams. "Where there is an open mind," he said, "there will always be a frontier." He looked at the world around him and asked, "How can I make it better?" He answered his own question with amazing inventions, such as the incubator for premature infants, the V-8 engine, the automobile self-starter, the storage battery electrical system, refrigeration and air-conditioning, as well as research in fields such as magnetism, which eventually led to imaging devices used to diagnose illnesses. The list of his inventions goes on and on. One of his most famous quotes speaks to the core of an open receptive mind:

"Nothing ever rose to touch the skies unless someone dreamed that it should, someone believed that it could, and someone willed that it must."

Once again, let's go to your action plan.

Your Action Plan Questions for Quality 3
OPENNESS

■ What can I do to be a more open person? Be specific. What actions will I take over the next month to improve my openness?

■ How would my company or organization benefit if I improve in this area?

■ How often—and in what ways—do I show my followers that I am interested in doing what is right rather than doing what merely looks good? Give some examples.

No matter where you are in your leadership continuum, it's important to think about your legacy. You can be the "someone" Kettering spoke of when you ask, "What do I want to leave to my followers, my organization, my country, and most important, to my children?" These significant questions deserve your serious consideration. Into what frontier will you move? The answer to that will depend greatly on your ability to be an open leader.

CHAPTER FOUR

Language Matters

CONNECTING RELATIONSHIPS

If I went back to college again I'd concentrate on two areas:
learning to write, and to speak before an audience. Nothing in life
is more important than the ability to communicate effectively.

—GERALD FORD, former U.S. president

Your words inspire or discourage, hurt or help, divide or connect, cause fear or give hope. As a twenty-first-century leader, you'll need to make the leap from having good communication skills to being a *wordsmith*, the owner of your language.

"Wordsmith!" That's an intriguing term that conjures up images of someone who can mold and shape words to influence others. To be called a wordsmith could be the highest praise any communicator could receive.

History books are filled with women and men whose words have influenced events. As children, for example, we all learned the words Patrick Henry spoke before the Virginia Convention of Delegates on March 23, 1775, when independence from England was being debated. "Is life so dear, or peace so sweet, as to be purchased at the price of chains and slavery?" Henry asked. "Forbid it! Almighty God! I know not what course others may take, but as for me, *give me liberty or give me death!*"

The power of an eloquent phrase is immeasurable. When we hear "I have a dream . . ." or "Ask not what your country can do for you . . ." we know immediately that Martin Luther King Jr. and President John F. Kennedy spoke these words. They are indelibly etched in history. You may not be pondering revolution, fighting for civil rights, or inspiring a nation in an inaugural address, but your words need to be equally expressive if they are to represent a passionate mission.

The power of language cannot be exaggerated. As you take on the duty of being a wordsmith, your language will be like a still pond into which you throw a pebble—the concentric circles will go out and out. You never know who will be touched by your words. You never know the impact you'll have on others. Be assured that when you speak in aspirational language, you lift minds and hearts. When you speak in clear, honest language, tasks will be completed in good order. When your followers hear and see your skill at communicating, you'll set an example for them to follow.

The Ken Blanchard companies released a study from a survey of 1,400 leaders, managers, and executives. They discovered that 43 percent said communication skills are the most important skill set to possess, while 41 percent said the inappropriate use of communications or listening is the number one mistake leaders make.

Words really matter. String them together artistically and sensitively and they become an inspired instrument by which you connect with your followers. Communication is your most critical tool for motivating your followers to take responsibility for creating a better future.

Variations

Look deeper into the definition of language and you'll find there's language of the heart, of the soul, of the mind, language of the culture, and language of society. We have business, science, legal, and political language as well as an entirely new computer-age language. There's the language of love, of war, of music, literature, and visual arts. So with all these variations, how do you as a leader build your skills to take advantage of both the opportunities and the challenges you face daily?

The best leaders I've seen or studied have been able to use words, in whatever form, to bring together people of differing agendas and backgrounds to form a team. That team can be as small as a family unit or as large as a nation. Without the ability to use language effectively, the other seven qualities that matter most won't have the impact they deserve.

The Highest Use . . . Persuasion

Kind words can be short and easy to speak,
but their echoes are truly endless.
—MOTHER TERESA of Calcutta

The capacity to persuade is one of the most significant elements of your success as a leader. Your language (words and actions) can move you up the pyramid of twenty-first-century leaders, from *Sustainer* to *Builder* and from *Builder* to *Creator*, even perhaps to being an *Enlightener* like Mother Teresa.

Your leadership establishes and communicates the moral tone of your organization. Your team is held together by the words its members hear and the actions they see. When you use your expertise to reinforce the organization's goals, values, ideas, and ideals in the minds and spirit of your followers, your communication becomes an art form.

But at times the impact of your presence—your personal power—will speak more powerfully than anything you could say. Knowing when to be silent is not easily learned or acted upon. It's so natural to want to speak and make your point. Yet leadership is often most influential when it's a quiet strength, shown and expressed with a few words said exceedingly well. As you seek to fulfill your mission and enhance your gift of connecting with others, remember that the persuasion of silence may at times indeed be "golden."

I don't know if you've seen the movie *Norma Rae*, starring Sally Field, but there is a scene in that film that wonderfully illustrates the strength of silence. Norma Rae is a textile worker subjected to intolerable working conditions, and an alliance with a New York labor organization motivates her to take a leadership role and push for the unionization of the workers.

Norma Rae

The year is 1978. Norma Rae (Sally Field in an Oscar-winning performance) is a naive Southern textile worker, widow, and mother in an Alabama mill town whose factory has intolerable working conditions. She's always been content to go along with the status quo, a powerless, down-and-outer whose life is destined to be a drab meaningless existence, like generations before her.

She meets and builds a strong alliance with Reuben Warshofsky (Ron Leibman), a New York labor organizer who recognizes her abilities. He mentors her to build the courage and skills to help him unionize the plant. They set out to accomplish what seems impossible.

After being jailed for protesting, she sits down with her children and says, "You will hear bad things about me. I'm not perfect. I love you, and you know I believe in you and will stand for you. What I am doing is right." Her language is down-home and basic.

She becomes empowered to stand up for her rights in the workplace. A tiny glimmer of hope bursts into a full-blown flame of resistance and resilience to unionize. At the climax of the film, defiant Norma Rae, with her big, sad eyes, her brown hair pulled back in a knot, wearing a sleeveless T-shirt and blue jeans, and with a tool belt around her waist, stands on a table, boldly holding a sign over her head on which she has scribbled one word: UNION.

For what seems like an eternity, she stands there scared, alone, and resolute amid several hundred workers on the factory floor. Everyone is shocked into silence. The only sound is the noise of the machines in the hot, humid workroom. The workers just stare at her in alarm. Fear is on their faces. Fear of the mill bosses. Fear of being beaten up by union busters. Fear of once again being locked out of their jobs, or the use of a "stretch out" against them, which means they only get paid for three days but must do a full week's work to keep their jobs. But Norma Rae's silence screams out the language of downtrodden mill workers everywhere: *"I have had enough! I am here to stay."*

In this highly charged atmosphere, the camera goes from

Norma Rae to a woman down on the floor; she's been persuaded by Norma Rae's courage. Her face reveals her internal battle: Should I or shouldn't I? She gathers her courage, wipes her sweaty face, tightens her lips, and pulls the handle that shuts down her machine. A big black man standing next to her slowly hits an off switch. An elderly, very tired-looking woman gathers all her moral indignation and pulls her off switch. The courage spreads from person to person. And there is Norma Rae, silently holding her sign high over her head.

The factory floor is now totally quiet, no mechanical noise, not a human voice. Just the palpable, silent resistance led by the once-passive follower turned rebel-with-a-cause, hell-bent on bettering the working conditions. Her "language" of actions, her attempts to enlist others, and her bold, daring, and courageous "stand of silence" cement her relationship with the workers, who previously had no leader and either would not or could not stand up for themselves.

She is dragged off the table by sleazy mill management and the sheriff.

The film ends with a scene showing a mill executive and a mill worker sitting at a table in the middle of the factory work floor. Everyone gathers around as they count written ballots for and against the union. When the results are called out, the union has prevailed, and everyone breaks into celebration. Norma Rae has won.

Director Martin Ritt caught the essence of what leadership language is truly about. It's not always eloquent words. In fact, language is so much more than just words. It's also action that exudes belief in a cause. Norma Rae's resilience and persistence are a kind of universal language. As you build your New Breed Leader skills and philosophies, think about the various ways you use language to connect people and how you can build relationships across the table and around the world.

People must trust you before they will trust your message. Language ties all eight New Breed Leader qualities together to create relationships built on belief and mutual respect.

The Language Puzzle Piece

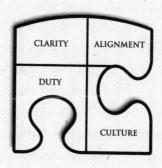

Clarity

All of us know what happened when Dr. Martin Luther King stood up and shouted, "I have a dream!" What do you think we'd remember if he'd said, "I have a strategic plan"?

—LOU HOLTZ, football coach

Clarity means being able to communicate in clear, simple, and precise terms. Clarity means you have given thought to what you say. All good leaders can communicate spontaneously; it is a great leadership asset. Even as you develop the ability to be a spur-of-the-moment thinker and speaker, it is vital to consider the impact your words have on others.

When your words are transparent, people can understand complex concepts and what, if anything, they are supposed to do or how to react to what you say. There is an old expression that says "if it's cloudy in the pulpit, it's cloudy in the pews." In other words, if you are clear in your various forms of communication, you will have a much better chance of engaging your followers. If you can explain things in uncomplicated language, you will get buy-in much more frequently; the more precision you have in your words, the more accurate the outcomes will be.

The terms clear, simple, and precise are the foundations of being a "wordsmith," and the development of highly effective "wordsmith" leaders is more important today than ever before. As a twenty-first-century leader, you must be able to be clear and precise, since this will be a major factor in solving problems and finding solutions.

As we saw in Chapter Two, "Accountability Matters," when James Burke, CEO of J & J, described the Tylenol crisis, he was clear, and every syllable he spoke rang with honesty and compassion.

> Clarity and simplicity gives your message the ring of truth that forges strong and long lasting relationships.

John Hamm, author of *The Five Messages Leaders Must Manage*, gave an excellent example of simplicity and clarity in his article in the *Harvard Business Review*:

One CEO always keeps communications about hierarchy admirably brief and to the point. When he realized he needed to realign internal resources, he told the staff: "I'm changing the

structure of resources so that we can execute more effectively."
After unveiling a new organization chart, he said, "It's 10:45.
You have until noon to be annoyed, should that be your reaction. At noon, pizza will be served. At one o'clock, we go to
work in our new positions."

That's an excellent example of a *Builder* leader (in our twenty-
first-century-leadership pyramid) whom people will follow. Not
only did he recognize the importance of telling his staff that he
knew they wouldn't all like the new policy, but he used humor to
minimize the stress or resistance.

Building Your Wordsmith Art

The language of truth is unadorned and always simple.
—MARCELLINUS AMMIANUS, fourth-century Roman historian

You, as A New Breed Leader, must make learning about words and
their fluid use a lifelong pursuit. The more you can simplify what
you're saying, the more receptive your listeners will be. But that
doesn't mean dumbing down what you say. It means breaking long or
difficult messages into parts so people can digest them more easily.

Thomas Friedman, a *New York Times* columnist and author
of *The World Is Flat*, and also one of our clearest communicators, said, "I am not the greatest thinker. I had low SAT scores.
What I do is connect the dots, take a bunch of disparate ideas in
finance, politics, technology, and geopolitics, and make a theory
around them. Then I explain it in a way the average person can
understand . . . and that average person is me."

If you're willing to work toward a more powerful command of language, a thesaurus is your new best friend. Either purchase one from a bookstore or have one installed in your software program. Look at what a thesaurus can do for a few of the eight qualities of A New Breed Leader:

Competence becomes expertise, capability, skill, proficiency, aptitude, or know-how

Openness becomes honesty, directness, frankness, sincerity, or candidness

Clarity becomes clearness, lucidity, simplicity, precision, intelligibility, or transparency

Power becomes authority, control, influence, command, clout, or sway

Not only can individual words be made to say more, but you can use groups of words to paint pictures. President Franklin Delano Roosevelt used groupings to create images in the minds of people who were demoralized by the Great Depression of the 1930s. He explained what the slogans meant to the average person who was trying to keep his or her life together. He then turned his words into action, which gave him enormous authenticity. He talked about:

"The forgotten man"

"A new deal for the American People"

"The great arsenal of democracy"

When Pearl Harbor was attacked by the Japanese on December 7,

1941, one of President Roosevelt's assistants was helping write the speech to be given to a stunned nation. The assistant wrote:

December 7, 1941: A date which will live in world history.

FDR substituted one word for two, and we have one of the classic lines in oratory:

December 7, 1941: A date which will live in infamy.

Another Enlightener leader, a communicator of equal skill, painted a word picture for us about equality: "I have a dream that one day on the red hills of Georgia the sons of former slaves and the sons of former slave owners will be able to sit down together at the table of brotherhood." Who would not recognize that as Dr. Martin Luther King Jr.?

Jargons, Slogans, and Gobbledygook

*We have too many high sounding words and too
few actions that correspond with them.*

—ABIGAIL ADAMS

I have revamped the old acronym KISS: My version is "keep it short and simple." Fuzzy phrases and jargon, as good as they may sound, don't give people the clarity needed to do their job. Fuzzy language leaves them scrambling for position and increases the likelihood of turf battles. When you communicate a clear vision backed by clear direction, you remove vagueness or uncertainty about your organization's mission and about you as the leader.

The Gobbledygook Test

To pass the test, answer three questions about the words you use:

1. Do people understand their meaning in terms of your purpose or vision?

2. Are they actionable, and if so, how?

3. Can you measure the results implied by the words?

Let's get away from the gobbledygook we hear every day. A major California bank, reporting on its financial standing, stated: "We have $1 billion in non-accrual loans." What does that mean? It means that they have $1 billion in bad debts caused by greedy and imprudent loans. An airline reported that it showed a profit from "one-time conversion of used equipment." That is, it received insurance payments for a plane that crashed. Business schools and corporate America have created unintelligible phrases such as "unlocking shareholder value" and "maximizing utility." To these I want to say, "Yes. And . . . ?"

New Breed Leaders need to make language more precise, not less, and build communication, not erect walls. We need to accept responsibility and accountability for our actions and let people know we do so by our honest, clear language.

We hear terms every day that are at best ludicrous and at worst deceptive:

Revenue enhancement and user fees = more taxes

Negative patient outcome = the patient died

Peremptory retaliation = we shot first

Decrease in the rate of inflation = it's still going up

Found to be redundant = you're laid off

He was neutralized = he was murdered

We use simple yet powerful language in our personal lives when we say things like "I won!" "It's a boy!" "We did it!" and "Play ball!" Let's be sure we also do so as leaders.

The art of simplicity doesn't mean speaking in one-syllable words, or disavowing the language of new technology, or forsaking sensitive, eloquent language. Simplicity means not purposely complicating how you communicate. If you're going to influence others, you need to be honest and clear in your speech. Messages put simply can make a critical difference in your ability to lead.

> The leader who understands the art and genius of simple language has a rare gift.

It doesn't take volumes to make an impact on people's lives. The Declaration of Independence has only 1,322 words. Lincoln's Gettysburg address has 268, and the Lord's Prayer has 56 words. The leader who understands the art and genius of simple language has a rare gift.

The great Supreme Court Justice Oliver Wendell Holmes was invited to give an after-dinner speech. His host gave him the following advice: "What we like is to gather, gobble, gabble, and git—in that order and about that fast." As leaders, we would be wise to get on with it also. Get to the point and then "git."

Clear Slogans and Messages That Work

One spring day in downtown San Francisco, I walked past one of the city's finest hotels, the Clift Hotel. I turned the corner, and within a few feet, I saw the employees' entrance. Above the door a big brass sign reads:

> THROUGH THESE DOORS PASS THE MOST COURTEOUS
> EMPLOYEES IN SAN FRANCISCO.

You might think that passing under that sign every day would blunt the importance of the message for the employees. However, it's obvious to guests that the sign is not just a slogan; it's an ingrained philosophy. Every employee from the general manager to the newest housekeeper knows that it's his or her personal responsibility to fulfill what the brass sign proclaims.

- Do you communicate as clearly to your followers as the sign at the Clift?

- Can you honestly say that your followers really understand your expectations?

- Do you think they have pride in fulfilling your organization's mission?

- What can you do to create slogans as clear and actionable as that example?

Here's another example of a clear message that works:

My husband, Bill, and I were driving home from a meeting with one of our clients. We'd agreed to prepare a complex proposal for a training program in sales and leadership and to deliver it to our client in time for its weekend executive retreat. It was Wednesday afternoon, and our deadline on the proposal was very tight.

We were driving along at 55 mph, discussing how to juggle our schedules, when a white van pulled up beside us. On its side in big red letters were the words EXPRESS IT. Underneath was printed COURIER SERVICE, 24 HOURS A DAY, 7 DAYS A WEEK, with a telephone number. "Wow," I said to Bill, "that's the answer to our delivery problem." I grabbed a piece of paper and started to write down the telephone number.

Just then the driver saw me, tooted his horn, and waved. I waved back. In sign language he asked, "Do you want us?" I nodded and showed him the piece of paper on which I was writing the phone number. He rolled down his window and, at freeway speed, held out a brochure. I was so excited that I started to roll down my window to take it. Bill said, "For heaven's sake, we don't want to get in a wreck. Wait!" So I signaled to the young man that I would call, by holding my cell phone to my ear. He smiled, tooted the horn, and off he went!

We called his company and have since used its services many times. When its employees would pick up packages at our office, we heard the same story repeatedly. They talked about the simple phrase that was posted everywhere in the company—on sticky tags for the van visors, signs in the lavatories, the employee kitchen, in the warehouses, as screen savers and mouse pads, anywhere the owner, Sal Grassia, could reinforce the simple slogan that goes to the very heart of world-class service:

> How do I make it easy to do business with me?
> —Express It

Whether service is given internally or externally, it's the word "I" that sets the tone of personal responsibility of each employee. Apparently, it worked well because a few years ago Sal sold the company for several million dollars.

Nice But Not Actionable

When invited to give a speech or conduct a seminar, I try to sit in on the executives' presentations. It often gives me last-minute clues to the direction, culture, and politics of the organization. I've heard many well-meaning people use clichés and slogans as a way to motivate their teams, such as:

"We are committed to our people."

"Customer service is #1 with us."

"This is a win-win for everyone."

"Let's give it 110%."

Unfortunately, they don't elaborate on the meaning. Such talk makes everyone feel good, but it ends there. The phrases are nice, but are they clear? If you heard them, what would you think you were supposed to do today? What policy or vision are you following? How do these types of phrases add to the other seven qualities like accountability, competence, perspective, and values?

FOUR SIMPLE STEPS TO BETTER COMMUNICATION

As a leader, strive to clear away extraneous issues and make language more precise, not less. Dedicate yourself to using words that communicate instead of obfuscate. Even bad news will go down better if you know what you want to say and have the skill—and the courage—to say it clearly.

Try these steps:

1. Improve your presentation power. Seize every opportunity to speak publicly. Join Toastmasters or a similar group to improve the ease and fluidity of your speechmaking. If the idea of speaking before a crowd makes you nervous, that's all the more reason for doing so. Speaking and making presentations are a big part of what leaders do. If the butterflies in your stomach don't disappear, at least they'll soon "be flying in formation," as an old speaking axiom has it.

2. Study the masters. Read widely, including biographies and collected speeches of the great communicators like Martin Luther King Jr., Eleanor Roosevelt, John F. Kennedy, and Ronald Reagan. Become a devotee of the apt quotation. When the admirable words of others can roll easily off your tongue and when those words are just right for the occasion, you're sure to inspire your followers.

3. Dedicate yourself to speaking plainly. Euphemisms and gobbledygook are epidemic. Be known as someone who speaks honestly and clearly, who says what he means and means what he says. Develop a bias for the honest phrase, such as "the patient died" (not "there was a negative patient outcome") and "laid off" (rather than "was found to be redundant").

4. Seek a mastery of words, written or spoken. "The difference between the right word and the almost-right word," Mark Twain famously observed, "is the difference between lightning and a lightning bug." Always keep a well-used dictionary and thesaurus handy.

A recent emergency room visit with my granddaughter underscored the stark contrast with fuzzy phrases. The minute we hit the front door of the hospital, everyone moved in unison, spoke seldom, focused on their specialty, and their language was precise, clear, and left no room for mistakes.

As you lead your teams through daily performance and emergencies, be sure to clarify vague language. Let everyone know where he or she stands, where the whole team is headed, and how it all fits into their personal part of the game plan.

Clarity Is Connecting Language

The great enemy of clear language is insincerity. When there is a gap between one's real and one's declared aims, one turns, as if it were instinctively, to long words and exhausted idioms, like a cuttlefish squirting out ink.

—GEORGE ORWELL

Simplicity is the key to all your language and messages. Be sure to put them through the gobbledygook test. As A New Breed Leader, the trademark of your communication skills will be the ongoing depth of your "wordsmithing." The world has become so complex that people everywhere long for leaders who can communicate with simplicity and clarity. The leaders I have met that are the most valuable are those who understand that being clear in their language builds bridges between them and their followers.

> Clear open language leads to trust, which builds relationships.

When you think of a leader you admire I would wager that he or she thinks carefully about what they say and how they say it. They have the skill of getting right to the kernel of a thought or idea. All of the leaders I interviewed in this book have the skill of clarity. It is what makes them exceptional people and strong relationship builders. Be courageous and take a close look at how these concepts about clarity apply to your thoughts and actions.

Alignment

Attunement to all stakeholders, and a sense of fit, or harmony—
so what we do and how we do it are reflections of who we are.

—AL WATTS, consultant

All language is about getting your point across. It can be the language of persuasion and influence or of intimidation; it's up to you to decide.

As you strive to form coalitions with others, it's helpful to have a definition to guide you. That definition begins as a question: What does alignment mean in terms of leadership language that matters most?

Alignment is the ability to bring disparate groups together around a common goal and shared values, through the use of personal, organizational, and cultural words, images, and a simple working philosophy.

Many excellent organizations fulfill this definition. One we all know is Starbucks.

HOWARD SCHULTZ AND STARBUCKS

Howard Schultz is not only the CEO, he is also the HCG (head caregiver), HTT (head truth teller), and HBR (head relationship builder) at Starbucks. His simple and connecting use of language not only ensures that what he says meshes with the promises of the Starbucks brand, but that it also makes him a superstar among New Breed Leaders.

He connects with his networks, partnerships, and alliances inside the company and with all external stakeholders, such as customers, suppliers, cities, and governments. He simply and eloquently communicates these principles, his "secrets of success."

1. Don't be threatened by people smarter than you

He's never hesitated to bring in expert opinions to help him make wise decisions, whether it is about coffee beans, employee benefits, store locations, or the global experience he's trying to create.

2. Compromise anything but your core values

In his famous public memo of February 2007, he said, "The Commoditization of the Starbucks Experience" has diluted the magic, replacing its mystic with unremitting commerce. For the first time in decades, it was losing business. Customers were saying that it had become "corporate," rather than the neighborhood gathering place, a home away from home, an extension of people's front porch, an urban oasis to soothe away the harsh realities of the daily grind (no pun intended).

3. Seek to renew yourself even when you are hitting home runs

In the winter of 2008, after a decade of breathtaking success and expansion, Schultz had to come back and take over. His task was to renew the company in the face of slow growth and increased competition. He said he wanted to refocus on the "customer experience." Many stores in the United States have closed, while he continues growth overseas.

4. Everything—and everyone—matters

He's soft-spoken, and his language is polite, with "please" and "thank you" firmly grounded in everything he says. This is a leader who knows what matters most. His values anchor his business and personal philosophies. The one that resonates with all his stakeholders is that everyone wants to be valued and respected. To Howard Schultz, that means everyone. He says that in America, working behind a counter is not viewed as a professional job. He wants to change that. At Starbucks, he wants to provide his people with dignity and self-esteem, not just clever corporate phrases, but tangible benefits.

Keep Your Audience in Mind

Just as Howard Schultz understands the critical issues of connecting with his networks, partnerships, and alliances inside and outside the company, so must you. You have many constituencies and stakeholders with whom you want to share your personal leadership and organizational message. Each has their own specific needs and agendas.

The Six Audiences of Every Leadership Message

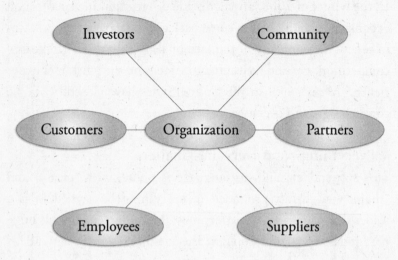

Keeping the six audiences of every message clearly in mind whenever you speak or act will help you be consistent as you build the all-important relationships you need to get things done.

With these audiences in mind, let's look at the best ways to build alignment and consensus with all your audiences.

1. Use inspirational language

The power to inspire people to think and then to act is your number one language tool. We can look to politics for some of the best inspirational language. Presidents and presidential candidates have speechwriters who help them construct their message. You may not have that luxury, but you can still learn from the best.

The late Tim Russert, host of the Sunday morning news talk show *Meet the Press* interviewed presidential historian and Pulitzer Prize–winning author Doris Kearns Goodwin about the use of aspirational language by various presidents such as FDR, JFK, and Reagan. She said that they had warmth and the capacity to create loyalty. "Their empathy gave them the ability to connect. It is an inherent gift of some leaders, you either have it or you don't," she said. But while she doesn't feel that's something that can be learned, she does think that a leader can work at language that inspires.

Among the most memorable phrases in modern times are JFK's "Pass the torch to a new generation" and Reagan's "A shining city on a hill." Each was a good speech, Kearns said, "not good just because of good words but because it touches something inside of people to mobilize them to do something."

The main purpose of FDR's fireside radio chats was to make the nation feel good in times of great despair, and it worked. Since then every president has had radio contact with the public. However, none has done it as well as FDR.

New York Governor Mario Cuomo's keynote address at the 1984 Democratic Convention is an almost perfect 10 on a scale of language that inspires:

We believe in firm but fair law and order.

We believe proudly in the union movement.

We believe in privacy for people, openness by government.

We believe in civil rights, and we believe in human rights.

We believe in a single fundamental idea that describes better than most textbooks and any speech that I could write what a proper government should be: the idea of family, mutuality, the sharing of benefits and burdens for the good of all, feeling one another's pain, sharing one another's blessings—reasonably, honestly, fairly, without respect to race, or sex, or geography, or political affiliation.

2. Narrow the choices

Take care to reject language that creates narrow or false choices. Every issue has multiple variations and shades. While simple language is important, a simplistic attitude of absolutes without the opportunity to expand thinking and actions can be disastrous to your ability to connect with other people. During the Iraq war people have used false language to sell their point, things like "stay and win" or "leave and surrender." Neither of these is true. There were many gray areas that were never examined before invading Iraq or during the occupation because of the emotions that these types of phrases elicit. Be smart enough to carefully examine your language and question narrow parameters and thinking.

3. Avoid playing the fear card

Never, ever, use the language of fear to get what you want. We must have language that binds us together, not language that triggers our rawest emotions in order to gain something by turning people against each other. When you make people afraid, they often react with anger—at someone or something—as a means to calm their emotions.

"When you make people angry, they act in accordance with their baser instincts, often violently and irrationally. When you inspire people, they act in accordance with their higher instincts, sensibly and rationally. Also, anger is transient, whereas inspiration sometimes has a lifelong effect." So wrote the Peace Pilgrim, a Quaker woman who walked all over Canada and the United

States from 1953 to 1981 to promote world peace. Her real name is Mildred Norman, but as she wrote on her twenty-eight-year journey, she wanted her message, not the messenger, to be remembered.

I was once the opening speaker at a small meeting of managers in the food distribution business. The plan was for the president to give a short message of welcome, then introduce me for a forty-five-minute pep talk. The company was in a downturn, and he felt that if I could start the meeting on a positive note, they then could get on to finding ways to solve their problems.

But instead of a quick greeting message, he went off on a tirade about how terrible business was. To this day I can remember his exact words: "Every person in this room is going to be fired. You are a bunch of . . . good for nothings. You failed at your jobs and your families are going to suffer. You had better spiff up your résumés, because each and every one of you is in big trouble . . . Now, here is our guest speaker!"

Gulp! I was so stunned that I simply stood in place and said, "We will take a short break before I begin." I knew I had to quickly rewrite my speech. The people were in desperate need of some recovery time from the tongue-lashing.

During the break, several of them picked up their belongings and left. I asked them why and they said, "We've had it. He rants, raves, and threatens all the time. We're going to do just what he said. Get our résumés out and get another job." Even more amazing to me was that the executive didn't understand why they left.

4. Be wary of "trigger" language

Be careful of what I call "trigger language," which is words or actions that set off a series of unintended consequences. For example, if something is urgent and you say, "Just do what you need to and get it done," that can be dangerous. Listeners can take that as a green light to do what's legally or ethically marginal or to go against the beliefs and values of the organization.

Certainly, you want to express initiative and encourage curiosity, ideas, opinions, and options. But be sure you set some boundaries to "getting it done."

5. Emphasize mutuality

The idea of mutuality—the sharing of benefits and burdens for the good of all—is sure to be one of the strongest global needs in this century. Language that's reasonable, honest, and fair without respect to race, gender, religion, or politics will be one of the greatest alignment tools in our new era.

> Be very careful how you use emotional language. It can backfire on you when you need your credibility most.

In our interview, I asked Dr. Donna Shalala about a leader's ability to align his or her message with all of the different audiences and how it will be different for A New Breed Leader. Here's what she said:

> I think there are different languages. We're going to have to talk more about collaboration and less about hierarchy and authority. We're going to have to be more nimble. Words like "nimble" and "collaborative" are going to be more important in this century.

As you become more aligned with your followers, you reinforce a bridge that can withstand pressure and problems. People will follow your lead if your language reinforces something in which to believe. They want to find fulfillment in their work. They want to be inspired and feel a part of something that matters and is even bigger than they are.

To energize your leadership, and establish the strongest alignments possible, these questions need to be answered and telegraphed as often as possible, in as many ways as possible:

1. What's our mission?

2. What's our overall purpose?

3. What are our goals?

4. What's their origin?

5. How and why did we adopt them?

6. What are our objectives?

7. What do we want to accomplish?

8. Are we emphasizing product and people in the right proportions?

9. What are our values?

10. What principles does this organization hold dear?

11. Are we focusing on the essentials of good business and best practices?

Let everyone know that you understand the questions and state the answers clearly and often. Shared values bring wholeness to individuals and organizations so they can weather the storms of change. Followers will stay longer, try harder, and care more if you give them a reason. They will follow you to hell and back if your philosophy speaks to their inner needs and values. We are what we value! Your leadership language can uplift, inspire, encourage, build consensus, forge a mission, build common bonds, and cement relationships.

Duty

Before you speak, think: Is it necessary, is it true, is it kind,
will it hurt anyone, will it improve on the silence?
—SRI SATHYA SAI BABA, Indian spiritual leader

Duty is a serious word. When you look it up in your thesaurus, you'll find that its synonyms include: responsibility, obligation, dependability, conscientiousness, reliability, and trustworthiness.

While a good manager has the need to continually work on communication skills, A New Breed Leader must go to a higher level. At that higher level, one grows into a wordsmith, one who accepts the "duty" of purposefully creating and managing his or her communications. Frequently ask yourself:

. . . Do my words fulfill my responsibility to my followers and stakeholders?

. . . What obligations do I have to further explain or define *what* I am thinking and *how* that thinking will influence our organization?

. . . Would my followers say that my language shows dependability and trustworthiness?

. . . Is my language consistent with my actions and does it communicate reliability?

As a leader, you wear many hats and play many roles. None is more important than your duty to give voice to the overarching purpose and mission of your organization. Then your primary focus is to communicate the importance and relevance of the other leadership qualities that matter most: building purpose, fostering trust, generating integrity, inspiring authenticity, forging community, establishing balance, and mastering influence.

An excellent reminder of what your duty is as a communicator is the quote at the beginning of this section from Sri Sathya Sai Baba. Refer to it often; it will never fail you as A New Breed Leader.

Global and Local

As A New Breed Leader, you're at a rare juncture in world history because you're being called on to lead people and organizations in new ways. You can achieve exciting and unique results through your use of language.

In the twenty-first century, leaders will need to foster a shared civic language to halt the widening gap between the myth of American life and its reality. We have an unprecedented window of opportunity to eliminate the divisions that exist here at home through words that describe the notion of a common good. Yet in a broad perspective, we can see both dangers and opportunities in our new global society.

Wordsmiths have existed throughout history, both good and

bad. Germany's Adolf Hitler, Russia's Joseph Stalin, and China's Mao Zedong, were all twentieth-century language masters, and each created a living hell for millions of people.

We're living in uncertain times, and your highest calling is to inspire others with authentic language. It's the key to leadership greatness. Thomas Jefferson wrote, "All tyranny needs to gain a foothold is for people of good conscience to remain silent." It's a moral duty not to be deaf to the perils of partisanship and ideology, to use language that is open to all ideas and sources. As a leader, you can use language that's factual yet doesn't harm people, cause fear, or divide.

Bruce Gordon, whom you met in Chapter Two, "Accountability Matters," has the gift of inspirational leadership language. He is an excellent example of understanding how the six audiences of every leadership message can affect all that you say. As a young executive, he worked very hard to develop the skill of using language in a way that connected to all of his audiences. When I called and asked him if he could share some of his expertise on leadership, communication skills were at the top of his list. I asked him, "At what point did you realize that you were a gifted speaker?"

There was a pivotal moment at which I realized that I had become an effective communicator. I was a sales manager in Wilmington, Delaware, early in my career. I was required, along with my other colleagues, to participate in an annual planning meeting. Each manager was called on to deliver a thirty-minute presentation on the subject of their choice. It was a really big deal. I prepared for that as intensely as I ever had. Every night when I came home from my office, I had dinner with my wife. I went downstairs with my charts, and I would practice that presentation for two or three hours. When it was time to deliver it, frankly, I don't want to sound immodest, but I was great. I mean, it was an amazingly successful presentation, and I surprised myself and I surprised my colleagues because no one had ever seen me speak that effectively. I could not recall in my life having spoken that effectively, and it simply told me that I could. I think that was the most significant thing that I found. That I had the capacity to speak and that, if I worked at it hard enough, I could be good at it.

I developed confidence. As you know, once you have confidence in your ability to communicate, one of the things that it allows you to do is to think on your feet. But stylistically my approach has always been to keep it simple. I sometimes think that speakers go out of their way to use complex phrases. They take simple ideas and make them difficult.

I don't think you have to dumb something down, but I do think that you have to speak clearly. I can think of a couple things that you can do that help. People relate to stories, so when you speak, if you tell a story around your point, they can follow the opening and the body and the close. I also think that you have to approach an audience with the mission not to impress them but to teach them. So I try to speak in ways that help people to learn and to understand.

My leadership has always been about how do I help my audience? How do I help my organization so that they can succeed? How do I help my customers so that they can accomplish their business missions? Or if it's a residential or consumer customer, help them achieve their personal objectives? I've always been about helping, and I believe that people are attracted to leaders who have their best interests at heart. If your leader seems to be interested in you and seems to want to help you, then you're far more inclined to follow their lead.

I learned it from my family. I grew up as a person who wanted to help, wanted to bring people along, so my leadership style, my speaking style, my approach to managing was always about how can I help the organization? How can I help my people? How can I help my community? How can I help my customer? And that is reflected in how I approached my roles.

Sticky Language

Certain types of words and phrases are referred to as "sticky" because we remember them so easily.

Both General Electric and DuPont used simple, positive, and powerful emotional language to get their message across with slogans that stuck for decades.

Last year, General Electric retired its legendary advertising slogan, "We Bring Good Things to Life," after a memorable twenty-four-year run. Although the tagline's demise was not particularly newsworthy, an entire generation grew up associating the phrase with GE.

The phrase "Better Living Through Chemistry" is a variant of a DuPont advertising slogan, "Better Things for Better Living . . . Through Chemistry." DuPont adopted it in 1935 and it remained such until 1982 when the "Through Chemistry" was dropped. Since 1999, their slogan has been "The miracles of science." It's nice, but it doesn't have the personal connection, the stickiness, of the old slogan.

One of my favorites was the "Nest Egg" commercials A. G. Edwards used in its national branding campaign until it merged with Wachovia. Each of the different stories in the ongoing campaign showed someone with an egg, from one small enough to hold in your hand to one so big it can hardly fit in the back of your SUV. In one story a man carries his egg with him to the barbershop; a couple takes theirs to the beach to be sure it's protected and with them at all times. One of the funniest "segments" had a businessman carrying a briefcase, some dry cleaning, and an unusually large "nest egg." As he opens the hatchback of his SUV, he sets the egg down and it rolls away. He is stunned and begins chasing it. Thus begins an epic journey. It rolls through the parking garage, into an elevator, and out onto the street, where pedestrians, surprisingly unimpressed by an enormous egg rolling down the street, watch it indifferently. The egg hops on an escalator, lands in a Dumpster, rolls out of that and then veers into traffic, where it causes an accident. Still chasing the egg, the man jumps over the hood of the cab, sprints through the street chasing it. He finally corners the egg in an alley, where it rolls to a stop and you hear a voice saying, "Don't let your nest egg get away from you. Get objective financial advice instead. A. G. Edwards. For 118 years, fully invested in our clients." The man, oblivious to the narrator's counsel, sighs and watches the egg roll away again.

That very funny and sticky message said: "Trust us to protect your nest egg. It is fragile and immensely valuable. You can trust us to make sure it's safe."

Do you and your organization have a message that sticks in people's minds?

Positive Actions to Take

Here are six positive actions you can take to produce better results because of your increased capacity as a wordsmith:

1. Avoid war language

I addressed a conference that used a theme of "war." At every opportunity, phrases and slogans were taken right out of Army manuals. Everyone was dressed in battle fatigues. They talked about attacking the enemy (competition) through stealth and with offensive battle plans. It felt as if I was in the middle of some kind of siege, or at least in the midst of a siege mentality.

When used in that fashion, war language makes people immune to the truth and horrors of real war, in which many people die or are injured and great suffering occurs. In an age of struggle worldwide, we cannot afford to become anesthetized to the realities of war.

2. Praise what's right—train for what's wrong

Your team-building success will soar if you can offer honest praise even as you define good performance. This is a bit of a dance: You want to praise generously but not so much that your kudos become cheapened by frequency. You want to cite substantial progress but not suggest a performance that can't be improved upon. So strive for a double-barreled approach. Remember: No great leader ever built a reputation on just firing or disciplining subordinates. But many have thrived by developing their followers with aspirational language. Legendary movie producer Samuel Goldwyn said, "When someone does something good, applaud. You will make two people happy."

3. Be careful of "win" and "lose" words

Be especially careful in using words like "winning," "losing," "fail-ure," and "success." Life isn't always—and shouldn't be—a "zero sum" game in which my gain is your loss, or vice versa. No one wins all the time, and winning isn't always the goal. True success usually involves collaboration and compromise, not the trouncing of the opposition.

4. Encourage feedback

Ensure that communication comes from the bottom up as well as from the top down. Ask open-ended questions, ones that can-not be answered with a "yes" or a "no." This will help you get real insight into whatever you need to know. Give feedback using encouraging words. Even criticism will be well received if the lis-tener knows you're interested in helping. If you let followers feel safe to discuss a problem or issue without fear of retaliation, you move the entire team forward.

5. Resolve conflicts

Conflicts are inevitable and can't be ignored. Conflict resolu-tion needs to be in every leader's arsenal. Begin to build this skill by identifying common ground. Rarely is a situation so bad that there's no area of agreement. Review whatever is agreed on. If the conflict is large and has many parts or people involved, work out little conflicts first before tackling the bigger issues.

6. Ask effective questions

One of the most important responsibilities of New Breed Leaders will be to question everything. Isidor Isaac Rabi, one of America's most famous physicists, tells the story of his childhood. When he came home from school, his mother would ask, "Did you ask any good questions today?" Not "Did you learn anything today?" He attributes a great deal of his success to his ability to ask good questions. We can learn from his example. Rather than always looking for answers, look for good questions. Remember the proverb that says, "If you know all the answers, you haven't asked all the questions."

Culture

That is true culture which helps us to work
for the social betterment of all.
—HENRY WARD BEECHER

When your organization's culture gives members reasons to be proud, a strong and exciting tie exists between leader and those willingly led—of common interest, of shared values, of mutual affection. Culture is your own personal language, the language of your organization, and a new language that encompasses our global village. Culture consists of your values, purpose, products and services, your people and the commitments and promises of your branding. To a great extent your culture is a reflection of your guidance and that of your leadership team, including a board of directors if you have one.

What are some examples of business cultures? If we look at General Electric, we see a tough, in-your-face, meat-grinder, arrogant culture . . . and a highly successful firm. Contrast that to Starbucks, with its more holistic approach to business, a much more caring attitude about employees, relationships, alliances, and suppliers . . . and it's also highly successful.

Some may say the two can't be compared because they're such different businesses. Yet the basics are the same: Both deal with people and products, nationally and globally, and with shareholder value, governments, and public perception. Neither is all bad or all good.

You can consider ideas from each company that will help with both your organization and dealing with your own issues. If you're not familiar enough with GE or Starbucks to make a good comparison, consider investing some time and energy to find out:

- What is good or bad about the culture of both of these highly successful global companies?

- What can I learn from them that I can apply to my organization?

- Could a hybrid of both cultures work?

- If a hybrid business model is possible, how would I structure it?

There are no clear answers. But you'll gain important insights by examining successful businesses and then applying what you learn.

A Culture of Clarity and Pride

We have talked about the other three parts of language, and of course, all of them flow into the issue of the culture you wish to establish or support.

Clarity—The clearer your values and purpose, the stronger your culture becomes.

Alignment—The better your alignment with stakeholders, the more robust and resilient your culture remains.

Duty—Your commitment to grow and become a wordsmith adds dimension beyond compare to your culture.

All four parts of the language puzzle piece unite people and support relationships, which is the overriding goal of *language that matters*.

Why is communicating culture clearly and accurately so important? Because when the culture supports a belief that the staff is part of an exciting future, you have a high degree of buy-in and loyalty. When your organization's culture gives members reasons to be proud, a strong and exciting tie exists between leader and those willingly led—of common interest, of shared values, of mutual affection.

When I spoke with Joe Driscoll, whom you met in Chapter Three, "Openness Matters," he spoke about the culture and pride he continually strived to build.

> One of the things we did over the years was make sure we would be best at what we did, that we worked at being the best, and we had established all along who our competitors were. Much of what we did was geared toward the employee's pride in the organization. We were the only ones that had certification from NCQA (National Committee for Quality Assurance) and from URAC (Utilization Review Accreditation Commission) for our medical-management services. No one else had that. It cost us some money and it forced us to put the controls in place that were beneficial to our business.

> The employees really took pride in the fact that we were an organization that wanted to be the highest quality [and] most competitive in the country. As a leader, you have to keep communicating with them; make sure they understand what you're doing and why you're doing it.

Leader as Teacher

As a twenty-first-century leader, you have the rare opportunity to build communities of interest, to gather and find answers, and to cross political, business, religious, and national borders to create a culture of commonality. One way you do this is by your example, which teaches others how to act and think. Henry Adams wrote, "A teacher affects eternity; he can never tell where his influence stops."

You also teach through your language. Leaders who create pictures with words that teach are those whom people will want to follow. But there are countless methods of communication: art, music, facial expressions, et cetera.

The Art and Wisdom of Storytelling

Those who tell the stories rule society.

—PLATO

Storytelling has been the mainstay of cultures since the beginning of time. Long before humans could write, we told stories. Today storytelling remains the most powerful tool you have to convey information and shape behavior. For a twenty-first-century

THE LANGUAGE OF MUSIC CROSSES CULTURAL BARRIERS TO TEACH

Yo-Yo Ma, the virtuoso cellist, is a twenty-first-century leader-teacher. He knows that his "voice and musical language" as a famous performer can open doors and minds. He created the Silk Road Project, a children's workshop that uses the sounds and instruments from the historic Asian-European trade routes of the ancient times as a way to build cross-cultural relationships.

He enlisted musicians from around the globe to use their artistry to help him share the richness of the musical experience. No one knew if the idea would work, so he relied on the inborn flexibility of musicians to find a way to communicate with each other with exciting new sounds, new skills, and new instruments.

This musical language is being used as a cultural ambassadorship around the world. His personal warmth and star power have helped him build the bridge and expand the knowledge of common heritage while celebrating local cultures. Colleague John Bertles says, "The sounds are strange, but they're only strange initially. If you look at the cultural connections, they're not so strange anymore. And that's where Yo-Yo's genius really lies."

leader, the ability to tell stories is imperative in order to connect people and influence a culture.

Chip Heath, a Stanford University professor, said, "Good corporate stories are more likely to conjure up tangible visible images than anything in a PowerPoint presentation." Your stories are everywhere. They can be a one-line statement like Eleanor Roosevelt made when she said and wrote, "It is better to light a candle than to curse the darkness."

Studs Terkel, author and broadcast personality, wrote, "People are hungry for stories. It's part of our very being. Storytelling is a form of history, of immortality, too. It goes from one generation to another."

One of our most successful big-box stores is Costco. I wrote about the CEO, Jim Sinegal, in Chapter Eight, "Humility Matters." Here's what he says about storytelling:

> What else have we got besides stories? That's what really hits home with people. It's what brings meaning to the work we do.

In Chapter One, "Competence Matters," you met Cathy Keating, First Lady of Oklahoma at the time of the Oklahoma City bombing. We also talked about using language to build relationships and a sense of community through storytelling.

> I think you build a sense of community with language. When I stood up to give my speech at the memorial service for the Oklahoma Federal Building bombing, I was so fearful that my speech wouldn't come out the way I wanted it to. The message I wanted to deliver was about hope and healing. But emotions can interfere with your ability to deliver the message in the way you want it to be received. It was important to me that my message be strong. The truth is, I got through all of my speech, which I had written, until I started talking about the children, and then my voice broke. But as it turned out, it was all right because everybody else was feeling the same way; we were all a community in grief.
>
> I'm an example person, I look at different examples and learn from other people's successes or failures.
>
> Language is sometimes so perfectly delivered through

storytelling that people go along with you when they shouldn't. Think of Hitler. He had the gift of communication unlike anybody else. And he fooled people into following him for such evil purpose.

Then there are the good stories. For example, Mothers Against Drunk Driving have used stories as an important role to get their message out to save lives. . . . Nancy Brinker—the founder of Susan G. Komen for the Cure, an organization named after her only sister, Susan, who died from breast cancer in 1980 at age thirty-six—has used language in story form to get the message out to change people's behavior to save lives for the Race for the Cure. And all those messages have been delivered very carefully so that they bring people along with them, and they want to join the effort. As a leader, you can't lead if you don't have people—if you're not communicating with people where you want to take them. They won't go with you, and they shouldn't go with you.

Life is built on lessons, and the lesson I learned at National Speaker's Forum by watching thousands of videotapes was that I found the most powerful speakers were those who would make a point and illustrate it with a story. Those were the messages I always remembered. Stories make the message real and believable, and it is something that people can take away. That's how you get buy-in because it's the real deal. It's not pretend. It's a message with a purpose. I really do believe storytelling is a powerful mode of communication.

I was thrown into the limelight when my husband was elected governor. He has the most unbelievable gift of extemporaneous speaking: He has a brilliant mind, speaks without notes, is quick-witted and spontaneous and funny. I work differently than that. I have to construct where I'm going, and the best way for me to get there is through storytelling. My five years at National Speaker's Forum prepared me to stand up in front of a group and give a meaningful speech.

If you want to improve your storytelling skills, consider reading the following books:

BOOKS

Words That Sell, Richard Bayan, Contemporary Book Inc., Chicago/New York.

Words That Work, Frank Luntz, Hyperion, New York.

Managing by Storying Around, David Armstrong, Doubleday, New York.

ONLINE

Evaluate Your Own Story, Evelyn Clark, www.corpstory.com.

Introduction to Corporate Storytelling, Hilary McClellan, www.tech-head.com.

The Ties That Bind

No culture can live if it attempts to be exclusive.
—MAHATMA GANDHI

As A New Breed Leader, your artful use of language is about connecting with others, building strong relationships, and inclusive communities. As John Ralston Saul wrote in *Reflection of a Siamese Twin*, "All the lessons of psychiatry, psychology, social work, indeed, culture, have taught us over the last hundred years that it is the acceptance of differences, not the search for similarities which enables people to relate to each other . . ."

The culture you create is a direct reflection of the stories you tell that support the mission and purpose of the individuals who work so hard to make it a reality. Our language is the tie that binds.

The Words They Hear and the Actions They See

Language is the light of the mind.

—JOHN STUART MILL

At the end of this chapter, it is important to reassure you there's no such thing as perfect language. As A New Breed Leader, you must continually strive to perfect your communication skills. As a leader, you must be able to clear away extraneous issues and get to core ideas.

Former Chrysler chairman Lee Iacocca wrote, "In crisis, language rises to a level of importance not realized before. Leadership is forged in times of crisis. It's easy to sit there with your feet up and talk theories and strategies for success. But when the rubber hits the road, as a leader you had better be able to communicate in a way that helps people understand their emotions and the power of what the crisis or emergency is."

The credibility and the moral tone of your organization are

established and communicated by you, its leader. Your team is held together by the words it hears and the actions it sees. When you use your verbal expertise to reinforce the organization's goals, values, ideas, and ideals in the minds and spirit of your followers, your communication becomes an art form. You serve your followers best when your mission is articulated by both what you say and what you do.

In the twenty-first-century leadership pyramid, each of the four categories of leaders—*Enlighteners*, *Creators*, *Builders*, and *Sustainers*—uses different language with different people in different situations. All four enlarge their sphere of influence when they have an abiding respect for words and appreciate the authority of language craft to build relationships and connect with people of every kind.

Your Action Plan Questions for Quality 4
LANGUAGE

1. Am I working on becoming an inspirational leader, using my words to motivate, inspire, and give hope?

2. Do I continually communicate the three vital messages that build strong long-term viable organizations: our mission, our objectives, and our values?

3. Am I using language to build communication rather than erect walls?

CHAPTER FIVE

Values Matter

FORGING COMMUNITY

*Personal leadership is the process of keeping your
wisdom and values before you and aligning
your life to be congruent with them.*

—STEPHEN COVEY

The Values Puzzle Piece

VALUES." WHAT A subtle, intangible, and elusive word. It has different meanings for different people under different circumstances. We have our cherished core values that give us a personal moral compass. Most companies and organizations have a set of values that represent them to their constituents. Even our communities have certain values that make them different from a nearby town or city. And the values of our global communities vary so widely that it may seem daunting to try to identify values at all. However, we've seen through the ages that values buoy the *Enlightener* leader, encourage the *Creator* leader, and provide guidance for the *Builder* and *Sustainer* leader to move forward.

Even with the enormous changes and challenges of the twenty-first century, reviewing your values is the right thing to do. Now is the right time to take a new look at your leadership standards and how you measure up. It'll take courage and self-confidence to do so, but you'll benefit by the authenticity you establish from a renewed set of principles. They will help you guide others as they navigate the sometimes-daunting issues of our new century.

Your Personal Values Come First

Whether we are consciously aware of them or not, every individual has a core set of personal values. Values can range from the commonplace, such as the belief in hard work and punctuality, to the more psychological, such as self-reliance, concern for others, and harmony of purpose. Whatever one's values, when we take them to heart and implement them in the smallest details of our lives, great accomplishments and success are sure to follow.

—ROY POSNER, author and philosopher

Charlie Plumb and Gerry Coffee were both Navy pilots shot down and captured by the Vietnamese. They were among the longest-held prisoners of war in Vietnam. They've both written books about their experiences and are popular motivational speakers. They both talk about how their core values got them though the worst of times.

Gerry Coffee

From 1963 to 1966, Captain Gerald L. Coffee was assigned to Heavy Reconnaissance Attack Squadron Three as a flight and reconnaissance training instructor in the new RA-5C Vigilante. From there he deployed to Vietnam in Heavy Reconnaissance Attack Squadron Thirteen aboard the USS *Kitty Hawk*.

On February 3, 1966, when his Vigilante was shot down over North Vietnam, he was captured and held as a POW. The seven years, nine days he spent in captivity—much of it in solitary confinement and enduring torture—served not to embitter him but to strengthen his faith, his love of country, and his belief in working together for a common good. He was released in the first increment of POWs on February 12, 1973.

Gerry says POWs in Vietnam saw their mission as "not mere survival but to go beyond survival; to survive and return home with honor. We lived with two mottoes in Hanoi: 'Unity Over Self' and 'Return with Honor.'" His book, *Beyond Survival: The Next Chapter*, is a warm, touching, and inspiring message about how the power of the human spirit buoyed by values can bring personal growth and triumph.

Charlie Plumb

Captain Charlie Plumb flew F-4 Phantom jets on seventy-four successful combat missions over North Vietnam. On his seventy-fifth mission, with only five days before he was to return home, Charlie was shot down, captured, tortured, and imprisoned in an eight-by-eight-foot cell. He spent the next 2,103 days as a POW.

During his nearly six years of captivity, Charlie distinguished himself among his fellow prisoners as a professional in underground communications, which he often credits with saving his sanity. He served for two of those years as the chaplain in his camp.

His autobiography, *I'm No Hero*, reveals how his values helped him as a POW to face an isolated world of degradation, loneliness, tedium, hunger, and pain; most significantly, it's a moving story of hope.

I've never seen an audience, no matter how young or old, keep a dry eye when either of these men tells his story and calls upon the audience members to find their own courage and values to give their life meaning. I've also seen people laugh with them at the ironies that even a prison camp can provide.

> Your personal values are the principles about what you believe is important, desirable, and true.

Jerry and Charlie both speak with deep emotion and are expert storytellers. At the base of everything they talk about are their core values. They talk about how their belief in what they were doing sustained them, about how their faith was the most important factor they focused on to survive, and how being true to your convictions can get you through unimaginable horrors. It is an honor to call them friends.

A Personal Values Exercise

Here is a "values exercise" that I have used all over the world. It contains 15 values toward which people commonly strive. It's neither a perfect list nor a static one. If you think something is missing, add it. I have updated it several times and will do so again as our world continues to change.

With a pen, prioritize the words 1 through 15. They will not be in numerical order. Number 1 may in the middle, 2 near the end, or 15 at the top, and so on. This is not a test with *right* or *wrong* answers. Any order you rank them in is right for you.

VALUES PEOPLE STRIVE TOWARD

Independence	[ ]
Good Health	[ ]
Acceptance	[ ]
Wealth	[ ]
Self-respect	[ ]
Accomplishment	[ ]
Power	[ ]
Fun	[ ]
Status	[ ]
Spiritual Wholeness	[ ]
Self-expression	[ ]
Recognition	[ ]
Security	[ ]
Relationships	[ ]
Simplicity	[ ]

©1980 Bethel Institute

After you have prioritized them, draw a line between the word and your top three values. Then write why that value is important to you. The simplicity of this list will help you quickly home in on the values that are important to you and so vital to the stewardship of your people and your organization.

Leading with Your Principles

True revolutionaries are like God—they create a world in their own image. Our awesome responsibility to ourselves, to our children, and to the future is to create ourselves in the image of goodness, because the future depends on the nobility of our imaginings.

—BARBARA GRIZZUTI HARRISON, author and essayist

Your principles are like a fixed beacon, giving direction and purpose to the other seven qualities that matter most to A New Breed Leader. The atmosphere in which you lead is determined largely by how you define and communicate your values.

Whether or not you realize it, every time you choose to do one thing as opposed to another, you make a value decision. In other words, your values are expressed through your actions. The better the result, the greater your integrity and credibility as a leader.

It's a worthy and honorable process to examine the standards that affect you, your organization, and your community. Ask yourself:

1. Where do I find the principles, ideas, and ideals that contribute to my personal values?

2. How do I build my leadership and move my organization forward with the leadership values that matter most?

3. How do I approach the complex task of defining, implementing, and sustaining a set of standards that forge community?

Our leadership puzzle gives us the opportunity to see how values affect the other seven qualities in the puzzle. If you took out the values piece, a significant part of what you need to lead would be missing. For example, power and accountability have major ties to values. When power is used wisely, it's because the person with the power is anchored to a strong sense of values. Accountability, as we've seen, is nonexistent when values are weak or ignored for personal gain.

As you define your values, you provide further clarity to the whole puzzle. When you execute well, based on those values, you lead by example and strengthen the significance of the other

seven qualities. Leading effectively with a consistent set of values helps forge a community among all your stakeholders.

Organizational Standards

Leadership begins with recognizing that everybody needs four things: something to do, someone to love, something to hope for, and something to believe in. Strategic plans don't excite anybody. Dreams excite people . . . And every employee, every team member, wants to know the same thing: Do you really care about me? Every successful organization shows its people that they genuinely matter.

—LOU HOLTZ, coach

Just as individuals subscribe to values, so do organizations and institutions. Examine any entity that has sustained long-term success and you'll find that it has a keen set of values that all its stakeholders see, understand, and believe in. Let's look at some examples:

PROCTER & GAMBLE

On Procter & Gamble's website, I found a description of what they call their "Purpose, Values, and Principles." This is an excerpt from the piece.

Purpose
We will provide branded products and services of superior quality and value that improve the lives of the world's consumers, now

and for generations to come. As a result, consumers will reward us with leadership sales, profit, and value creation, allowing our people, our shareholders, and the communities in which we live and work to prosper.

Core Values
P&G is its people and the values by which we live.

- Integrity
- Leadership
- Ownership
- Passion for Winning
- Trust

These are the principles and supporting behaviors which flow from our Purpose and Values.

- We Show Respect for All Individuals
- The Interests of the Company and the Individual Are Inseparable
- We Are Strategically Focused in Our Work
- Innovation Is the Cornerstone of Our Success
- We Are Externally Focused
- We Value Personal Mastery
- We Seek to Be the Best
- Mutual Interdependency Is a Way of Life

EISENHOWER MEDICAL CENTER

This medical center, located in Rancho Mirage, California, describes its values in terms of commitment:

Our Commitments:

- *Safety.* Ensure that our patients, their families, friends, and our staff are always secure from harm or danger.
- *Clinical Excellence.* Ensure that measured outcomes meet/ exceed agreed-upon expectations. Respected clinical practice policies, procedures, and other standards are practiced 100% of the time. Tests, treatments, and procedures are thoroughly explained to patients and are understood.
- *Courtesy/Caring.* Staff always practice good manners, are friendly, polite, and emotionally sensitive to each individual whether patient, family, visitor, or fellow employee.
- *Healing Environment.* A supportive setting is developed and maintained that embraces the physical, emotional, and spiritual aspects of health and healing.
- *Efficiency.* Services are provided effectively with a minimum of waste.

IBM

Insert the words "IBM Values Statement" in your Internet search engine, and you'll find a message from Samuel J. Palmisano, IBM's president and CEO. Its candor and openness say volumes about the future sustainability of this global giant. Here's an excerpt:

Business value and a company's values

Last year [2003] we examined IBM's core values for the first time since the company's founding. In this time of great change, we needed to affirm IBM's reason for being, what sets the company apart and what should drive our actions as individual IBMers.

Importantly, we needed to find a way to engage everyone in the company and get them to speak up on these important issues. Given the realities of a smart, global, independent-minded, twenty-first-century workforce like ours, I don't believe something as vital and personal as values could be dictated from the top.

So, for 72 hours last summer, we invited all 319,000 IBMers around the world to engage in an open "values jam" on our global intranet. IBMers by the tens of thousands weighed in. They were thoughtful and passionate about the company they want to be a part of. They were also brutally honest. Some of what they wrote was painful to read, because they pointed out all the bureaucratic and dysfunctional things that get in the way of serving clients, working as a team or implementing new ideas. But we were resolute in keeping the dialog free-flowing and candid. And I don't think what resulted—broad, enthusiastic, grass-roots consensus—could have been obtained in any other way.

In the end, IBMers determined that our actions will be driven by these values:

- Dedication to every client's success
- Innovation that matters, for our company and for the world
- Trust and personal responsibility in all relationships

Where will this lead? It is a work in progress, and many of the implications remain to be discovered. What I can tell you is that we are rolling up our sleeves to bring IBM's values to life in our policies, procedures and daily operations. . . .

And we have to do all this by taking personal responsibility for all of our relationships—with clients, colleagues, partners, investors, and the public at large. This is IBM's mission as an enterprise, and a goal toward which we hope to work with many others, in our industry and beyond.

If you were to give a presentation on your values and those of your organization, could you be as clear as IBM, P&G, and the Eisenhower Medical Center?

Remember, when followers feel that their work is satisfying, it's usually because it's compatible with their values. For some people, money, power, prestige, and status are what make a job rewarding. Others must experience meaning and purpose in the work itself.

Shared meaning energizes people. It yields stability and, like ballast in a ship, produces a counterbalance in good times and bad. It builds community and brings people together. It motivates followers to create good things for everyone involved. Part of the reason for that is because we're more inclined to trust people when we understand their values and see that their actions match those values. We understand we can rely on how they will act.

An Organizational Bioswale

My friend Muriel is an architectural landscaper. I was talking to her about some of the ideas I had for this book. She, in turn, discussed a challenge she faced in designing a proper bioswale in a building and parking lot where pollution from cars collects on pavement, then is flushed by rain. A bioswale—a slanted drainage course with gently sloped sides filled with vegetation, compost, and/or loose and broken stone—effectively treats runoff before releasing it to the watershed or storm drain. As Muriel described it, I saw an immediate application on how a long list of values could be filtered to end up with the most important ones.

Let's take the quality/value of openness and put it through our organizational bioswale. Just as vehicles in a parking lot leave residue, daily life and business leave a residue in your mind, the minds of your followers, and in the culture of your organization.

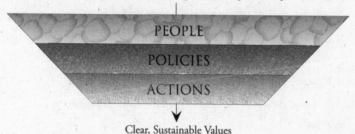

OPENNESS

Residue from events, decisions, issues, challenges, failures, practices, procedures, successes

PEOPLE

POLICIES

ACTIONS

Clear, Sustainable Values

As you can see, everything that happens filters first through people; then, through policies; and finally, what's left works its way into actions that reflect our values. Take, for example, the Hurricane Katrina disaster. *People* in authority in Louisiana and Washington, D.C., were largely unprepared for the magnitude of the disaster. Thus, they didn't have the needed *policies* (such as flood protection, warning systems, evacuation plans, recovery and rebuilding efforts) in place. So when it came time for *action*, what resulted was too little and too late. They weren't open in dealing with their preparation for the crisis. And the residue? Suffering and outrage on an epic scale, so much so that millions of Americans saw that a basic national value had been shortchanged: the desire to help out fellow citizens, whatever their color or economic level, in a time of emergency. This painful process led the country to underscore and redefine that core American value.

ASSESSING THE OPENNESS OF YOUR RECENT PROJECTS

Using the bioswale idea, focus on the quality of openness. Try these two assessments.

A successful project

- Name a recent project or task that went well.
- How did people react? Were they excited to see the benefits of openness?
- If so, how?
- What policies were strengthened, updated, or improved by the positive result?
- How can you as leader help yourself and your organization exhibit greater openness?

A less-than-successful project

- Name a recent project or task that did not go well.
- Did openness threaten some "power towers"? Were people hoarding information and knowledge to enhance themselves?
- If so, what did this do to the policies and outcomes for the project? What happened?
- What policies impeded the effort or even caused a breakdown?
- Which policies needed changing to foster a community attitude?
- What can you do to create a core value of openness?

Drawing on your answers to this assessment, describe how openness is and can be more valued in your organization.

Now, take the other seven qualities that matter most and put them through your own organizational bioswale. As you do, ask:

- How do our organizational values help people stay focused with all this residue?

- What policies need updating to filter unnecessary or harmful outcomes?

- Do our actions in response to the residue reflect our mission, purpose, and values?

The answers will give you a renewed opportunity to test the values to which you subscribe. This could have a huge impact on your effectiveness as A New Breed Leader.

Values and Conviction

We can look back at history and see many examples of how a person's strong values can define a community and generate social change. This story is one of the best examples. It illustrates how individual principles shaped the slave trade in 1800. Nations and communities worldwide were affected by their values.

Amazing Grace

The film *Amazing Grace* (2006) is based on the true story of British antislavery pioneer William Wilberforce. It has three intertwining values themes: salvation, redemption, and the power of an enlightened leader with deeply held core values.

Throughout the film, you hear the hauntingly familiar hymn "Amazing Grace." Time and again you see the moral and ethical battle between right and wrong, between good and evil, and the inhumane results of greed when money trumps values.

The story within the story is about the hymn "Amazing Grace," written by John Newton (played by Albert Finney). He had been captain of a slave ship for many years until he underwent a dramatic religious conversion while steering his vessel through a storm. Repenting and regretting the misery he'd inflicted on thousands of slaves, he devoted his life to the church and wrote the lyrics to many hymns still popular today. In 1780, Newton went to London to become rector of St. Mary Woolnoth, where he drew large congregations and influenced many, among them young William Wilberforce. Haunted in dreams and in his waking hours by images of the terror the captive Africans endured on their long journeys, Newton imbues Wilberforce with his passion to abolish slavery.

Wilberforce is a newcomer to the world of politics. He must learn to operate in a world of skillful deception and cunning one-upmanship in order to attain his unpopular goal: the abolition of slavery. Wilberforce has many enemies who will stop just short of bodily harm to prevent him from achieving his goals. He knows that he needs a powerful older member to help shepherd his bill. After voting against him, Lord Charles Fox (Michael Gambon), aptly named for his astute manipulation of power, experiences redemption and secretly joins forces with Wilberforce.

He and his group amass a wealth of evidence to support their case and show how the trade is an affront to Christian values and common humanity. They wage the first modern political cam-

paign, using petitions, boycotts, mass meetings, badges, and slogans. An abolitionist bill has been introduced year after year and
every time roundly defeated by members of Parliament voting to
preserve either their personal vested interests or those of the mon-
eyed class they represent.

Lord Fox works the levers of power and gets a member to speak
in support of the bill. But as they listen, the panic on their faces
tells you they realize that a key member has been bought off by the
pro-slavery members. He tells them that he's for the bill but they
should not rush into it. Instead, he suggests, they should implement it slowly over a period of years so no one's hurt financially.

Wilberforce and Fox are crushed. They've failed.

Fast-forward eighteen years. The fire of Wilberforce's dreams
will not be extinguished. He cannot give up. He musters all his
strength and decides to try one last time. He finds an archaic law
that could put an end to slave ships plying their trade, and his
friend, William Pitt, now Prime Minister, says he will support a
sneak attack on the intransigent members.

Lord Fox rigs the voting in their favor by giving all the opposition members free tickets to a horse race. As the innocuous-
sounding bill is being presented, few members are in the chamber,
except for their most powerful adversary. As their opponent listens, he sees one of the abolitionists in the balcony and realizes
what's happening. He rushes out to find the absent members and
runs into Lord Fox, who, smiling, says, "I gave them all tickets to
the race." The head of the chamber asks for a vote, and the measure
passes. The hymn rises in the background. Wilberforce has been
aged by the battle, giving him dark circles under his eyes. He looks
around in astonishment. He can't believe that after so long he's
achieved abolition. He sees his wife's face in the balcony. Newton

is there, too. Now blind but waving in his direction, Newton is crying. The tears run down Wilberforce's face.

This story of idealism and idealists reaffirms that there is something inordinately moving and dramatic about a person of great conviction and clear values who stands up for what is right.

Values in Harmony and Balance

People must believe that a task is inherently worthwhile if they are to be committed to it.
—EDWARD DECI, University of Rochester

The combination of harmony and balance in your personal and organizational values makes it so much easier for people to follow your lead. Harmony is key in forging community, and balance provides the stability to keep it together. At times one or two values may take precedence over others, but generally, when your stakeholders understand that a few deeply rooted values are in balance with theirs, you get the buy-in you need to get things done. You not only attract good people to strengthen your organization, but you increase sustainability. And sustainability will be one of our most vital leadership results in the twenty-first century.

As A New Breed Leader, you'll find it increasingly important to ask:

- What are the specific behaviors that represent the things that I value?

- How do I exemplify them to my followers?

Having worked with hundreds of companies and organizations around the world, I've seen several core behaviors in the most successful. Let's look at a few:

Commitment

Nothing resists a human will that stakes its very existence upon the achievement of its purpose.

—BENJAMIN DISRAELI, former British Prime Minister

Commitment ranks high at every stage of your leadership development. Total commitment separates the great from the near-great. It's an intangible ingredient, an inner strength that binds the eight qualities that matter most. It gives them enormous power.

You might recall the old story about the chicken and the pig. They're walking along a country road early one morning when they pass an eatery with a sign in the window reading, BACON AND EGGS, $1.79.

"Well, well—will you look at that!" the chicken says proudly. "What would breakfast be without my contribution?"

The pig replies, "That's easy for you to say. For you, it's a contribution; for me, it's total commitment!"

When you believe deeply in what you are trying to achieve for the organization and believe that its mission is noble, that mission rises to the level of a calling. It's hard to show

To put the world in order, we must first put the nation in order; to put the nation in order, we must first put the family in order; to put the family in order, we must first set our hearts right with a clear set of values to which we are committed.

commitment if you aren't really committed. In fact, it's impossible. Commitment can't be faked.

People follow leaders who display their commitment in many ways, including the vision they pursue, the competence they display, the ethics they follow, the perseverance they exhibit, the change they seek, and the risks they take.

Try critiquing your sense of commitment:

COMMITMENT SELF-ASSESSMENT

1. Think of a leader you greatly respect. Indicate the ways he or she demonstrates commitment:

____devotion to people   ____demonstration of competence

____intensity of vision   ____acceptance of responsibility

____strength of ethics   ____integrity of decisions

____pursuit of change   ____other (list: _____)

2. List the ways in which you show commitment to those you lead.

3. Compare your areas of commitment with those of your respected leader.

4. Cite the areas in which he or she excelled that you could improve in.

New Breed Leaders will change the world through deep and abiding commitment. "Anyone can dabble," wrote comedian Bill Cosby, "but once you've made that commitment, your blood has that particular thing in it, and it's very hard for people to stop you."

In olden days, military leaders sometimes burned their boats after making an assault from the sea. Why? Biographers often say they did it to give their followers no choice but to fight on and win. Maybe. But as retired Air Force Major General William Cohen has pointed out, the rank-and-file still could have surrendered. Perhaps instead the act demonstrated the leader's unflinching commitment to the objective.

Remember the Founding Fathers' commitment of "our lives, our fortunes, our sacred honor" to the cause of the American Revolution? You don't need to burn boats or risk treason to show commitment. But you do need to fervently believe in what you're doing and what your organization is about. To your very marrow, you must believe in your mission and act accordingly.

That commitment, that passion, must be genuine and unrelenting. If it is, followers will respond. Then when there's doubt about an action, they will say, "I know her heart is in the right place. She's been right before. I have every reason to trust her, so I'm going to go with her." Your commitment will have given you the leader's edge.

Take a moment to reflect on the ways you show commitment:

- How have I shown my commitment today in words?

- How have I shown my commitment today by example?

- If my leadership were to be judged solely on the basis of my actions tomorrow, what would I do differently than I did today?

Michael Maccoby, author of *The Leader*, wrote, "Without a commitment to culture that supports the practice of life described in the great humanistic religious traditions, people find meanings in idols of self, possessions, technology, or organizations. They put their faith in bureaucracies rather than the divine spirit in each other, and the self remains childish and undeveloped."

Do all you can to make your followers feel aware of the higher purpose of their work, and you'll create in them—and you—an inner strength that can work miracles.

Courage

In a crisis, you can't manage by manual; you
have to manage by values and beliefs.
—KENNETH CHENAULT, CEO, American Express

Courage: The state or quality of mind or spirit that enables one to face danger with self-possession, confidence, and resolution.

It's dangerous to put yourself on the line and stand up for your beliefs. However, the world has always been a dangerous place. And the world has always had leaders who had the courage to lead in spite of the dangers.

Danger is obviously relative. It's dangerous just living in this nuclear age. But as the late M. Scott Peck, a psychiatrist and best-selling author, wrote, "There can be no vulnerability without risk; there can be no community without vulnerability; there can be no peace, and ultimately no life, without community."

There's a saying that courage is "fear that has said its prayers." We're all afraid of something. At some time, we have all overcome fear and displayed bravery. But there's more to courage than bravery in the face of danger or hardships. While physical courage is admirable, mental and moral courage are just as meaningful. Courage also means being able to keep going when the burden is heavy and there's no end in sight. Courage can be the willingness to live one day at a time, doing the best you can.

Kenneth Chenault

Kenneth Chenault has been CEO and chairman of American Express since 2001. He was the third African American CEO of a Fortune 500 company. *Fortune* magazine named AmEx one of the nation's best companies for leadership development.

On September 11, 2001, he was in Salt Lake City on a conference call with his headquarters that overlooked the World Trade Center. As the 9/11 tragedy unfolded, he knew that he and his leadership team would need to call on a special kind of courage to help employees, victims of the disaster, the people of New York City, and the firm's customers, the credit card holders.

Known for his integrity, discipline, and drive, along with a pleasant personality, Chenault had to tackle multiple problems. AMEX had lost eleven employees in the tragedy. He put his telephone operators to work making sure that all AMEX employees in the vicinity were located and that their families were safe. The company went to work to assist the distressed customers, waived late fees, and raised credit limits. He set up a crisis center in Phoenix and sent staff members to three other states to help manage the crisis. He has said that his job at the time was "to define reality and give hope."

Nine days after the disaster he brought the entire New York City staff to Madison Square Garden for a company team meeting. He told them that it would take courage and hard work, but he was confident that the company would come back bigger and better and stronger than before. His calm demeanor and quiet grace, his steady hand and courage under fire, gave his followers the confidence and courage to carry on. Chenault is A New Breed Leader.

Unlike many of the other leadership qualities, courage is not a set of skills. You can't study it or train for it the way you can for, say, team building or decision making. There are no guidelines to adhere to, no step-by-step plan to follow, no acronym to memorize and heed. Instead, you become more courageous by *doing*, by looking deep within yourself, deciding what is important to do, and then trying to do it. Much like finding your vision, finding your courage may mean starting out small, then building upon that base.

First, you discover the "why" of courage—what do you need to be courageous about? Then the "how" will show itself to you. Situations that require courage pop up with frequency. As Eleanor Roosevelt said, "You gain strength, courage, and confidence by every experience in which you really stop to look fear in the face."

Christa McAuliffe

January 28, 1986. The space orbiter *Challenger* took off in the bright morning sun. Aboard the spaceship, the crew was excited about its mission. Christa McAuliffe believed with all her heart that the value of her mission to "teach" from space was worth all the risk and hard work. Her dedication and courage had won her a place on the mission.

It's a terrible moment in space history: The horrific sight of the *Challenger* exploding, killing the entire crew. Even amid the national grief for this brave crew and for Christa, the message of having the courage of your convictions came back to Earth in ways that will live on in the annals of teaching. Christa was posthumously awarded the Congressional Space Medal of Honor.

As we've done before, think of someone you admire or admired as courageous, perhaps Christa or one of the other crew members. What was it about that person that was so laudable? Was it his or her persistence in the face of hardship and long odds? Was it his outspokenness when there was a penalty for candor? Was it her humility when, in truth, she had reason to be prideful? Did he or she act ethically when, all around that person, others were less than circumspect?

WHAT I LEARNED FROM
A COURAGEOUS LEADER

Reflect on a leader you know or knew who showed courage.

Specify how he or she showed that courage.

What effect did that show of courage have on his or her followers?

What can you learn from that experience to help you become a more courageous leader?

Courage to Hold Everyone Accountable

To see what is right, and not to do it, is want of courage.

—CONFUCIUS

You may not remember the name "Sherron Watkins," or remember what she looks like, but you probably recall her. She was vice president of corporate development at the now-notorious Enron Corporation in Houston. She testified before Congress about the shenanigans of partnerships and the accounting tricks that eventually led to the downfall of Enron executives and also sparked revelations about similar corporate scandals.

She'd been with Enron for nearly a decade and had risen high enough on the corporate ladder to send her bosses a hard-hitting, no-nonsense, seven-page critique of their Ponzi scheme. (A Ponzi scheme is a fraudulent investment operation that involves promising or paying abnormally high returns to investors out of the money paid in by subsequent investors, rather than from net revenues generated by any real business. It was named after Charles Ponzi, who spent five years in jail for his scheme.)

Sherron also notified Enron's accounting firm, the now-defunct Arthur Andersen.

Cynics may say she was just giving herself cover in case of problems, or giving then CEO Ken Lay time to do the same. But in the end, when her letter was made public five months after she wrote it, history was made. Others at Enron came forward to support her claims. At the same time over at WorldCom, Cynthia Cooper stood up and talked about CEO Bernie Ebbers and the financial fraud that eventually got him convicted and sent to prison.

It's sad that we call people with this kind of courage "whistle-blowers." How contemptuous. Why don't we call them "heroes"? How do we teach the new, young leaders about accountability, honesty, and lack of arrogance if we don't honor those who have the courage of their convictions? As A New Breed Leader, your job will be not only to prevent these kinds of fraudulent actions, but to respect those who defend high values and standards and hold everyone, even their bosses, accountable.

The Quiet Voice of Courage

Courage doesn't always roar. Sometimes courage is the quiet voice at the end of the day saying, "I will try again tomorrow."
—MARY ANNE RADMACHER, author

We all know that Rosa Parks was given the title "Mother of the Civil Rights Movement" after she refused to give up her seat on the bus to a white man on December 1, 1955. The rest of Parks's story is American history: her arrest and trial, a 381-day Montgomery bus boycott, and finally, the Supreme Court's ruling in November 1956 that segregation on transportation is unconstitutional.

What gets lost in the telling is that this quiet but determined woman had the courage to try again and again. Prior to her arrest, Mrs. Parks had a firm and quiet strength to change injustice. She served as secretary of the NAACP and later as adviser to the NAACP Youth Council, and tried to register to vote on several occasions when it was still nearly impossible to do so. She had run-ins with bus drivers and was evicted from buses. Parks recalls the humiliation: "I didn't want to pay my fare and then go around the back door, because many times, even if you did that, you might not get on the bus at all. They'd probably shut the door, drive off, and leave you standing there." Even before that fateful day, Parks had quietly but persistently showed the courage to fight inequality. She was committed to instigating change and resolutely acted on this commitment throughout her life.

"Courage is not limited to the battlefield or the Indianapolis 500 or bravely catching a thief in your house," Pastor Charles Swindoll wrote. "The real tests of courage are much quieter. They are the inner tests, like remaining faithful when nobody's looking, like enduring pain when the room is empty, like standing alone when you're misunderstood."

> *What you risk reveals what you value.*
> —JEANETTE WINTERSON,
> author and columnist

Defining Your Courage

To become a more courageous leader, it's vital that you evaluate your capacity for courage. The more clearly you define your list of courageous qualities, the stronger you will become. Ask yourself:

- Do I have the courage to speak out for my beliefs and values?

- Am I brave enough to examine my courage and try to see myself in a true perspective?

- Do I encourage others to be bold and act in courageous ways?

- Do I have the courage to inspire my followers even when the trek is long and the odds seem longer?

- Do I have the strength of character to tell them the facts they need to know rather than the illusions they may want to hear?

- Am I willing to sacrifice immediate satisfaction for future gains?

- Am I willing to seek out the truth even though it makes my life much more complicated?

In today's business climate, it's not easy to maintain your values when the ambition to succeed at all costs is so prevalent. It takes real courage to hang on to your morals, ethics, and values. While Howard Schultz, CEO of Starbucks, faces some business uncertainties, he doesn't lack clarity about his values: "We have to be careful not to let our values be compromised by ambition to grow. Being a great leader means finding the balance between celebrating success and not embracing the status quo. Being a great leader also means identifying a path we need to go down and creating enough confidence in our people so they follow it and don't veer off course because it's an easier route to take."

Integrity

I will not cut my conscience to fit this year's fashions.

—LILLIAN HELLMAN, playwright and author

"Do it, just don't get caught" is often the prevailing mantra when values and money collide. Putting aside the values of openness and honesty is very tempting. It may seem easier to "rule" rather than lead, or to yield to the instincts of power and control rather than being open and cooperative. But the twenty-first-century leader must drastically change the thinking about how things have always been done, things like the blind striving for money, the lobbying, the "You scratch my back and I'll scratch yours" attitude that's so prevalent. As A New Breed Leader, you can change the environment in which the loss of integrity has occurred. It won't be easy, but abiding by some simple values of truth and honesty will eventually help turn the tide.

Do you think this story would hold sway with business leaders today?

When the Jews returned from captivity to rebuild their land, their holy city, and their temple, there lived a Jew in Egypt named Nittai, who was a gatherer of books. He prepared to go for a trip one day and sent his servant to buy a camel and a saddle. The servant returned, and when the saddle was removed from the camel, a fortune in rare diamonds was discovered hidden in a pouch. Nittai sent the diamonds back to the camel dealer with the message: "I bought a camel and a saddle, but not these jewels."

The grateful merchant came to thank Nittai. "Had you kept them," he said, "I could not have brought you to court."

"That is true," Nittai replied, "but had I kept them, I would have lost my integrity. One can enter the heavenly kingdom without diamonds, but not without honesty."

Or how about this nineteenth-century example of integrity?

Henry, a nine-year-old, helped his mother grow and sell vegetables from their Pennsylvania garden. He worked hard, and by the time he was sixteen, he was supplying nearby Pittsburgh markets. His business expanded further—until, at age thirty, he made a disastrous investment and was forced into bankruptcy.

Although he had no such legal requirement, Henry got a notebook and wrote on the cover, "The Moral Obligations Book of Henry J. Heinz, 1875." He set about earning enough to repay those who'd trusted him. That done, he began yet another company, which became famous for Heinz's 57 Varieties.

Two critical questions to ask:

- Do I, as a leader, and my organization as a whole exemplify these kinds of personal ethics?

- If not, what can we do to redefine, retrain, and reintroduce personal accountability around ethics and matters of integrity?

A Loss of Shame

As a nation, we seem to have lost our capacity for shame. The "shame factor" in the past provided a strong motive to do right and be accountable. But it's been so weakened that we take bad people and give them television time and exposure as if they were examples to follow.

- Serial killers write books in jail and do television interviews, and we regard it all as entertainment rather than depictions of murder and crimes against not only the victims but society as a whole.

- We debase ourselves with phony "reality" shows on television. Talk show hosts try to increase their ratings by giving people their fifteen minutes of fame through exposing their most intimate neuroses. We're voyeurs to their pain.

- Television networks spend untold hours covering unfounded claims and supposed details of tragic events such as kidnappings and suspicious deaths of wives and husbands. They must fill twenty-four hours with something, so they often just make things up. They are not giving news; they are giving opinions, which are often misleading and wrong.

No Blame, No Shame

Sometime in the last twenty-five years we have developed a rampant corporate entitlement mentality in a free market run amok. We give outlandish signing bonuses to incoming executives and even more outlandish golden parachutes for their departure, even when they have failed to be good stewards of their company and its financial resources.

The recent Wall Street financial meltdown is a perfect example of the problem we have with the No Blame, No Shame attitude of some leaders. We still do not know the full global consequences and ripple effects of the meltdown and government bailout of these huge institutions.

It is astonishing to watch these so-called financial titans go before Congress and testify with absolutely no shame about what they have either done personally or furthered through not doing what should have been done.

Angelo Mozillo, former CEO of Countrywide, took $121.5 million by exercising his stock options and $22.1 million in compensation in 2007 at the height of the housing slump and subprime mortgage debacle. The Securities and Exchange Commission is investigating the details of his stock sales.

Lehman Brothers' Richard Fuld was unrepentant and coolly arrogant as he testified before Congress about his 2007 salary of $45 million ($17,000 per hour), earned while he steered his company into oblivion.

The winner of the worst of the worst goes to AIG and Joe Cassano, president of their financial products division. His unit lost $11 billion. When he was fired, he received $34 million in bonuses and was kept on as a consultant at $1 million per month. Even when the government, using taxpayers' money, stepped in and gave AIG an $84 billion line of credit and a $38 billion loan to save it from total bankruptcy, AIG had a lavish conference at a southern California resort to the tune of $400,000. When it was revealed and all hell broke loose, did the notoriety do anything to their entitlement mentality? Apparently not, because two weeks later, four of the top executives and four guests went to England on an $86,000 luxury hunting trip.

The important question to ask is, does all the money and power these executive have corrupt their perception, values, and sensitivity? Or are they corrupt to begin with and then take advantage of the situations where they can manipulate the system to earn massive amounts of money?

Apparently going to prison for corporate shenanigans is no deterrent. We just went through the Enron and WorldCom scandals, and now we have a new batch of robber barons who accept no blame for what they do and have absolutely no shame about their outlandish lifestyles and financial remunerations.

Boards of directors and hiring committees use the excuse that they have to pay this kind of money to get good people. That is beyond ridiculous. I know many excellent leaders, both men and women, who still believe in earning their pay with no signing bonus and no guarantee of riches, no matter how well or how badly they perform. They would be glad to have their performance determine the amount of bonuses or annual pay they receive.

We used to be a country that accepted blame. Shame was a real motivator. We valued success and didn't reward failure. We have gone way off base. We need a new breed of leaders to guide our ship back onto the right course.

When standards and performance don't match, we lack authenticity, confuse our followers, and set bad examples. Our people must be able to trust us, or the consequences can be detrimental, not only to profits or success but to attitudes and actions. If you're a leader who combines high ethics with a genuine concern for others, personal competence, and fairness in the exercise of power, you'll inspire trust and build community by your values.

> The leader's first task is to be the trumpet that sounds a clear sound.
> —PETER DRUCKER,
> management expert

A Simple Integrity Test

Shame is a powerful incentive to do what's right. Do you remember how your parents or grandparents would talk about not bringing shame to them and to the family? I remember wondering as a kid how I would face my parents or withstand the scrutiny of my neighbors if I did something contrary to our family or community values.

A simple set of questions could go a long way to reinstate the value of shame. Think about a recent incident or action you took and ask yourself:

1. What would my mother think if she saw this on the front page of the newspaper or on the evening news?

2. Would I want my children to know about this? Would I have a hard time explaining my actions or behavior to them?

3. If all my counterparts in other organizations knew about this, what would they think?

4. If everyone in my field of work did what I do, what would the world look like?

5. When telling the truth is embarrassing, awkward, and inconvenient or even threatening to my job or position, what do I do?

High Ethics—A Value Worth Working Toward

A young executive recently said to me, "How can I worry about ethics when our company is involved in a hostile takeover and we're fighting for our very existence?"

My answer was, "You don't have to put ethics on the shelf while doing corporate battle. Without ethics, even if you win, you lose." Every time we say or do something unethical, we chip away at the foundations of our moral character and the reputation of our organization.

Yes, the prime purpose of businesses is to make a profit. But when profits become the only measure of success, we've lost sight of our shared values. When unethical business practices create unfair situations that go beyond a healthy competitive environment, we're in deep trouble. Business competition often involves beating out the other guy, getting the best of the deal, turning, say, $1 million into $5 million. In this adversarial climate, clear definitions of ethics can be difficult. How do you know when an action is a brilliant tactic or an unscrupulous double dealing? One way is to ask yourself: Will this action bring harm to an individual or a business?

No one ever said that being ethical is easy. We live in a world with more and more ethical gray areas. Circumstances pull at us every day, urging us to take the easy way out, to twist something just a little, or to close our eyes for just a second. Acts of omission can be just as unethical as acts of commission. Saying and doing nothing can be just as unethical as the committed act.

Business problems are ultimately human problems, so human values must be applied to their solutions. These human values and solutions come from you and me. The good news is that the profit motive and social responsibility can coexist and prosper when we operate with high ethical standards and compassion. The stronger our ethical behavior, the better leaders we become. Harry J. Gray, former chairman of United Technologies, said, "How we perform as individuals determines how we perform as a nation."

Situational Ethics

Each of us makes daily decisions about how to behave in various situations; thus, we live with situational ethics. Because we aren't perfect, we rarely operate consistently at the highest ethical level. Instead, the best we can do is to try to develop the wisdom and judgment to get as close to perfection as possible. For example, absolute honesty means never lying. That sounds good. But all of us have told "white lies" to keep from hurting someone's feelings.

Let's say a friend asks if you like his or her new clothing. If you don't, there's little point in saying so. If you find a neutral comment that didn't tell the absolute truth, are you unethical? Most of us would answer no. So we use our experience (wisdom and judgment) and our conscience (moral character and integrity) to tell us how far we stray from absolute honesty.

Situational ethics or not, if something is ethically or morally repugnant on a personal scale, it's equally repugnant in your job and profession. In both your personal and your business lives, one of your biggest challenges as A New Breed Leader will be to set high standards, try to live by them, and communicate the same expectation to others.

Integrity is about your actions based on an internally consistent framework of principles. Someone is said to have integrity to the extent that everything he or she does is based on the same core set of values. While those values may change, it's their consistency with each other and with your actions that determine your integrity.

The real test of any leader or company's ethical fiber is to ask:

- What happens when we are under pressure?

- How do I stand up, how does my organization stand up, to those pressures?

When circumstances tempt you to drop your standards, you must reach down inside and find your consistent set of values and then act accordingly. As Frances Perkins, a social reformer and former U.S. Secretary of Labor, said, "Most of man's problems upon this planet, in the long history of the race, have been met and solved either partially or as a whole by experiment based on common sense and carried out with courage."

Values Forging Community

We were born to unite with our fellow men, and to join in community with the human race.

—CICERO

One of the things for which we can be proud is how fast our shared values forge communities in times of disaster or a crisis.

On August 29, 2005, Hurricane Katrina hit with a fury. The tidal surge was equivalent to a Category 3 hurricane, causing more than fifty breaches in drainage and navigational canal levees. Eighty percent of New Orleans was flooded, with some parts under fifteen feet of water. It was the worst engineering disaster in U.S. history. The city was in chaos. We all saw the human suffering flashed across our television screens.

What you may not know is that at New Orleans's leading newspaper, *The Times-Picayune*, a new kind of leadership was emerging. The paper had planned for hurricanes and had given warnings in many articles about a possible levee disaster. However, like other New Orleans observers, it hadn't truly appreciated the possible devastation that could be wrought by such a catastrophe. Editor Jim Amoss said, "It became immediately apparent that our very survival as a publication depended on collaboration and cooperation."

On August 30, he loaded more than 200 staffers and family into a convoy of the paper's delivery trucks and headed across the Mississippi River to one of the suburban bureaus. The staff crowded into a room whose power came from a backup generator. Any hierarchical levels of leadership were quickly leveled by the enormity of the disaster, and collaborative leadership emerged instantly. People took responsibility for all sorts of jobs: the business manager delivered equipment to colleagues, for example, and reporters distributed newspapers and kayaked to get supplies. Leaders appeared everywhere.

Many who'd never worked together before were planning and implementing how to get the paper out to the citizens. Passionately, the staffers worked as a team, a community of people who shared the same goals and love of their city.

In addition to their commitment to their jobs, they were all dealing with the same personal problems as other New Orleans residents—finding family, trying to save homes, and figuring out what their insurance covered, what was left of their neighborhood, and how to put lives back together.

The core values that bind people together in crises quickly came to the forefront. They were all "family." They were an integral part of forging a new identity among themselves and their fellow citizens. A new sense of collaboration and distributed leadership remains at the paper. It has become a new and different community.

The moral fiber of people, leaders, organizations, and a nation is determined by the courage to define what we value, personally, organizationally, and in our communities, whether the latter span the neighborhood, the nation, or the world. The team at the *Times-Picayune* found and cemented its moral fiber.

Elie Wiesel, Nobel laureate and Holocaust survivor, wrote about the terror of Nazi Germany and the termination camps. His words are just as meaningful for the New Orleans disaster:

> *This is the duty of our generation as we enter the twenty-first century—solidarity with the weak, the persecuted, the lonely, the sick, and those in despair. It is expressed by the desire to give a noble and humanizing meaning to a community in which all members will define themselves not by their own identity but by that of others.*

We don't have to look far to see nonprofit groups bringing personal, organizational, and community values together. They often collaborate with businesses to respond to the needs in their cities and towns. Starbucks and organizations such as the Bill and Melinda Gates Foundation seek ways to be good community citizens locally and globally. They have strong values statements and encourage others to follow suit. Organizations with character, like people with character, get results; they do it with integrity and a respect for others.

At Home and At School

Leadership begins at home. A parent speaks to a newborn baby in warm, loving tones, and the child comes to trust the parent. As the child grows, the parent's words, actions, and examples give the child direction and a sense of themselves and how they should act and respond to the world. The only place to establish

the foundation of values that hold a person in good stead throughout their life is in the home.

Arnie Palmer's Childhood Lessons

Arnie Palmer did not win a U.S Amateur Championship, four
Masters Championships, two British Opens, and a U.S. Open
Championship by accident or a casual approach to make the most
of his immense talent. He attributes his success to many lessons
he learned from his father. He writes about them in his autobiography, *A Golfer's Life*.

In a recent interview with Arnie, I asked him how his father
helped shape his values. I said, "Arnie you have such a strong reputation for openness and integrity. In your book you wrote how
your father taught you values that helped you become the success
you are." He answered, "Absolutely. Values are the most important thing." I asked, "Could you talk about a couple of the values
that served you well in your career? Perhaps even helped you get
through something in which you might have otherwise stumbled
or failed?" "Integrity and honesty are those things that you are
talking about, and the fact that he taught me to be up-front about
anything that I did or things that I did wrong. He was very much
in favor of being open and honest. If I did something wrong, he
taught me not to hide it. That's how he wanted me to conduct
myself. Does that make sense?" I said, "Yes, it does. I guess the
basic word is just being honest." "Right, and having integrity. I
try to keep his policies intact in my life. I'm in business and I like
to be up-front in my business dealings."

We talked at length about parental influence and I said,

"Parents can be such strong leaders in their children's lives." I asked him, "Is there some golf incident in which your dad taught you a lesson that has been with you through life? An incident where it is almost like you can hear your dad saying, 'Now, son . . .'" He chuckled and answered, "It was an incident that happened when I was a junior and he was watching me play and I missed a little putt and I reeled and threw the putter over a row of poplar trees. On the next hole I laid about a ten-foot putt to win the match, and of course I was elated. I was as happy as I could be. I went in and changed and got in the car to drive home with my parents and there was total silence. Here I'm a real happy guy 'cause I've won and I'm getting the quiet treatment. Finally I said, 'Isn't anybody going to say anything?' and my father laid into me and he said, 'Boy, if you ever do that when I'm watching you again, you'll never play golf as long as you live in my house.' He didn't tell me never to show some temper but he told me what the rules were and it's a lesson that I've never forgotten and have tried to pass on."

Parental Values Lessons

I think Arnie's dad would have liked my parents. They had a rule: Never use the excuse "everyone is doing it" to justify something you know is wrong. Apparently it stuck, because when I was raising my two sons, I told them the same thing.

When my eldest son was in high school, he and his closest buddy cooked up some nutty scheme that involved going somewhere that my son knew I would disapprove of. So the friend came along as my son's "lobbyist" and gave me all the reasons why I should say yes. He was very persuasive. But when he was finished, I said "I guess you don't know the rule around here. If you say, 'Well, everyone else is going,' you've just absolutely guaranteed that it will not happen." I was not a popular mom that day with my son or his friend.

During the trying years of raising teenagers, I often recalled my mother's advice as a parent-leader:

She had another piece of wisdom that she taught me early in my parenting days. She said, "Love them unconditionally; teach them discipline so

> Parenthood is not about being popular with your kids, it is about giving them the values they need to get along in the world.

they have the inner strength to get through the good and bad. Then give them the best education you can. The rest is up to God." I have tried to live up to those three simple values lessons: love, discipline, and education. She's gone now, but I often think of her simple, quiet wisdom on many things, but especially about being a good parent.

As A New Breed Leader, you'll need to take integrity all the way back to its starting place, which is not only in your own home but in the homes of your neighbors. Is there some way you can support or establish programs in your community that teach good parenting skills?

Meet Frank Keating

Former Governor of Oklahoma Frank Keating (1997–2003) is currently president and CEO of the American Council of Life Insurers. He has a wise sense of history and a deep and abiding respect for the values inherent in our constitution. You'll hear more from Frank in Chapter Eight, "Humility Matters."

When we spoke, one of the subjects he wanted to discuss

was what we can do to educate our children and prepare them to become future leaders.

I just finished a children's book entitled, *The Trial of Standing Bear*. It is about a Native American Indian whose case established that Indians were [considered] people under the Constitution. Remember that in 1858, the U.S. Supreme Court ruled that blacks were not people in the Dred Scott decision. That was greeted with some outrage. And [as a] matter of fact, it was one of the reasons for the march toward civil war, but there were a lot of people who just didn't see the threat to themselves in that awful decision.

In the 1879 Standing Bear case, the chief of the Ponca tribe was arrested for leaving Oklahoma. The Indians were outraged because according to the government they were not people entitled to constitutional protection. In this case, white people had nothing to gain and a lot to lose by asserting that this red man, this fellow American, was a human being, not just a wagon or a piece of property. Four white men were particularly outraged; one was the general council of the Union Pacific Railroad, one was a newspaper man, a third was a lawyer, and one was an Army general; and of course, Standing Bear. They won the case and established that a Native American Indian was a human being, and he had a right to travel where he wanted to, just like any other American.

I believe [that] in schools we have to start teaching the young people about having less hubris, having a little more humility, [and] understanding that they can learn from others, from their past experience. Young people need to understand that the moral challenges they will face will be the challenges that they don't recognize frequently for the long-term historic implications. Whether it's to protect a down-trodden segment of society or to be open to the views of others, or whether it's to be humble in listening to guidance and advice from people who didn't go to the school that they did or don't have the social background that they do, that's the great challenge: to recognize that in every relationship you need to view it as a peer relationship and not as a superior or inferior relationship.

How can you, your followers, and your organization partner with schools to exemplify high integrity as a value worth learning?

What values lessons and language will we use in the twenty-first century with the youth of our nation and around the world? Will our government and our organizations send a message of inclusion, sensitivity, and tolerance along with strength? Will we relay a sense of who and what we are as a nation and as people, and what we can become? The world is waiting for us to lead again. Not dominate, invade, or dictate, but bring nations and peoples together to solve our shared problems.

The *Tao Te Ch'ing*—the writings of the ancient Chinese philosopher Lao Tzu—often describes evolved people. Whether you're a leader in the making, one who's improving your skills, or a high-level leader reassessing your values, you may find this list from a page in the *Tao* entitled "Noncompetitive Values" worthy of consideration:

The value in a dwelling is location.

The value in a mind is depth.

The value in relations is benevolence.

The value in words is sincerity.

The value in leadership is order.

The value in work is competence.

The value in effort is timeless.

As A New Breed Leader, your highest value will be to forge a community with all your stakeholders and all the communities in which you operate. There could be no higher calling. Anthropologist Margaret Mead put it best: "Never doubt that a small group of thoughtful, committed citizens can change the world. Indeed, it is the only thing that ever has."

Your Action Plan Questions for Quality 5
VALUES

1. How do I define and communicate my values? Be specific. What actions will I take over the next few months to demonstrate—in word and deed—my values to my followers?

2. How does my company or organization proclaim its values? How can I help it do a better job of communicating those values?

3. How clearly are my values congruent with those of my organization? What steps can I take to bring the two into alignment?

CHAPTER SIX

Perspective Matters

ESTABLISHING BALANCE

*There are no extra pieces in the universe. Everyone is
here because he or she has a place to fill, and every
piece must fit itself into the big jigsaw puzzle.*

—DEEPAK CHOPRA

IN OUR LEADERSHIP jigsaw puzzle, perspective is part of the whole, connecting directly to power.

If you approach leadership power without first addressing the balance that perspective brings, you are robbed of the insight needed to harness all the qualities in the puzzle and keep them glued together. Thus, a true-to-life perspective is key to maintaining the values necessary for leading others.

If you are a student of history, you gain a much broader perspective from which to make wise decisions. You've come to learn from the mistakes and lessons of others, and can discover how it plays into your life and life situations. Being on target with your viewpoint of a present situation can spell the difference between failure and success. Most important, if you have the counterpoint

A PERSPECTIVE LESSON
WELL LEARNED

My husband, Bill, and I went to Poland as unofficial volunteer ambas-sadors for President George H. W. Bush's new Leadership Corp. We conducted seminars across Poland and were fortunate to be there the week Lech Walesa was elected the first president of a new free Poland. The old Eastern Bloc nations were emerging and were very excited to participate in the free world.

Bill's seminars were about how to form joint ventures with Western companies, and mine were on leadership and how it would apply in their new post-communist world.

The newly formed Chambers of Commerce arranged the venues and seminars. They assigned several translators to us as we went to dif-ferent parts of the country.

One morning I was working with a group of about 200 managers from the manufacturing sector of a central region. Andrzej (Ange) Chrapek from Bielsko-Biala, Poland, was standing right beside me, simultaneously translating every word I said.

It was a strange feeling of stop and start, but we were doing pretty well . . . we thought. People had laughed at some of the humor and they were taking notes and asking questions. When I began talking about the importance of "delegation," all of a sudden the body lan-guage came screaming at me. They sat back in their chairs, folded their arms, put down their pens, and I could see the wall go up between us.

I was stunned and told Ange to tell them that we would take a short break.

I asked him, "What on earth did I say that brought on such a closed, unhappy reaction?" Ange replied, "Well, can you tell me a little more about this delegation idea?"

I explained why a leader must be able to assign work to others in order to accomplish more. His face lit up and he laughed.

"Oh, I see," he said. "But that word is a real problem here, because when you talk about delegation, they automatically think of a 'delegation' that would come from Moscow to inspect their factories. When that happened, it was not a good thing!"

We brought the group back and I apologized for frightening them. Between Ange and me, we were able to explain the term in more comfortable language. A few smiled and some even laughed because they saw my distress at their reaction. The walls went down and we were back on track.

The participants had a harsh past to get beyond, and I had a new appreciation for the fragility of language between cultures. As Bill and I look back on those two weeks, we realize we learned more from the wonderful Polish people we met than they learned from us. Our perspective on Communism, World War II, their deprivations and hardships, along with their incredible determination and courage, moved us more deeply than any group we have worked with in any country.

of past and present to use as a transition into the future, you're ready to be A New Breed Leader.

Our Leadership Pyramid

How does perspective influence the four levels in the pyramid?

ENLIGHTENERS . . . have the highest degree of perspective.

CREATORS . . . apply perspective to fuel their creativity.

BUILDERS . . . draw on perspective to explore growth.

SUSTAINERS . . . relate perspective to their long-haul value.

Wherever you are on the pyramid, a steadiness of viewpoint will inspire your followers. Your growth kindles theirs. There's just no substitute for a workplace or organization where followers feel comfortable—even secure—because you provide a perspective and balance with which they can identify and believe in.

In this chapter, you'll hear from three wise leaders—Former China Ambassador James Sasser, Donna Shalala, and U.S. Army (ret.) Colonel Bill Smullen—who have always been people of perspective. Their varied and interesting viewpoints result from the deep thought they've given to where we've been, where we are now, and where we are going. Such views are critical in solving our global problems and making this a century of community and connectedness.

> We are at times too ready to believe that the present is the only possible state of things.
> —MARCEL PROUST

As you read their remarks, pause and ask:

- What are the thoughts, actions, and outlooks I need to have a vibrant, realistic perception of leadership in the twenty-first century?

- How can I bring my followers along for the exciting ride this century promises?

- What are the issues and important aspects on which I need to focus to maximize the other qualities that matter most?

- How can my perspective build a sense of community and shared purpose?

When faced with current challenges, we can easily forget that all of us on this planet have more in common than we have differences. We become more connected and have a better perspective when, as President Barack Obama said, "We value the constellation of behaviors that express our mutual regard for one another: honesty, fairness, humility, kindness, courtesy, and compassion."

Judith Lewis Herman, M.D., and professor of clinical psychiatry at Harvard Medical School, wrote, "Commonality carries with it all the meaning of the word *common*. It means belonging to a society, having a public role, being part of that which is universal. It means having a feeling of familiarity, of being known, of communion . . ."

It's imperative that, as leaders, we move away from the past into the future with a new perspective and come together to rediscover and confirm our commonalities. Using Dr. Herman's term, let's have a national and global "communion" of reconciliation.

The Perspective Puzzle Piece

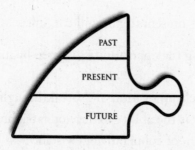

The Past

It is useful occasionally to look at the past to
gain a perspective on the present.
—FABIAN LINDEN, author

History is one of the most useful guideposts for A New Breed Leader. When you learn from past failure, you're less likely to make the same mistake again. When you gain insight from past success, you can preserve your strengths and build on them.

To say that we need to learn from the past seems like such a commonsense thing. But as the great American humorist Will Rogers said, "Just because it's common sense doesn't mean it's common practice."

As beneficial as the past can be there are three common traps that will keep you and your followers in some of the negative, dead-end thinking of the past:

1. Believing that yesterday's solutions will solve today's problems.

2. Assuming present trends will continue.

3. Neglecting the opportunities offered by future change.

These traps block innovation and breakthrough thinking. Your value as a leader is the ability to develop farsighted prospects and a constant stream of cooperative new solutions. Important questions to ask are:

- At what level are we hanging on to the past?

- Are we even aware that we're still operating under outmoded ideas and policies?

- What can I do to move us forward?

Letting go of the past can be difficult for some of your team members and nearly impossible for others. As leader, your vision, values, and communication skills will come into play as a major part of helping others through these transitions and gaining new perspective.

Leadership Tools for Perspective

In God we trust; all others bring data.

—DR. W. EDWARDS DEMING

In previous chapters, I've quoted from books I find inspiring, informative, challenging, and even provocative. I hope you'll read them all or, at the very least, go online to find reviews that give you the major points and themes.

Because I feel so strongly about the significance of perspective and

> Live as on a mountain top.
> —EMPEROR MARCUS AURELIUS

the balance it brings to life and leadership, I'd like to recommend five specific, oft-used volumes from my bookshelf. Add them to your collection, and you'll wonder how you ever managed to lead without them. (I have no financial investment in any of them, but simply respect and admiration for their insights and wisdom.)

These books will help you gain new perspective and "live as on a mountain top," which is difficult but important to do amid the daily crush of events and the demands of leading others. These books are filled with not only wisdom but practical ideas that will give you fresh insights so that it seems you're looking at life and business from the highest point.

1. *The Hidden Persuaders*, by Vance Packard, first published in 1957. You can find it on Amazon.com and at used bookstores. There's a recent update by another author, but I recommend the original because it strikingly explores the use of consumer motivational research and other psychological techniques. It looks at the psychology and subliminal tactics used by advertisers to manipulate expectations and induce desire for products. It's about media manipulation, including the manipulative ways politicians are marketed to the electorate. Packard questions the morality of using these techniques, and he crafted a powerful read.

2. *The Seven Sisters: The Great Oil Companies & the World They Shaped*, by Anthony Sampson, 1976. This book will open your eyes as to how we got into the oil mess we're now in. The Seven Sisters consisted of three firms formed by the government breakup of Standard Oil, along with four other major oil companies. Because they dominated oil production, refining, and distribution, they were able to take advantage of rapidly increasing demand and create immense profits. Well organized and negotiating as a cartel, the Seven Sisters were able to have their way with most Third World oil producers. It was only when the Arab states began to gain control over oil prices and production—mainly through the formation of OPEC (beginning in 1960 and really gaining power by the 1970s)—that the Seven Sisters' influ-

ence declined. Then the Seven Sisters went through a confusing series of acquisitions and mergers, name changes, and divestures and redivestures for which we have all paid dearly.

3. *Corporate Cultures: The Rites and Rituals of Corporate Life*, by Terrence E. Deal and Allan A. Kennedy, 1982. Deal and Kennedy proposed one of the first models of organizational culture. When the book was published, it had many supporters, although many also felt the idea of corporate culture would be just a passing fad. Now, the notion of corporate culture is widely accepted as an important business concept for financial control and employee satisfaction.

Corporate culture is one of the key drivers for the success— or failure—of an organization. A good, well-aligned culture can propel it to success. However, the wrong culture will stifle ability to adapt to a fast-changing world. So how can you understand your corporate culture? And what steps can you take to create a strong corporate culture that will best support your organization's activities? This book will help you find the answers. Its theories are applicable to any organization, not just the corporate world.

4. What the Great Religions Believe, by Joseph Gaer, 1963. It can be found on Amazon.com and at used bookstores. *The New York Times* is quoted on the back cover of the paperback edition: "Across the world and throughout history men have sought to fathom the meaning of their existence by heeding the words of various spiritual leaders and following the ways of many faiths. This is the story of the great religions of mankind: how they began, how they evolved, and how they are practiced by the faithful. This is a book which is at once compact, lucid, readable, and unbiased in its appraisals."

The world needs to reconcile its differences and people need to value one another's religions and customs if we're going to make progress in our societies and civilization as a whole.

This small book of 182 pages gives you a quick and meaningful grasp of the great religions, along with many "how" and "why" insights into what you are dealing with as A New Breed Leader. On top of that it is a fascinating read!

5. *The Lessons of History*, by Will and Ariel Durant, 1968. I've saved the best for last, and this one, too, can be found on Amazon .com and at used bookstores. Husband-and-wife team Will and Ariel Durant were giants in the study of civilization. Among their other writings was the unbelievable ten-volume *The Story of Civilization*. I wish I could say I've read all of it, but I can't.

Upon completion of that series, Will stated that he and Ariel "made note of events and comments that might illuminate present affairs, future probabilities, the nature of man, and the conduct of states." (I have never seen a larger understatement in all my studies.) So they wrote *The Lessons of History*, which provides a summary of periods and trends in history they'd noted. The book presents an overview of the themes and lessons observed from 5,000 years of world history examined from thirteen perspectives, consisting of geography, biology, race, character, morals, religion, economics, socialism, government, war, growth, decay, and progress.

To give you a taste of the power of this little book (117 pages), here is an excerpt from the inside cover leaf describing the contents of the book:

. . . they looked back at what history has to say about the nature, the conduct, and the prospects of man, seeking in the great lives, the great ideas, the great events of the past for the meaning of man's long journey, through war, conquest, and creation—and for the great themes that can help us understand our own era.

I discovered *The Lessons of History* at the beginning of my business career. At that point, I was a sponge. I had long lists of books to read. However, something about the title intrigued me. I read it immediately, and it has been my constant companion for twenty-five years. There's no volume that's had such an impact on my view of the past, the present, and the future. I guarantee it will do the same for you.

This little gem teaches us that we've been here before and gives us perspective in our turbulent times. Though written sixty years ago, it'll awaken your instincts and help balance your emotions, intellect, and New Breed Leader skills.

When I conduct leadership seminars, I always bring my copy with me, carefully protected in a special cover (and I never, ever ship it inside checked luggage). There's never been a time when I couldn't find a line or paragraph that applied to the subject at hand, regardless of what country I'm in or what group I'm working with.

Of course, I don't think these are the only books about history that you should read. The classics, both prose and poetry, give you an understanding you can find nowhere else. For example, in the twentieth century we thought bigger was always better. In the twenty-first century, we are learning that less is often more. In 1854, Henry David Thoreau wrote *Walden; or, Life In the Woods*.

His shrewd observations about what can happen when organizations get too big could help you look at things differently.

In 1884, Mark Twain wrote *Adventures of Huckleberry Finn*, in which young Huck learns some very important life lessons as he travels the Mississippi River. He is faced with the entrenched thinking of the past, especially racism. If you did not read it during your school years, it is worth reading now and asking yourself, How far have we progressed? What can I, as a leader, do about racism and other harmful entrenched thinking?

Homer's *Iliad*, an ancient Greek epic poem, dates back to the eight or ninth century B.C. It is one of the greatest classics of all time and fascinating reading today. What Homer wrote all those centuries ago is still a valuable guide for following a true path in today's complex business environment.

You will never run out of wisdom to tap if you have a library of the classics. The most effective leaders I know always have several books they're reading at the same time. It is their curiosity that keeps them searching for past insights, present solutions, and visions of the future.

We Are Part of History

One of the most enlightening television interviews Charlie Rose has conducted was with biographer/historian and bestselling author David McCullough. You may remember some of his many books, such as *The Johnstown Flood*, *Truman*, and *John Adams*, all brilliantly written and historically accurate.

> To not know what came before you is to remain forever a child.
> —Roman proverb

Charlie and David were discussing the importance of historical writing and understanding history in general. McCullough said, "History is not something in the past. You and I are part of history . . . we are history. Fifty and a hundred years from now people will say, 'How did they comport themselves? How did they handle the pressing issues of their times?'" His questions and the possible answers they can produce struck me as a very important element for A New Breed Leader.

Here are a few questions that came to mind to help to begin your own inquiries about our role in this new century. Add your own questions to the list and share it with your leadership team. The answers could very well give everyone a new and better perspective.

- What will people in the future say about the New Breed Leaders who come forward in this new century?

- Did we stand up to the test of time?

- Were we insular and looked only at what is in it for us today?

- What have we left to our progeny?

- Did we have the courage and foresight to view our action as something that our grandchildren will have to grapple with?

Every action you take and every word you speak will affect the future and will soon become the past. Putting our actions into the context of how we "comported" ourselves makes that a formidable leadership test.

Wisdom from the Past

*Democracy is not an easy form of government, because it is never
final; it is a living, changing organism, with a continuous shifting and
adjusting of balance between individual freedom and general order.*

—ILKA CHASE, American actress/novelist

On April 16, 1953, President Dwight D. Eisenhower delivered
his famous speech, "The Chance for Peace," before the American Society of Newspaper Editors. It's been known for nearly
sixty years as the "A Cross of Iron" speech because of his brilliant
allusion to William Jennings Bryan's famous phrase, "a cross of
gold." Eisenhower was seeking some concrete way to dramatize
the futility of the Cold War. He hit upon the idea of comparing
peaceful expenditures to those being incurred in the armaments
race.

He spoke of hope rather than fear and of putting our resources
to their best and highest use. We can translate his examples to current dollars and still come away with the power of his insights.

*The worst to be feared and the best to be expected can be simply
stated.*

The worst is atomic war.

*The best would be this: a life of perpetual fear and tension; a bur-
den of arms draining the wealth and the labor of all peoples; a wast-
ing of strength that defies the American system or the Soviet system or
any system to achieve true abundance and happiness for the peoples of
this earth.*

Every gun that is made, every warship launched, every rocket fired signifies, in the final sense, a theft from those who hunger and are not fed, those who are cold and are not clothed.

This world in arms is not spending money alone.

It is spending the sweat of its laborers, the genius of its scientists, the hopes of its children.

The cost of one modern heavy bomber is this: a modern brick school in more than 30 cities.

It is two electric power plants, each serving a town of 60,000 population.

It is two fine, fully equipped hospitals.

It is some 50 miles of concrete highway.

We pay for a single fighter with a half million bushels of wheat.

We pay for a single destroyer with new homes that could have housed more than 8,000 people.

This, I repeat, is the best way of life to be found on the road the world has been taking.

This is not a way of life at all, in any true sense. Under the cloud of threatening war, it is humanity hanging from a cross of iron.

This Government is ready to ask its people to join with all nations in devoting a substantial percentage of the savings achieved by disarmament to a fund for world aid and reconstruction. The purposes of this great work would be to help other peoples to develop the underdeveloped areas of the world, to stimulate profitability and fair world trade, to assist all peoples to know the blessings of productive freedom.

The monuments to this new kind of war would be these: roads and schools, hospitals and homes, food and health.

We are ready, in short, to dedicate our strength to serving the needs, rather than the fears, of the world.

Again we say: the hunger for peace is too great, the hour in history too late, for any government to mock men's hopes with mere words and promises and gestures.

The test of truth is simple. There can be no persuasion but by deeds.

The comparisons of President Eisenhower ring true today. The lack of priorities and long-term perspective could lead our nation or any nation into insolvency and indebtedness to others. This, in turn, leads to a type of bondage.

In the mid-1800s, John Alexander Tyler wrote about democratic societies' evolution:

SOCIETAL EVOLUTION

The average longevity of formerly great civilizations was about 200 years . . . and each of them passed through the following evolutions:

- From *bondage* to spiritual faith,

- From *spiritual faith* to great courage,

- From *courage* to liberty,

- From *liberty* to abundance,

- From *abundance* to selfishness,

- From *selfishness* to complacency,

- From *complacency* to apathy,

- From *apathy* to dependency,

- From *dependency* right back to the bondage where it all started.

How far along this cycle have we moved? Can we profit by the lesson of history?

As A New Breed Leader, you would be wise to give it some hard thought.

The past is our roadway to the present. Let's all work together to build leadership skills that go beyond limits of every kind. The twenty-first century can be a wondrous place if we find our commonality and equilibrium as people, organizations, and nations.

The Present

People think focus means saying yes to the thing you've got to focus on. But that's not what it means at all. It means saying no to the hundred other good ideas that there are. You have to pick carefully. I'm actually as proud of many of the things we haven't done as the things we have done.

—STEVE JOBS, CEO, Apple

As important as it is to be a diligent student of the past, the reality of today is all we really have. So with a good understanding of the past, you can focus on what you need do to bring competence, accountability, openness, humility, language, and values into the present state of your organization and your personal leadership style.

> Yesterday is our teacher, tomorrow is our dream, and today is our reality.

Meet Bill Smullen

When I met General Colin Powell in 1998, he was chairman of the national youth movement America's Promise. We were both speaking at an event in Washington, D.C.

The next day I visited their headquarters in Alexandria, Virginia, and met Colonel William Smullen (U.S. Army, ret.). Bill had been General Powell's chief of staff at the White House when Powell was chairman of the Joint Chiefs of Staff, and he was acting in that same capacity at America's Promise. You know about General Powell. But let me tell you a little about Bill Smullen so you can fully appreciate his comments.

F. William ("Bill") Smullen III reshaped Army media relations. He became the chief of the Army Public Affairs Media Relations Division when interaction with the civilian press was frayed and trust was nearly nonexistent. Nearly five years later, Smullen had reversed that climate so that reporters genuinely strived for balanced news stories and came out to the field instead of reporting from inside the Beltway (Washington, D.C.).

Bill served as the special assistant for public affairs to two chairmen of the Joint Chiefs of Staff, General Powell and Admiral Bill Crowe. He was the first public affairs officer to hold this position. Powell respected him so highly that he made Bill his chief of staff when he became the Secretary of State. In 2006, Colonel Smullen was inducted into the U.S. Army Public Affairs Hall of Fame.

Bill is currently Maxwell Senior Fellow in National Security and director of National Security Studies at Syracuse University. Even with all of his stature, he's one of the most approachable and responsive leaders I have met. You will meet his wife, Lieutenant Colonel Mary Lou Smullen (ret.), later in the book. They are quite a team!

I knew Bill would have some very clear thoughts on how we bring leadership from the past into the present. Here's his perspective:

Being a leader in the new millennium is really no different than being one in any time past. What is different are the changing times and the urgency of finding the best leaders available to face what lies ahead. If ever there was a time our nation needed leaders who could make an impact, it's in this, the twenty-first century. The challenges have never been greater for leaders. In response, they need to have certain qualities and to do certain things that positively influence those they ask and expect to follow them. Here are six qualities of leaders who have the right stuff:

1. They need to establish and practice a clearly stated set of values that will motivate others to reach and maintain high standards.
2. They need to inspire others to serve the organization, the institution, the nation, or others in selfless ways.
3. They need to bring people together around a meaningful purpose they can commonly share and be proud of.
4. They need to pursue that position with positive energy, optimism, and a passion that is infectious.
5. They need to get the best players on their leadership team and inspire them and those who work for them to strive for success.
6. They need to mentor others at all levels and not just those who look like or sound like them.

I learned early on, and it was reinforced at virtually every experience level, that having a sense of purpose and of place can set a tone for being who and what you are in life. Moreover, while living every phase of life, you should seek and take advantage of opportunities for friendship, leadership, and learning. With respect to the latter, make lifelong learning a way of life, and in so doing, nourish a spirit of curiosity and develop a desire for intellectual growth. Use whatever experiences life provides to follow your passions, to aim high, and to remain committed to excellence. Take every step with a sense of dedication and purpose. At the same time, take along an open mind and a sense of humor on this journey of life.

For those interested in public service, there has never been a more important time for making commitments to military service, national security, or public diplomacy. The needs and the challenges in these areas are incredibly high. So are the opportunities to make a positive impact on the welfare of the nation. Develop the requisite skills, find the proper niche, and invest your time and talent on behalf of the nation and the American people. The rewards may not be as high in treasure as much as they are in making a difference in life, the best gift of all. As you study leadership, you'll find many views of what it'll take to make this new century and millennium work well. For example, in my first leadership book, *Making a Difference*, I outlined the twelve qualities that make you a leader. Bill Smullen lists six; John C. Maxwell describes *The 21 Irrefutable Laws of Leadership;* Barbara Kellerman's *Bad Leadership* cites five categories; Jim Collins has Five Levels of Leadership in *Good to Great;* and the father of modern leadership, Robert K. Greenleaf, has eleven categories of *Servant Leadership.* We could also mention lists and categories and attributes cited by Ken Blanchard, Rosabeth Moss Kanter, Warren Bennis, John Kotter, and James Kouzes and Barry Posner.

So there's no end to the variations on the themes of leadership. Nor should there be. You are a unique person, with your unique style of leadership. None of us is 100 percent correct. We each bring our leadership versions and viewpoints to the table so that you can assimilate as much as possible and then build and update your tool kit of New Breed Leader skills.

Common Sense

I always try to balance the light with the heavy—a few tears of human spirit in with the sequins and the fringes.
—BETTE MIDLER, singer and actress

Your leadership will be at its best when you apply some good, old-fashioned common sense. No matter how difficult today may seem, a dose of common sense is a great leveler. It will get you and your team through the worst of times and make the good times even better.

> It ain't over 'til it's over.
> —YOGI BERRA

Legendary baseball figure Yogi Berra's offbeat humor has always been a favorite of mine. I have this quote on a Post-it on my office wall to buoy me when I have "one of those days!"

A much longer version of this popular eulogy to common sense was flying around the Internet for several years. As of today there are 56,000 entries with no attribution or who the originator was. I think this is the best part:

Today we mourn the passing of a beloved old friend, Common Sense, who has been with us for many years. No one knows for sure how old he was since his birth records were long ago lost in bureaucratic red tape. He will be remembered as having cultivated such valuable lessons as: Knowing when to come in out of the rain, why the early bird gets the worm, life isn't always fair, and maybe it was my fault.

Common Sense lived by simple, sound financial policies (don't spend more than you earn) and reliable parenting strategies (adults, not children, are in charge).

Common Sense was preceded in death by his parents, Truth and Trust; his wife, Discretion; his daughter, Responsibility; and his son, Reason.

When you have done your best, let common sense tell you that it'll never be perfect. Try to let go and just keep moving toward your goals and vision.

The Future

All truth passes through three stages: First, it is ridiculed.
Second, it is violently opposed. Third, it is
accepted as being self-evident.

—ARTHUR SCHOPENHAUER, German philosopher

Moving followers from the present across the wobbly bridge to the future is not easy. New ideas often run into brick walls of rejection. And that's okay. The "new" must go through the fire of examination, of testing, and of hammering out, before the fresh, strengthened structure is in place. It will take all of your leadership skills to be a change-master leader able to move from the present to the future.

BRIDGE TO THE FUTURE

The Five F's of a Change-Master Leader

Effective change-master leaders and their organizations are characterized by what I call the Five F's:

Fast . . . You have a culture that can adjust and move quickly.

Focused . . . Each person knows clearly what their job is and how to do it.

Fluid . . . Processes and procedures move smoothly from one department to another.

Flexible . . . You are supple and changeable to handle the needs of all your constituents.

Futurized . . . You always have your eye on great future opportunities.

Those are the simple keys, and as you think about them, remember that simple does not mean easy, and these are no exception. They are and will be difficult to achieve as you move your organization forward.

As you build your leadership skills, you will need to examine your heart and your mind to define what the Five F's mean to you. How can you use these concepts? How can you help your people understand them? How do you identify core values, core principles, keys in learning and capabilities? What are you going to have to do? How are you going to have to act?

You must take those five keys and then break them down, saying, "This is what we need to do. Now, how are we going to do it?" Because in this century it's critical that A New Breed Leader be able to break down major factors and identify them so that they are trainable, actionable, and measurable.

There are several basic principles that can help you begin using the Five F's to become a change-master leader:

DEVELOP FOLLOWERS

> Some leaders develop followers. Other leaders develop other leaders.
> —ZIG ZIGLAR, author, motivational speaker

Executives have told me numerous times that very little is more rewarding than watching followers blossom and grow. Seeing their faces when they accomplish a new task and sharing their excitement when they do what they thought was impossible—these are the rewards of a change-master leader. When you help others change, grow, and discover their own potential, you've added to the quality of their life. You've made a difference and served them well as leader.

DEVELOP PATIENCE

Even in times of accelerated change, everything takes longer than you think. Try not to succumb to frustration. You live in a world that's always advertising perfection as an attainable goal. But in truth, there's no perfection in this world. So begin taking perfection out of the equation

> The key to self-empowerment is to always strive to do the best you can with what you have at hand.
> —EDGAR CAYCE

and instead strive patiently to do your best with what you have, right where you are. If you like simple and thought-provoking proverbs, as I do, think about these:

A handful of patience is worth more than a bushel of brains. (Danish proverb)

With time and patience, the mulberry leaf becomes a silk gown. (Chinese proverb)

DEVELOP STEADINESS

Keeping change in perspective is a major task for modern leaders. You can't become overly excited or depressed by events. This doesn't mean you should fail to enjoy life. Go for the best you can imagine; fulfill your potential. But while you're enjoying life, keep your priorities and reactions in balance. You don't want to go through life like an emotional yo-yo. As a leader, you'll take everyone else with you on that roller coaster, and when you do, you'll obliterate productivity. Yes, we'll always have winter, but to provide balance, we can remember that spring is just around the corner.

> Slow and steady wins the race.
> —AESOP

DEVELOP A REALITY CHECK

> Man is the only animal that laughs and weeps; for he is the only animal that is stuck with the difference between what things are, and what they ought to be.
> —WILLIAM HAZLITT, English literary critic

It's not easy to stay in tune with what's actually happening. The smoke and dust of constant change, adjustment, and transition can cloud your leadership vision.

Every so often, go through the mental exercise of taking a fresh look at any situation. Take it back to its basics, look at it as it is today and then try to project it into the future. As you go through this exercise, ask:

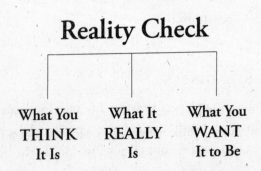

Reality Check

| What You THINK It Is | What It REALLY Is | What You WANT It to Be |

- What's the single most significant thing I can do to be sure I'm in touch with reality?

- Who can help me clarify what I *think* it is and what it *really* is?

- Is what I *want* it to be still applicable, clear, and supportive of our overall mission?

- Is this current situation real progress or just different?

You may not like all the answers, but the point is to try to get a clearer perspective. Then you can begin to change and grow where you should. On the other hand, some of the questions may surprise you with a clear, positive response. Either way, you are better off and on a road to a more productive outcome in any situation.

DEVELOP A SENSE OF HUMOR

We'll cover more about the importance of having a sense of humor in Chapter Seven, "Power Matters." However, I can't write about perspective without a word or two about the power of humor to help your followers grow and change.

> A sense of humor is part of the art of leadership, of getting along with people, of getting things done.
> —President DWIGHT EISENHOWER

When things are changing quickly, a sense of humor keeps you sane and allows your followers to develop their own sense of balance. Humor can counteract the pain of change. A good sense of humor sustains people when life becomes difficult. It gives everyone a momentary "emotional vacation" so they can recharge and get on with the job at hand. Kahlil Gibran wrote that humor "gives us a sense of proportion."

These basics to using the Five F's effectively make good discussion points with your team of leaders.

Change and growth are never easy. As you become a more effective change-master leader, your roots will go deep and you will become stronger.

The sixth-century Chinese philosopher Lao Tzu advised us to be like the willow tree, whose roots go deeper than other trees. When the storm comes, the willow tree bends with the winds of time and change and remains standing while the other trees crack and break. The ability to keep change in perspective represents the strong roots of your leadership as you calm and strengthen followers while showing them how to bend with change.

A Global Perspective

Events occurring in one part of the world are viewed
as a matter of concern for the whole world in general
and lead to an attempt at collective solutions.

—WALTER ANDERSON, *All Connected Now*

Gandhi

The 1982 movie *Gandhi*, starring Ben Kingsley and directed by Richard Attenborough, both of whom won Academy Awards, portrays Mohandas ("Mahatma") Gandhi not as a saint but as a self-searching, sometimes fallible human being with a sense of humor and a deep sense of historic perspective.

As the epic film opens, we see an elderly Gandhi (Ben Kingsley) wearing his simple loincloth and "homespun" shawl around his shoulders, his little round glasses perched on his nose. He is walking with his arms draped over the shoulders of his nieces as they go out to greet the people who have come for afternoon prayers. He is smiling and speaking softly to people with a kind word and with hands together in prayer fashion at chest height. The faces surrounding him are filled with reverence and great love for this "little brown man."

The film portrays the decades of struggle he went through to bring independence to India. When asked his motives, he says, "If you are a minority of one, the truth is still the truth."

There is a faction within the movement that breaks off to form Pakistan, with its majority Muslim population. Blood runs hot over the same issues with which they struggle today. Elderly Gandhi knows this but goes out to walk among the people anyway.

As he walks into a group, a young man comes up to supposedly lay some food at his feet, and as he bends over, he brings out a gun and fires point-blank at Gandhi, who falls to the ground and dies.

The film cuts to the procession at his massive funeral, attended by dignitaries from around the world. There are 300,000 people jammed into the square. An old-fashioned newsreel comes on the screen showing the huge gathering and you hear the reporter say, "General George C. Marshal, U.S. Secretary of State, said, 'Mahatma Gandhi was a man who made humility and simple truth more powerful than empires.'"

A flashback shows the horrible massacre at Amritsar, where the British kill over one thousand men, women, and children who have gathered for a peaceful protest. In response to such unfathomable brutality, Gandhi begins his famous water fasts as a personal protest to the violence. He says, "An eye for an eye makes the whole world blind."

The movie rolls out the years of struggle, imprisonment, despair, disappointment, and the resurrection of commitment.

Gandhi spends his last days trying to bring about peace between India and Pakistan. He angers many dissidents on both sides, and the man who assassinates him is one of the protesters.

A voice at the end of the movie repeats the most powerful and far-reaching words of Gandhi: "Whenever I am in despair, I remember that all through history there have been tyrants, despots, and murders. And for a time they can seem invincible, but in the end always quit, always fail, always. The way of truth and love has always won—always."

While watching the movie, what struck me most was the perspective his simple language gave to the way life was in the past, what he was dealing with in his time, and how it applies to our life and struggles today. His words were harbingers of the future for other leaders fighting against prejudice and injustice.

Nelson Mandela, fighting against the Afrikaner-dominated National Party with its apartheid policy of racial segregation, frequently credited Mahatma Gandhi for being a major source of inspiration in his life, both for the philosophy of nonviolence and for facing adversity with dignity.

Dr. Martin Luther King Jr. and the American civil rights movement took roots from Gandhi's nonviolent leadership. He was an *Enlightener* on our twenty-first-century leadership pyramid. He was a man of deep simplicity, openness, humility, accountability, and competence that fueled his vision. His language, both in actions and spoken, gives us a perspective that we would do well to study and emulate in the twenty-first century.

There have been many world leaders who have talked about

living together in peace, but none so eloquently as Mahatma Gandhi. Above all things, he led by example.

Mutual Benefits from Interdependency

As far back as we can study history, the best societies have been based on the principle of mutual aid. We see that we have always been interdependent. We eventually learn to limit our selfishness, our pursuit of and preoccupation with self-interest, in order to enjoy the benefits gained from living in peace and harmony with our fellow world citizens.

To be A New Breed Leader, you will have to go beyond being worldly and move to being global, in both thoughts and actions. After all, our problems are global. Our neighbors' walls are on fire, and we must work together to stop the flames from spreading. That doesn't mean build more or bigger walls; it means taking them down so we can easily reach one another across the office, the company, the country, and the world. We must learn to understand one another and our cultures.

New Breed Leaders must be open to new insights and a new perspective in order to align their leadership with other cultures. As we become more and more connected globally, our world shrinks but our opportunities expand. We can reach across old boundaries and connect with people from a much wider range of experiences. We can learn from them and apply the lessons to our own leadership. When we do, we add a depth of knowledge and richness of understanding that never existed before. Technology is our greatest tool to build these new alliances and partnerships in the far places on the globe.

A CULTURE LESSON
LEARNED

I recently conducted a seminar in London. I worked carefully with the meeting planners to anglicize the approach while keeping true to my beliefs about twenty-first-century leadership. The conference was simultaneously broadcast by satellite to a group in Cape Town, South Africa, so I took that into consideration also.

At the conclusion, the London executive told me it went very well and that they were pleased. When I returned home, I received an e-mail from one of the participants in London. She wrote that the seminar was helpful and she was already using ideas from my book with her teams. She also liked the inspiring aspect of the presentation.

Then she wrote, "I must admit to being very typically British. At the start in the first piece of group work, shaking hands with a stranger was a bit disconcerting, but I coped."

As I read her comment, I realized I had just relearned the lesson that Americans are often overly friendly at first and that the British can be more conservative. I was so happy to have her e-mail. It was an important reminder that once again I must carefully evaluate interactive exercises that seem natural in the United States but may not be received in the same manner in other cultures. I really like her comment, "but I coped." I think we both grew as a result of the experience.

My husband, Bill, is very Irish! He loves to sing Irish songs and tell stories and jokes with an Irish brogue. We were discussing leadership perspective, and he said, "Remember the Irish story? Someone said. 'Will all the leaders stand up?' and everyone stood!" Sometimes it really is a cultural perspective! It certainly was for me in London.

University of Miami president Dr. Donna Shalala talked about recognizing the fact that we operate on a world stage now, and that New Breed Leaders will be wise to maximize this innovative abundant reality. She elaborated on what challenges she thinks leaders will face in the twenty-first century.

> I think that the major [challenge] is that you have to understand different cultures because we're going to have to manage in a multiethnic, multicultural situation; that you're not going to have a homogeneous workforce or negotiate with people that are just like you or hire people that are just like you or buy things from people that are just like you.

Cultural diversity is here to stay. As you move your organization forward, you will need to capitalize on the differences, cultures, ethnicities, and languages of your followers. It may take a lot of work to lead effectively in our new world, but it can also be one of your most exciting and rewarding missions.

President Eisenhower had five rules about peace and living together in the "Cross of Iron" speech:

1. No people on earth can be held, as a people, to be enemy, for all humanity shares the common hunger for peace and fellowship and justice.

2. No nation's security and well-being can be lastingly achieved in isolation but only in effective cooperation with fellow-nations.

3. Any nation's right to a form of government and an economic system of its own choosing is inalienable.

4. Any nation's attempt to dictate to other nations their form of government is indefensible.

5. A nation's hope of lasting peace cannot be firmly based upon any race in armaments but rather upon just relations and honest understanding with all other nations.

Consider that your enhanced global perspective will help you lead your followers in ways that give everyone hope for the future; learning to live together is our greatest connective goal.

Speaking the Global Language

Learn a new language and get a new soul.

—Czech Proverb

The need to sustain international relationships increases daily. According to the Council of Graduate Schools, 29 percent of U.S. graduate schools have dual or joint degree programs with international universities. Almost 25 percent more plan to add such programs in the next two years.

Universities from Maine to California are offering minors and majors in global studies with a strong language program attached. Many language departments are expanding their scope to incorporate cultural components that go beyond language fluency. Students who participate in programs that incorporate language and international studies say, "We support each other, rather than compete with or undercut each other. We ask questions, share information, and help each other."

MEET JAMES SASSER

Jim Sasser knows the importance of taking leadership skills beyond the confines of an organization and recognizing that leaders must operate on a world stage.

I first met Jim in the mid-1990s when he was a U.S. Senator from Tennessee. As I outlined this chapter, I could see that Jim's experience, both as a Senator and as U.S. Ambassador to China (1995–99), would be informative and helpful.

Jim is a highly respected and trusted consultant in all things Chinese. In 1999, during his term as ambassador, NATO and the United States were involved in stopping the violence in Bosnia. In the process, we accidentally bombed the Chinese embassy in Belgrade, Yugoslavia. To China, this was an act of aggression. Hundreds of Chinese protestors clashed with police as riots broke out at the American embassy in Beijing. It lasted for many days before it was quelled. Jim's deft handling of the dangerous situation won him the respect of the Chinese authorities.

When I asked, he kindly agreed to share some of his perspective on leadership and our new, global society.

> The Chinese economy has been growing in double-digit rates for about twenty-five years. This is probably the most rapid economic expansion in the history of the world; certainly in the twentieth century. In the last ten years, I've seen the economy grow very, very substantially. There is a disparity in wealth that now rivals the disparity here in the United States.
>
> There is a striking self-assurance on the part of the Chinese that was not present when I went there as ambassador in 1995. At that time, there was a chip-on-the-shoulder attitude

on the part of Chinese officials and diplomats. There was a hypersensitivity to any real or imagined slight. It was, I think, the result of a sense of inferiority to the West and also of the distrust that came from the view that the West had exploited the Chinese people unfairly for over the last 150 years.

Many young Chinese have now been educated partly in the United States or Europe, and the cultural gap has closed. There is greater understanding. At the same time, more Americans and Europeans are living and working in China. There are Western businesses almost everywhere in China, particularly in the coastal areas and in southern China. The Chinese now see themselves as a rising power and no longer second-class citizens of the world.

As China continues to emerge as a powerful player in the global market, Western leaders will have to understand and interact with the new leaders of twenty-first-century China. When Jim and I spoke in 2008, he was engaged in many consulting projects involving China. All of the lessons he learned as ambassador, as well as his experiences during that time, have enabled him to understand China in ways others do not.

While China has fully entered the new century, its values and ways of operating are deeply tied to their past. Jim talked about how the past and the present have merged. His insights will help you understand how to better interact with a Chinese businessperson, if you have the opportunity.

I think it will be much easier to interact. Because fifteen years ago there was a huge cultural gulf between the leadership of the West and East. I refer to the U.S. and Europe, and the industrialized West, including to a lesser extent, the Japanese.

The average Western leader and the average Chinese leader would have difficulty communicating with each other, not because of language—although that is a big problem—but just different cultural mores, different ways of acting. Some of our actions would be perceived as discourteous, and some of their actions might be perceived by us as being vulgar.

Now, a young leader in the U.S. or from England meeting with a young leader from Shanghai or Beijing or Guangzhou will find they have many similarities. The cultures are coming together in the sense that they understand each other better. The young leader from Beijing or Guangzhou has probably been watching CNN or even Star Television from Hong Kong. The young leader from the United States or the U.K. is now reading in the *New York Times*, the *Washington Post*, or the *Financial Times* in London extensive reporting of what is going on in China.

Then you have so many American and Western firms that are operating in China in a big way. So you have this flow of people back and forth. The young leader in the West now and the young leader in China find that there is more of a common ground between them, and they can communicate much better and they don't have such a huge cultural gulf to bridge.

I asked him if there is a particular skill that a Western leader should develop to better interact with a Chinese leader. This is his advice:

Many times I would observe American CEOs after I arranged meetings with the president or the premier of China or one of the very important heads of one of the ministries.

The American CEO would first compliment and flatter the Chinese for just a few moments, and then they would make their pitch and were then ready to leave. They did all the talking. That is not the way the Chinese operate.

It's always very helpful to build the relationship, because the first thing you've got to do with the Chinese is to establish a basis of trust and approach them very carefully. They've got to get to know you first. Even discuss things with them on personal terms.

As I said earlier, there is in the Chinese psyche a sense that they have been tricked and betrayed by Westerners over a period of at least 100 or 150 years. And they can be very xenophobic and suspicious of outsiders. That suspicion has declined rapidly in the last 10 or 15 years; however, it is still there.

But once you gain their trust, then you can do business, and that trust is really more important than the contract you sign.

Transcendent Challenges of Twenty-First-Century Leadership

We all have possibilities we don't know about. We can do things we don't even dream we can do.

—DALE CARNEGIE, self-improvement writer and lecturer

It's a time of transcendence, a time of limitless possibilities. As A New Breed Leader, you may find that the unlimited possibilities for the future are both exhilarating and unsettling.

Past, present, and future—volumes have been written on each. This chapter has only scratched the surface. However, in thinking about how to tie them together, I remembered what John Adams wrote about all three of these stages. He was well aware of why our country was founded in the first place, what his role was, and what he was building for future generations:

> I must study politics and war that my sons may have liberty to study mathematics and philosophy. My sons ought to study mathematics and philosophy, geography, natural history, naval architecture, navigation, commerce, and agriculture in order to give their children a right to study painting, poetry, music, architecture, statuary, tapestry, and porcelain.

Adams's words of wisdom about our being broad leaders with a broad perspective is key to studying the past, being completely aware of the present, and trying to put into place ideas and actions that will lead us into the future.

As A New Breed Leader, it is time to fill your leadership toolbox with as much intellectual, emotional, and physical perspective as you can gather for your journey to the new horizons of the future. Perspective and balance seem so well summed up in Ecclesiastes 3:1-8:

> *For every thing there is a season,*
> *And a time for every matter under heaven:*
> *A time to be born, and a time to die;*
> *A time to plant, and a time to pluck up what is planted;*
> *A time to kill, and a time to heal;*
> *A time to break down, and a time to build up;*
> *A time to weep, and a time to laugh;*

A time to mourn, and a time to dance;
A time to throw away stones, and a time to gather stones together;
A time to embrace, and a time to refrain from embracing;
A time to seek, and a time to lose;
A time to keep, and a time to throw away;
A time to tear, and a time to sew;
A time to keep silence, and a time to speak;
A time to love, and a time to hate,
A time for war, and a time for peace.

You're leading with your heart as well as your head when your perspective—and the balance it generates—yields a sense of promise, a sense of a better life, and a sense of progress that builds community and connectedness. When you do, followers will recognize you as A New Breed Leader.

Your Action Plan Questions for Quality 6
PERSPECTIVE

1. Have I been a good student of history to give me a better perspective about the twenty-first century?

2. Have my followers and I discussed the implication of how our current actions could affect our future?

3. If I could step back ten years and change an important unsuccessful decision, how would today be different?

CHAPTER SEVEN

Power Matters

MASTERING INFLUENCE

Come to the edge.
We can't, we are afraid.
Come to the edge.
We can't, we will fall.
And they came to the edge,
And he pushed them,
And they flew.

—CHRISTOPHER LOGUE, English poet

HOW MANY OF your followers have "flown" because of your wise use of leadership power? As A New Breed Leader, the answer to that question will be a gauge of your leadership. After all, shepherding, guiding, and channeling the skills, talents, and abilities of others are your calling.

What is power? A thesaurus offers these synonyms: direct authority, influence, strength, hierarchy, rank, superiority, clout, prestige, sway, mastery, and persuasion.

No matter how you define it, you recognize power when you see it. You know a powerful person when you're with him or her. And you know you need power to lead. Yet the exact nature of power can be elusive. "Being powerful is like being a lady," former British Prime Minister Margaret Thatcher said. "If you have to tell people that you are, you aren't."

> We thought because we had power, we had wisdom.
> —STEPHEN VINCENT BENET,
> *Litany for Dictatorships*

Power is inherent in leadership. You can't lead effectively without it. Leaders who make the greatest contribution use power wisely.

The essence of power and leadership wisdom is summed up in a statement about the legendary jockey Willie Shoemaker: "He was the best because he had the lightest touch on the reins. They say the horse never knew he was there unless he was needed." Do you have a "light touch on the reins"?

A key to being A New Breed Leader is understanding that the best leaders neither shrink from power nor seek it unnecessarily. They know that having clout often intimidates others, so they use their power carefully to promote cooperation and mutual respect. Cultivating the wisdom to use power wisely takes time and energy, but the benefits are well worth the effort.

Such judicious use of power takes wisdom, restraint, and patience. As Lao Tzu wrote in 2,600 B.C.:

Water is fluid, soft and yielding. But water will wear away rock, which is rigid and cannot yield. As a rule, whatever is fluid, soft, and yielding will overcome whatever is rigid and hard. This is another paradox: What is soft is strong.

As A New Breed Leader, you'll need to be strong but gentle—strong enough to tackle the tough issues but gentle enough to keep the solutions humane. You'll need to be demanding enough to challenge others not to settle for easy answers but patient enough to know that all progress will take longer than you think.

The Benefits of Wise Power

With power, you can accomplish much; without it, very little. Power well used holds the other seven qualities together and gives you the authority and clout you need to accomplish things. The primary benefit of using power wisely is that it shows followers you can be trusted because they see that

> The higher up you go, the more gently down you reach.

you're honest, open, accountable, and competent and won't take advantage of them. Earn that kind of trust, and you also gain loyalty and respect.

When you accept the responsibility of power, you'll quickly find that it's a delicate instrument. Like the sharpest surgical knife, it can destroy and cause pain, or heal and create new life.

As you use your power more and more, you will find that it can never be underestimated. Followers react to all of your actions and words. They are greatly affected by how you use authority. General Dwight D. Eisenhower understood judicious use of power. Not only did he "pull rank" only in emergencies, but he often counseled his commanders, "You do not lead by hitting people over the head. That's assault."

When you're forced to use your power to correct a difficult situation, try to employ what I term the "velvet hammer." You may need to bring the hammer down. But when you do, wrap it in velvet. Be careful and very aware of what your power can do, both positive and negative. I have always liked what Indira Gandhi, former Prime Minister of India, said as a warning about the wise use of power: "You cannot shake hands with a clenched fist."

Truly great leaders understand the power of leading by persuasion. You bring others along with good ideas, facts, arguments, and vision of a better future. Actor and former Carmel, California, mayor Clint Eastwood went right to the core of power when he said, "It takes tremendous discipline to control the influence and power you have over other people's lives."

Management guru Peter Drucker adds, "The leader sees leadership as responsibility rather than rank and privilege." When viewing power in terms of developing others, a wise leader says, "My greatest responsibility is to use all my energy to fulfill the potential of my followers."

The Power Puzzle Piece

If you want to build a boat, do not instruct men to saw wood,
stitch the sails, prepare the tools, and organize the work, but
make them long for setting sail and travel to distant lands.
—ANTOINE DE SAINT-EXUPERY, French writer and aviator

A personally powerful leader is like a multifaceted diamond: he or she shines in every direction and upon all who come near. When you commit to being A New Breed Leader and design your individual version of the eight qualities that matter most, you set the

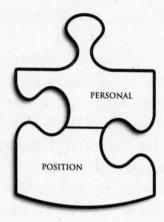

example and send the strongest possible message to your follow-ers. You're telling them that they, too, can build their own power as they "long for setting sail and travel to distant lands."

Paradoxically perhaps, personal power strengthens when you use it less. That's because most power is given to you by others; it's not something you take. Because people give it to you, it doesn't have defined limits; it's as great as they think it to be. When you exercise it wisely and less frequently, their estimation of its strength and scope becomes greater. If you use it unwisely and too often, though, you reveal your limitations.

Personal Versus Position

Personal power comes from within you. *Position power* comes from holding a particular place. A New Breed Leader combines both.

Your personal authority is what makes the prestige of your position meaningful. It is the real "horsepower" of your leadership. It's the magnet that draws people to you, the dynamic force that gets things done.

Position power is only minimally effective without personal power. And lack of both leads to many a downfall. In fact, "how the mighty have fallen" is a constant human theme since biblical times, the subject of Greek tragedies and Hollywood potboilers alike.

Historian Robert A. Caro, when discussing current corporate leaders, noted, "There are many examples of senior managers who could not make the switch from ambitious executive to corporate leader because they did not know what to do with the power they had so expertly accumulated."

If you ever need to choose between the two, always choose personal power, because no matter what happens, if you're a well-grounded person with a strong sense of self, emotional intelligence, and humility, you'll be able to handle change and difficulty. Your personal power will outlast position power every time.

Eleanor Roosevelt, PBS—American Experience, 2000

Eleanor Roosevelt was the most influential woman in America for three decades. Few people had neutral feelings about her. The most admired and most controversial woman in the country, she evoked great love or distinct dislike. This PBS documentary takes you through a fascinating journey of the life of a shy little girl who became a commanding figure in American and world politics.

When Eleanor Roosevelt died in 1962 at age seventy-eight, she was mourned around the world. On screen, her grandson tries to explain why this unlikely woman became such an extraordinary icon of power. ". . . she transcended politics and religion. Her name was not on any U.S. legislation, yet her touch was everywhere. It was the essence of who she was that echoes through time."

The story shows her struggle as an unattractive, bucktoothed girl who spent her entire childhood searching for love. She came from one of the wealthiest families in the country (her uncle, Theodore Roosevelt, had been president), but her beautiful and socially skilled mother didn't like her because she was ugly, and she didn't hesitate to tell Eleanor so. Her alcoholic, adventurer father was the light of her life, but they were seldom together because he often went off on alcoholic benders or on some exotic escapade.

Her mother suffered from migraines, and Eleanor would sit for hours rubbing her mother's forehead to help ease the pain. In so doing, little Eleanor learned a deep lesson: to be useful to others is of value.

Tragedy filled her childhood. Her family committed her father to a mental institution, and her mother died four months later. Eleanor went to live with her stern, deeply religious grandmother, whom she eventually came to love for the stability she brought to Eleanor's life. She went to a progressive girls' school in England, where for the first time she was valued for her intelligence. She blossomed and began a metamorphosis from caterpillar to butterfly. After graduation, she returned to New York and began a lifetime of working with the downtrodden. She fought against sweatshops and child labor and championed labor progress, women's rights, and civil rights.

When she and Franklin Delano Roosevelt, her distant cousin, fell in love and married, she felt true love for the first time. Though he quickly moved from serving in the New York Senate to being the Assistant Secretary of the Navy, polio soon crippled him for life. During his recovery, she was at his side.

As FDR continued to move up in the world, Eleanor moved with him. While not well suited to the limelight and political life, she adjusted and learned to be an excellent speaker.

When FDR had an extramarital affair with Lucy Mercer, Eleanor was crushed. They never again lived as husband and wife. His overbearing mother dominated her life and told them they couldn't divorce. So she and FDR settled into a "partnership" that would last his whole life. As she would say, "We became best friends."

She quietly exercised her enormous personal power as a tireless fighter for causes. A one-woman "War on Poverty" during the Depression, she visited coal mines, hospitals, and squatters' camps all over the nation. Despite painful shyness, she also traveled around the world speaking with equal enthusiasm to kings, presidents, and the destitute. During her husband's presidency, she acted as unofficial ambassador to the world as well as devil's advocate to his conscience and the conscience of a nation.

She often suffered from depression, and her life was a contrast between dysfunctional personal relationships and successful public accomplishment. Through it all, she never stopped growing. She became an influential counselor not only to her husband but to other prominent leaders. Even people who didn't like her gave her credit for being an indefatigable force for good.

When FDR died in 1945, Eleanor no longer had any official responsibilities. However, she continued to be a spokesperson for dozens of causes. In 1945, President Truman appointed her to the new league of nations. When she arrived, she learned that they had assigned her what they thought was an inconsequential committee concerned with human rights. It was a perfect platform from which to launch her worldwide fight for fairness and equality. Establishment politicians ignored her and tried to minimize her. Everywhere she encountered barriers that would have discouraged a less passionate person. But she cajoled and compromised, pleaded and demanded, and everyone she met felt the power of her convictions.

A summation of her growth to power-broker leader comes when she stands in front of the international body and confronts the Soviet Union's objection to her call for freedom and equality. Her years of political infighting served her well because the Soviets finally agreed. Her leadership in favor of the "Universal Declaration of Human Rights" for the newly formed United Nations came to fruition after four years of arduous effort. To date, this document has been used as the basis for the constitutions of sixty nations. Eleanor Roosevelt's personal power has made a major difference in our world.

Eleanor Roosevelt's entire life is an example of growth from within. She faced her crucible moments, learned from them, and applied them to her daily activities.

If you are currently in a position of authority, work constantly on your personal power to be an effective leader and to reinforce your authority. As you increase your skills and shape your leadership style, opportunities will arise for you to move up to an even weightier position.

The Enlightener leaders in our leadership pyramid evolved, grew, and took humanity to a better place. The fires of experience, as described in the Introduction, tested them. Their "crucible moments" gave them depth, intensity, vigor, and a command of the best leadership skills.

While few people are in the Enlightener category, those people can make a huge imprint with a good balance of both personal and position power. When you learn from the examples of great leaders, you can then adapt their methods to your own style. Being A New Breed Leader is not about *adopting* the styles or traits of other successful leaders. It is about *adapting* examples of good leadership for your personal style.

Assess Your Life for Leadership Effectiveness

We are living in a new age that requires you to seek a deeper balance between your professional and your personal life. In our complex and fast-moving world of the twenty-first century, keeping that balance involves staying in sync with the times and keeping a clear, open mind about future possibilities.

These possibilities open to you when you take the time to assess your life. When your life and work are congruent, your inner spirit fills and gains meaning.

This inward exploration is the key to finding the *why* of your personal power, and can even help you through a crucible moment or event because of the clarity it brings to both life and business.

You'll find that the Pie of Life is a helpful tool to begin finding better life balance, which in turn will increase your leadership effectiveness.

As you begin to fill in your Pie of Life, don't be too hard on

Your Pie of Life

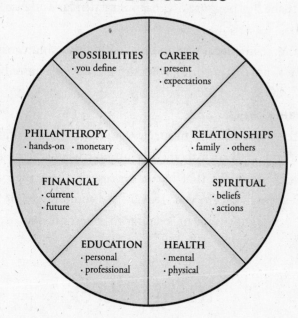

yourself. Attaining equilibrium isn't easily accomplished. No matter how hard you work, you'll never achieve perfect balance between your leadership responsibilities and your personal ones. Here's how to make best use of this self-assessment:

1. Place, time, and tools

Find a quiet place to sit without too many distractions. Perhaps drive to the beach or a park. Go to the library or even a coffee shop. The point is to go somewhere you will be alone, uninterrupted, and able to focus on this personal inner journey. Leave all your electronic devices at home. (The world really won't come to an end if you can't be reached.) Set aside about one and a half hours in the first session of working with your pie. You don't want to feel rushed or pressured. Clear your calendar and just focus on yourself.

Take a yellow legal pad and pen, sit quietly, and work on one slice at a time. Begin with any sector; there's no required order.

2. A reality check

Describe what each slice means to you. At this point, don't worry about what you think it should be; just note what it actually is. For example, "health": If that means staying healthy, then describe what healthy means to you. If you have some illness or impediment, "health" may mean keeping to a certain diet or exercise regimen.

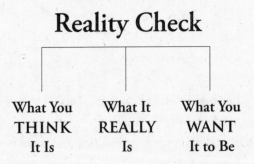

Reality Check

| What You THINK It Is | What It REALLY Is | What You WANT It to Be |

As you go through the descriptions in each slice, use the subtitles as starting points. In health, perhaps "mental" means you take a brisk twenty-minute walk at lunchtime to relieve the emotional stress of your work. The word "physical" could be the time you spend at a gym or exercise class or a stretching program you perform at home.

Use the reality check to help clarify your thinking and give you more accurate assessments of the time and definitions of the meanings of each of the seven pieces of Your Pie of Life.

Consider the health slice in terms of your stamina and sustainability. If you put it through the filter of the reality check, it could give you a much better perception of your long-term physical ability to lead.

While "sustainability" is usually spoken of with regard to organizations, it's also an important part of your personal power. As you grow personally and move your organization forward, you, too, will need to think about, plan, and execute for the long haul. Can you withstand the challenges and sometimes daunting tasks you'll face?

Katsuaki Watanabe, president and CEO of Toyota Motor Company, is often quoted and interviewed about his company's approach to their "Long Drive" philosophy and their principles for enduring success. He talks about strategy, exploration, sustainability, and change, among other things. While I read a recent article about him, it occurred to me that Toyota's emphasis on stamina for the long term is an excellent analogy for New Breed Leaders.

Being able to stay for the long term, when others fall by the wayside, requires your personal health, energy, vitality, stamina, and physical sustainability. When your mind and body are not in tip-top shape, you're not able to function at your best. As a twenty-first-century leader, you'll need to do some serious introspection about your health and lifestyle. Staying mentally and physically fit is like money in the bank—it compounds and you end up with more than what you began with. Your return on investment is well worth the cost!

If everyone in a position of leadership would start a dialogue about healthy living and then lead by example, we'd greatly reduce the cost of health care and go a long way toward preventing our current epidemic of illness caused by poor lifestyle choices.

Stress Is Literally Killing Us

USA Today wrote a major article on how stress is affecting our lives. It quoted from a recent survey by the American Psychological Association revealing that stress has increased dramatically in the last five years and is affecting everyone.

More than a third of all U.S. workers take fewer than seven vacation days a year. Most other industrialized nations have far higher numbers and have healthier people. Perhaps when we brag about our competitiveness, we should look at how long we work. Based on the number of hours worked, we're not as productive as we think.

> *The core problem with working longer hours is that time is a finite resource. Energy is a different story.*
> —TONY SCHWARTZ, founder of the Energy Project

We're fond of phrases like, "Work hard, play hard" and "working vacations." But these are terrible messages. We can tie part of our soaring health costs to our inability to unplug, let go, and take time off. As A New Breed Leader, you must set new examples of balance between hard work and relaxation.

In Chapter Eight you will hear from chef Graham Kerr about humility. He and his wife, Treena, are leaders in the Global Healthy Life Movement. They recently celebrated their fifty-second anniversary, calling themselves "Partners in Purpose" whose goal is "M.Y.T.C."—More Years to Contribute. "It doesn't matter how *long* we live, it's really how *well* we live it," Graham says.

Treena and I now celebrate a series of lifestyle choices that result in time to facilitate wellness, which allows more real time and energy to be spent upon the object of our individual passion. The end result has the potential of creating stronger communities—"the common good is the good we do in common"—with a lessening of the injustice caused by the painful awareness of our increasingly two-tiered availability of health-care system.

Both Treena and I want to collaborate with organizations that share our goal of finding solutions on the preventative side of our health-care services. We have created a plan and theme we call The Ate Ball: a search for a solution to the disease of excess consumption! "You are not what you eat . . . you are what you ATE."

We identify the need as lifestyle choices leading to over-weight and obesity-related disease of the heart, adult-onset diabetes (insulin resistance), and cancers that may be preventable through lifestyle changes leading to permanent weight loss.

Treena and I know the key is to make it easy for people to become engaged in the process of ATE. We have identi-fied eight words (each ending with "ate") that help give a plan to construct a healthy living lifestyle, and work with others to build a "healthy city."

1. Compassionate: Moved to *consistent action* to meet a need.

2. Evaluate: *Correctly measure* why the need is not being met.

3. Innovate: Search for a means to fill the gap with a *specific remedy*.

4. Educate: Help both those in need and those who serve to *understand the remedy*.

5. Motivate: Understand in depth what various *reward factors* can apply.

6. Consolidate: Provide supportive choices to reinforce and *make sturdy* the decision to change.

7. Celebrate: Gather together all the people who have served another . . . to celebrate their *shared success*.

We're very excited about the plan and believe strongly that by honestly reviewing our past (what we ate) we can better inform our future and in doing so we can celebrate the difference in every year we are granted the opportunity to make a contribution to our fellow man. Now that's a lifetime!

3. Action plans, growth steps, and review

Outline three steps you'll take to achieve better balance in the amount of time you give to each slice in Your Pie of Life. Take one slice of the pie per week and work on it. Plan to review and update your life pie on a regular basis. These are the basics of life and leadership. I have never know any leader or organization that has reviewed the basics too often. However, I have known many people and entities that have gone astray because they did not review their basics, their Pie of Life, often enough.

Do's and Don'ts

Here are two important Do's and Don'ts that go along with Your Pie of Life:

Do: Relax and enjoy the process. It'll be as rewarding as you allow it to be.

Don't: Get stressed over the process. It's not a test but a gateway to a better future.

Notice that I have left the eighth slice open to possibilities that are unique to your life. Making the slices more in line with your life goals does not mean you'll automatically achieve them. Nevertheless, it's a great place to begin and gives you a path to follow to a better-balanced life. Setting the

> Build a career, and design a life!

example of actively designing your life as well as building your career can never be overemphasized to followers. If all of your followers would use the Pie of Life, you would go a long way in building a healthy, strong, and sustainable organization.

Just as for the Action Plans at the end of each chapter, you may go to my website, www.anewbreedofleader.com and click on "Resources." You will find a full-page PDF of the Pie of Life for your personal use or to share with others.

The Great Balancing Act

Sallie L. Krawcheck, chair and CEO of Citigroup's Global Wealth Management Division, speaks frankly about not being able to have it all, or do it all. In fact, she warns: "Don't kid yourself. Leadership at the top is about unrelentingly hard work." Though she doesn't yet have any regrets, she says she's very aware that she makes sacrifices that affect her family and herself.

You may not be willing to make the same kind of personal sacrifices for professional success as Sallie. But that's not to say that you can't make a concerted effort to reach your ideal life and business balance. One of the greatest benefits of working on equilibrium is to avoid the "I could've" or "I should've" regrets of later life that plague many who have been in leadership positions and didn't try to balance their life.

In Chapter Six, you met Colonel Bill Smullen (U.S. Army, ret.). In our conversation we also discussed the importance of balancing one's time:

> Early in my Army career, I was a first lieutenant at Fort Benning, Georgia. The demands of the job were so great, I knew that I needed to get a better perspective on managing my priorities. I would work twelve-hour days and still feel that I couldn't get everything done, and I just felt I needed to manage my time better.
>
> Columbus College in Columbus, Georgia, was offering a night course in speed-reading. I thought that if I could read faster, I could have more time and I could do more in the course of a day. The first night of instruction the professor said, "Okay, we're going to take a couple of minutes here to think quietly about what is most important in your life. I'm not talking about family or monetary things, just what you think is the most important thing to you personally."
>
> I picked my eyesight. If I didn't have my sight, I wouldn't live this well. I wouldn't be able to do as much. I would be

unhappy with my life. Everyone gave an answer, and he said we were all wrong. He said, "The most important thing each of you has is a common commodity; it is your time."

He told us: "I'm going to help you with that and you are going to have more of it available to you as you go through each and every day. As you have quiet time, you're going to fill it in different, more productive ways."

I took him seriously and have taken that lesson of perspective through life. My wife laughs at me because we may be going to a basketball game. I know there's going to be time before the game and at halftime that I either have to sit there and stare at the relative inactivity around me or use it productively. I've always stuck a magazine or book in my pocket, and I've always used that available time to read.

I find quiet time can be used not just to read but to work through things that are going on which are difficult for me. Time is really something that I have valued so much. Not just since that course, but, I think, my entire life. So when I find time in the morning to steal away to the kitchen and it's all quiet, it's just me frying the bacon and the eggs and making the coffee and having the juice and all of the other things that go with the breakfast, that's my quiet time. My mind is working not on what I'm going to eat so much as what I'm going to do that day. If I've got a problem or a challenge that needs some inner strength, then I'll take the time to work through it on my own, in these quiet times. I always get a better perspective on how to proceed.

Even during the Civil War, President Lincoln went to the theater many times. President Reagan went to his ranch to work and relax. FDR's "Happy Hour" with Winston Churchill during World War II was legendary. If these men, who were embroiled in monumental issues of war and peace, could take time to clear their minds and gain a better balance, so can you.

Relax, step back, and take the time to get a better perspective. Find a hobby that takes you away from daily issues. We all know we need time for both work and play. As A New Breed Leader, taking that time will win you a much better perspective on how to move forward. Since the topic of life-and-business balance has taken on such importance, many universities now include courses on this issue in their business school curricula. There's a new weighing scale on which making money and seeking celebrity status are balanced against having a meaningful life, while still being an effective leader.

Begin to grapple with these philosophical questions, and you'll see leadership is no longer about gaining financial worth but building *self-worth*—that is, how much and how well can you serve others. If you've had the privilege of a good education, have built strong people skills, and have combined experience with knowledge, and then can balance all of that with humility, you have the potential to be a great leader.

Good Listening Means Good Leadership

Listen. Listen. Listen. You will learn what people think the problem is, and maybe you'll learn what the solution is.

—MEG WHITMAN, founder, eBay

Chapter Four, "Language Matters," was about the use of language to connect with others to build strong relationships. The topic wouldn't be complete with some thoughts about the power of being a good listener. The first time I met presidents Bill Clinton, Jimmy Carter, and Gerald Ford, as well as publisher Katharine Graham and General Colin Powell, I was struck by a supreme leadership skill they all shared: an intense listening ability that builds great loyalty in their followers.

When you're talking with them, they focus every ounce of their attention on you. For that short period, they make you feel as though you're the most important person in the world. They actually create a space around you and them that others back away from and won't breach. These leaders have an aura of power stemming from their ability to concentrate, to get every word, to *hear*—not just listen to—what you're saying. It's a visceral force when you're included in their circle.

I learned a lesson from these powerful leaders: If you are going to speak with truly powerful people, have your thoughts in order, because you won't hold their attention with unclear or wobbly language. Even if they disagree with you, that's okay; they'll still listen *if* you speak with precise language and offer thoughtful ideas.

Are You a Good Listener?

Here are some questions to consider regarding your listening attitudes and the way you listen:

- Do you like to listen to other people talk?

- Do you encourage other people to talk?

- Do you listen even if you do not like the person who is talking?

- Do you listen equally well whether the person is man or woman, young or old?

- Do you listen equally well to friend, acquaintance, or stranger?

- Do you put what you have been doing out of sight and out of mind?

- Do you look at the person talking to you?

- Do you ignore distractions around you?

- Do you smile, nod your head, and otherwise encourage the person to talk?

- Do you think about what the person is saying?

- Do you try to understand what the person means?

- Do you try to understand why he is saying it?

- Do you let the person finish what he is saying?

- If he hesitates, do you encourage him to go on?

- Do you restate what he has said and ask him if you got it right?

- Do you withhold judgment about his ideas until the person has finished?

- Do you listen regardless of the person's manner of speaking and choice of words?

- Do you listen even though you anticipate what the person is going to say?

- Would your followers describe you as a good listener?

When you have examined these questions, have someone you trust answer them about your listening habits. Compare your answers to theirs. It could be an important step to enhancing your wise use of power through better listening habits.

Real Power Versus Quasipower

Sometimes we are mistaken in believing that wealthy or famous people automatically have leadership qualities. Today, fame and status come and go like the changing winds. True personal power must be judged on a longer track record. Today's headliner can be tomorrow's has-been. The much-lauded financial whiz or political genius can pass quickly into oblivion, never having understood or acquired personal power.

How do you distinguish quasipower from real power? The

characteristics are relatively easy to spot. People with quasipower do not admit mistakes, rarely apologize, and would never ask for forgiveness. They are frequently rude and discourteous.

While we all play the hero in our own movies, the trick is to be sure we're in touch with reality and are humble about our contribution. Of course, there's nothing wrong with a healthy ego. As A New Breed Leader, you'll need it to get you through the tough times, the lonely times that inevitably come your way. However, a key to using your power wisely is to recognize your limitations. Here are four wise but crucial sentences that confirm your self-esteem and humility:

"I don't know."

"Maybe you could help me."

"I'm sorry."

"I was wrong."

When you are secure in using those words appropriately, doors open, barriers fall, and your influence takes a quantum leap. Quasipower often enters what I call the "kingdom of the power pigs."

Power pigs and their piglets are everywhere. They flourish in every sector of our society. They go to the trough of avarice, subversion, dominance, greed, ego, arrogance, self-interest, and force. They thrive on yielding raw power.

Power pigs exist for one purpose and one purpose only—to accumulate and wield as much raw power as possible. Intoxicated and obsessed with their own importance, they attract unsuspecting piglet-followers because they usually possess all the trappings of power.

They have an abundance of the five deadly power pig traits. To be sure you have not become a power pig, review the traits and see where you stand.

Five Deadly Power Pig Traits

- Arrogance—overvaluing yourself, having a condescending attitude toward others

- Vanity—intensely craving admiration and applause; having excessive pride in yourself and your accomplishments

- Disloyalty—violating the trust of your followers; being unfaithful to your values

- Intemperance—immoderately or excessively indulging your appetites and passions

- Presumption—assuming superiority and privilege where they are not warranted

Check yourself periodically to be sure that you never slip into these weak, destructive behaviors of power pigdom.

We've seen power pigs come and go. They usually destroy themselves. Unfortunately, they also destroy many piglets. When we watch quasipower and power pigs in action, it may seem unfair that these people receive the rewards of real power without having any. It's important to understand that these people have insatiable appetites and these rewards never satisfy them. They are not fulfilled as true-servant leaders are.

Power can bring out the very best and the very worst in people. It's up to each of us to stand guard at the door of our desire for power. "Power tends to corrupt," Lord Acton noted, "and absolute power corrupts absolutely." Frank Herbert, author of *Chapterhouse: Dune*, wrote: "It is not that power corrupts, but that it is magnetic to the corruptible. . . . We should grant power over our affairs only to those who are reluctant to hold it and then only under conditions that increase the reluctance."

Networking, Alliances, and Partnerships

Your next client, partner, investor, employee, or job

may be waiting for you on MySpace or LinkedIn.

—DANNY BRADBURY, freelance journalist, networking expert

During the writing of this book, I often came to the office early for some quiet time in which to write. I closed my e-mail so I couldn't even see it arrive, and I didn't answer the telephone.

However, very early one morning the phone rang, and I automatically reached over to pick it up. When I answered with our standard greeting, a warm, friendly, very Southern-accented man said, "This isn't State Farm, is it?"

"No, I'm sorry, it's not," I replied. "You have the wrong number."

After a pause, he said, "Well, I sure don't want to waste the call. I'm single and looking for a new girlfriend. You sound real nice. Are you available?"

I laughed and said, "No, I'm afraid not. I have been happily unavailable for twenty-five years."

He sighed and said, "Well, no harm in trying. I like to network anytime I can."

I asked, "By any chance, are you in sales?"

"Yes, ma'm, I am," he said. "How did you know?"

I laughed and said, "Oh, just a wild guess!"

"Well, ya'll have a great day," he said and hung up.

Now, as much as I believe in networking, you probably don't have to take it as far as my Southern caller did. But the most productive and effective leaders create and use social and professional networks, alliances, and partnerships to increase their ability to get things done. They have an instinct and a nose for opportunities. These successful leaders include their networks, alliances, and partnerships as part of the mix to surround themselves with the brightest and the best. They also use their networks to quickly expand their knowledge base, find solutions to problems, and share important information. These networks cover many areas—internal and external people, customers and constituents, even competitors.

Your networking is of great strategic value to your vision and goals. As you reach out to kindred spirits, you multiply your knowledge and glean valuable information with which to make decisions. Your networks can even help you through a "crucible" period.

Susan RoAne is a bestselling author of *Face to Face: How to Reclaim the Personal Touch in a Digital World*, and an expert on networks, alliances, and partnerships. She shared some of her thoughts about the power of building networks and alliances:

> If you read the backstories of almost every leader, every CEO, every executive, you will find out what got them in that position was generally that they knew someone. They may have known someone who was a fellow alumnus. They may have known someone from one of the organizations they are in. The thing that struck me the most is when Robert Nardelli got bounced from Home Depot and he showed up as chairman and CEO of Chrysler. The reason was one of his former employees, whom he had mentored, was now there and brought him over to lead the company.

What I think is important in twenty-first-century leaders is having these networks of people who are peers. They stay allied with people who might be above them or preceded them. They also stay in touch with the people they've mentored because that is the generation which, as it moves on, is going to include people in the network who recommend them, like Mr. Nardelli, for a new job. And that, to me, is why the smart people, the leaders, have always had a significant network of people with whom they stay in touch.

When I wrote *The Secrets of Savvy Networking*, it was one of the first books with networking in the title. Women in the late seventies looked at all these men in power and thought, "I'm just as smart. I'm just as skilled." It was the women who said, "This is like the old boys' network." The old boys never called themselves that, and we tried to model ourselves after them for a couple of decades. Now it's turning around. Women are now becoming experts at networking, support, information, and sharing. The twenty-first-century leader will always network because it is basically a safety net.

Their network may be the people that go to Davos [the World Economic Forum in Davos, Switzerland] and the people who might go to TED [the Technology, Entertainment, Design conference] or the people who go to some of these upper-level leadership institutes and retreats. They also are active in their universities as alums.

People at that level often meet each other on the golf course. But now you are finding the leaders, the people who are moving up, do other things as well. They will be the honorary chair of the local United Way campaign or some other major charity.

If you think that everyone is going to be age forty-five or fifty-five, go to the Silicon Valley. Mark Zuckerberg, who started Facebook, is twenty-three. He brought the newest woman to his team as a senior leader executive . . . He met her at a Christmas party. These new leaders also have a social life, and they know that connecting with people socially is something that they need to do.

Any leader, even if you're starting out, should make alliances in other divisions of a company. Be active in your professional association. Many people meet through their professional associations some of the people they end up working for and working with (and, by the way, recruiting) on their teams as they move up.

And if you're going to be active in the twenty-first century, you have to network online as well as off-line. If you really want to be effective and have relationships with those go-to people, you've got to put some effort and time in there.

I do want to say we still do have to be online and have online networks. The global companies are having virtual meetings and virtual space on Second Life [an Internet virtual world] so that they can stay in touch and communicate, and all that is well and good because so much is happening. There is now podcasting and the webinars and the virtual reality, but the real reality is that the twenty-first-century leader has a face-to-face, personal network that they see, that they talk to, that they stay in touch with because that really makes the relationship go deep rather than just having many shallow relationships.

I'm going to give you the other twist, which is, when you're a leader, part of your responsibility is to be the go-to person for other people. So while you could say, "I'm busy and I can't take the time," make the time because that person might be the person that you will need for a project, has the information you need, might recommend you for consultancy or the next position, or be on your board. So it's a two-way street.

The Power to Say "Yes"

When you have the courage and foresight to let go of the reins of power and say yes to other people, it multiplies your own power. It may not feel like it in the beginning; however, you will quickly find that when you empower others, you actually enhance your own. Followers feel rewarded and appreciated when you say yes to their use of power.

One of the most important aspects of being A New Breed Leader is knowing when to say yes. Yes to enhance a project, yes to impact the potential of a team or a person, yes to move your organization forward, and yes to expand your leadership around the globe.

As you move up the ladder within your organization, you can make a major impact by having the ability to say *yes*. A case in point: Earlier, I recounted our 1990 trip to Poland as volunteer ambassadors for President George H. W. Bush's Leadership Corps. In the city of Opole, Poland, we had several extraordinary meetings with the region's governor, with whom we discussed the possibility of establishing the first business-training center in what was then the old Eastern Soviet Bloc. The governor said he had people who would staff the training center, and he donated a big room in the basement of a city building.

When we returned to the United States, we contacted all of the best trainers, training organizations, and business authors and asked them to donate material for this new Opole center. Their generosity overwhelmed us—more than a thousand pounds of books, videos, training manuals, and audiocassettes quickly filled our warehouse.

My husband, Bill, had originally bartered with Lufthansa airlines, training its sales staff in return for round-trip tickets to Poland. When he contacted the airline again and explained what we were doing, Lufthansa quickly donated another ticket for him to go back to Poland and transport all the training material, which filled two huge pallets.

Bill worked with our Polish translator in the Opole area, and the materials were delivered and a training program was established. On that trip Bill serendipitously met the head of the Peace Corps for Poland at the Marriott Hotel in Warsaw. They talked, and eventually a dozen Peace Corp members went to work with the Polish staff of the business center.

Then we had the challenge of how to fund the business center. I thought that some of my American corporate clients might be interested in donating to the project. I immediately thought of Bruce Gordon at Bell Atlantic. I explained the project, and asked if he'd be interested in a barter in which I would give a presentation to a group of his people and he would donate my speaking fee directly to the Polish-American Fund that would administer the money for the training center. I remember how he clearly, with no discussion or hesitation, said, "Yes."

I also contacted John Bowell, an IBM manager with whom I'd worked, and he quickly agreed to the same arrangement. Between the two companies—Bell Atlantic and IBM—

we covered the initial funding of the Opole Business Training Center.

As A New Breed Leader, you have the power to say yes. It's one of your most significant tools to move your organization forward and to enable people to use their creativity and initiative.

The Capacity to Influence

When Bruce Gordon and I spoke of the various leadership skills needed for the twenty-first century, he described his approach to influence and power. He's compiled what he calls "Bruce's List," nineteen leadership principles he's developed over the course of his career. On the list are some clues about the use of power and how to influence others. Bruce had this to say:

> I believe that the world is made up of two kinds of people, givers and takers. I think that when a group of people is listening to their leader who is trying to motivate them, some leaders come off as takers. The audience listens and thinks, "You know, all they're trying to do is advance their own career at my expense. They're just trying to take from me."
>
> Other leaders stand in front of their team and approach them in a way that clearly tells them, "My leader is trying to help me to be successful. My leader is trying to give of himself or herself whatever they can to help our team succeed." They see these people as giving to them, not as taking from them. Leaders who are able to accomplish that prove to be more inspirational and are more successful at getting a team to align with their approach to the business.

Another concept Bruce recommends to twenty-first-century leaders is "Think Yes."

> We have all sat in meetings where somebody says, "I have an idea." It's been my experience that people hear the idea and are more inclined to say it's a bad idea: We've tried that before, so it's not going to work. They "Think no," and I say that you always need to be a "Think yes." person. I establish a rule in my meetings. If someone puts an idea on the table, the only responses that are acceptable for the first five minutes are "yes" responses. I would say, "Tell us why this will work," though we may get around to talking about why it won't work.
>
> Another item on my list is "Do the job you have." My bosses would say here is your next job, and I'd say fine and I'd go do that job. Then they would say, "You know, you did well, so we have another assignment for you." I followed the opportunities as they came to me. I find that a younger generation is more strategic, planning their careers and mapping it all out. They say, "I should be in this job, and in the next eighteen months I want to have this job." They have laid out this whole plan. Sometimes they lose sight of doing the job that they have and making the most of it.
>
> The next item on my list is, "Make your boss successful." Too many times folks are asking what am I going to do to be successful and what is my boss going to do for me, instead of saying what can I do to make my boss successful. Because if he or she is successful and I've been a major contributor, then it's going to come back to me.
>
> There's a lot of talk about mentors these days. Everybody thinks they need to have a mentor, so they go out looking for

one. I don't believe that you can go get a mentor. I think that mentors find you. There's an item on "Gordon's Principles" that says, "Mentors find you." If you are exceptional, if you work hard at what you do, if you demonstrate the qualities that are appealing to folks, then a mentor will seek you out and take on the role.

There is another item on my list that says, "Build bridges, not walls." I think that probably speaks for itself. Another item is "Create positive energy." You can always tell in a group of people those who are negative versus those who are positive. We all like to be around people who create positive energy, and we tend to stay away from people who create negative energy.

I think you have to look at yourself constantly and say, "When I walk in the room, what do the other folks feel? Do they feel positive energy when I arrive? Or do they feel negative energy when I arrive?"

The Future of Collaborative Leadership

Leadership in a modern organization is highly complex
and it is increasingly difficult—sometimes impossible—
to find all the necessary traits in a single person.
—JONAS RIDDERSTRALE, Stockholm School of Economics

The "go it alone" mythical hero riding off into the sunset to save another day was never real, and certainly is not real in our new century, which has a plethora of challenges and issues you and other leaders face. As A New Breed Leader, you wear many hats and play many roles as you serve your followers. A tight span of control no longer works. Too many changes have affected all organizations. Nowhere on the globe can any society fall into the trap of thinking that one person, in any position of power, can or should have all the answers.

Your role is to find the best people you can and seek their collaboration and contribution to your teams. That includes the informal leaders that you have within those teams. Woven throughout any successful organization are people who have no title or formal authority, yet who are respected and have influence in subtle and important ways. They have an aura about them that attracts, excites, and directs others in ways that go beyond any job description. These informal leaders have influence and can sway others. Because they impact and shape policy in quiet, unnoticed ways, they can become some of your most valuable people.

These informal leaders play a vital role in building a cooperative spirit among various teams. Keep an eye out for them and regularly ask yourself:

- Do I recognize the informal leaders in my organization?

- Have I acknowledged their contributions?

- How can I maximize their energy and spirit for the benefit of everyone?

- Do I have training processes in place to help them take on a more formal leadership role?

The more collaborative and nonpolitical you are about finding and forming your leadership teams, the less isolated you will be— which, of course, is one of the key ingredients in your leader-

COMPLEMENTARY AND COLLABORATIVE STRENGTHS AT XEROX

For seven years, Anne Mulcahy and Ursula Burns worked together saving and growing the Xerox Corporation. In 2007, it was time for Anne, the CEO, to turn over the reins of management to her successor, Ursula. It was the first time a Fortune 500 company female CEO would be succeeded by another woman. This wasn't an easy task. Even in the best of circumstances, the sharing of power is a delicate balance between egos and wills. And these are both strong, highly effective leaders.

The question is always how much power to give up and how much to retain. To solve this problem, Anne and Ursula decided to divide the workload by dividing problems instead of the processes. Burns is tackling the complex business of centralizing Xerox's IT business in Europe, while Mulcahy is spending more time with customers. Because each had very specialized skills, the answer to sharing power was for each to concentrate on her individual strengths.

Both Anne and Ursula have a deep commitment to apply the rules of complementary and collaborative leadership—a shared vision, open and constant communication, fair compensation and incentives, and trust.

Other major organizations have survived the stress of developing a highly collaborative leadership team: Bill Gates and Steve Ballmer at Microsoft come to mind, as do PepsiCo's Indra Nooyi and Steven Reinemund.

Such collaboration doesn't come without hazards. If you embark on shared power, you must send a strong, continual message to all your followers about your shared skills, talents, and visions that include their best interests.

ship. Being in touch with your followers, encouraging and openly acknowledging their value and creating an environment of collaboration and openness, keeps "power towers" and turf battles from destroying your organization.

Building Successors

I look to hire people who I think have the
potential to take my job at some point.

—SUSAN LYNE, former president/CEO, Martha Stewart Living Omnimedia

When I began working with an executive from a Midwestern company I first introduced you to in Chapter One, he told me he was looking for his successor. I was quite surprised to hear him take such an open, down-to-earth approach. In my experience, not many people walk into a position of power and immediately begin looking for an heir.

> If you could do it all yourself, that would be great, but you can't. Anne has taught me that 90 percent is getting the rest of the organization to line up.
> —URSULA BURNS

When I asked him about it, he said, "It is one of my top priorities. I want to build a team of other leaders I can work with to help move the company forward quickly. Hopefully, at least one or two of them will be ready to take my place when the time comes."

I knew that he had done well at two other companies. So I asked him where he had learned the importance of empowering people in that way. "Early in my career, I had a boss who was effective, respected, and had done well. But she knew that she had gone as far as she was going to go. One day she invited me to lunch and told me that she felt I had the talent to go further than she had and that she was gong to help me reach my full potential. I'll never forget her. She played a very meaningful role in my career."

The wisest leaders use power to develop successors. This is rarely easy. It's like allowing a child to grow up and leave home. As a parent, you stand at the door and wave good-bye, hoping and praying that what you've given your children will get them through the obstacle course of life. True servant-leaders give up positional power with the same hope, that they've done the best they could and now their replacement will carry on with courage and commitment. If the retiring leader has used power wisely, the chances of a successful succession are great.

Sharing and Giving Up Power

Two U.S. presidents have given us very meaningful examples of sharing and giving up power. At end of the Revolutionary War, for example, President George Washington reassigned the power of war to Congress. Dr. Martin Luther King Jr. said that Washington's ability to give up his war powers was "one of the greatest events in history."

During the Civil War, President Lincoln did something unheard of: he appointed to his cabinet his most skilled rivals and most vociferous adversaries. William Henry Seward got the top spot as Secretary of State, Salmon Chase became Secretary of the Treasury, Edward Bates was appointed Attorney General, and Simon Cameron was the Secretary of War.

Later, when asked why he'd made these appointments, Lincoln

said, "We needed the strongest men of the party in the cabinet. These were the very strongest men. Then I had no right to deprive the country of their services."

Seward said of Lincoln, "His magnanimity is almost super-human. The president is the best of us." Indeed, in the final analysis, it was Lincoln who emerged as the strongest among them.

- Whom do you know who has given up power?

- Do you think you could give up power?

- Could you willingly give up your power if it benefited others?

Servant Leadership

A leader is one who serves.

—LAO TZU, sixth-century Chinese philosopher

Of all the examples you set as a leader, perhaps the wise use of power has the most obvious impact. If the basis of your desire for power is one of service, then your leadership acquires an aura of dignity. Your charisma is increased a thousandfold.

The majority of a good leader's time is spent on people problems and issues. Here your power is essential to direct and empower others to act. Whether you are a young developing leader, an established leader, or a major public figure, the examples you set will have enormous impact on those who watch and make judgments about how they should live and act. The person who understands the "power of power" will do the most menial job when necessary, and since they demonstrate that willingness, they rarely have to do it.

Bill Pollard, former CEO and board chairman of The Service-Master Co., reportedly spilled a cup of coffee at a board meeting. Instead of calling for someone to clean it up, he simply grabbed some paper towels and did it himself. It was an important piece of Leadership Theatre.

Some might say it's demeaning for a leader to do that. But is it really? In the servant-leader environment, it's important to send certain messages, such as: Never ask your people to do something you would not do yourself.

> Never ask your people to do something you would not do yourself.

Certainly, you have to keep such efforts in perspective. If that had been a crisis meeting, for instance, cleaning up spilled coffee would not be the wisest use of a leader's time. Perhaps Pollard felt it would be good to send a message about serving. Or maybe taking responsibility may have been so ingrained in him that he just did it naturally without thinking. In either case, it was a terrific way of illustrating the point of servant leadership.

Historian Robert A. Caro said, "Today, when CEOs have acquired more and more power to change our lives, they become like presidents in their own right, and they, too, need to align themselves with something greater than themselves if they hope to become truly great."

When your motives for power are to serve, your followers respond quite differently than when you seek power for self-aggrandizement. True power can be lonely, the responsibilities heavy, and the pleasures few. But when you understand the wisdom of losing yourselves in service to others, you no longer need to seek power; it comes automatically.

Being a good leader isn't about who has the most power. It's about who earns power by motivating and inspiring others, showing them how to make their lives better. Real service has a high value for you and for your followers. When you contribute to the well-being of others, your joy and fulfillment become immeasurable. We need a new group of heroes to inspire us to be better than we are, to encourage us to make a difference. Heroes have always inspired us to advance and perform far beyond our limited expectations. Arthur M. Schlesinger Jr. wrote in *The Decline of Heroes*, "A free society cannot get along without heroes, because they are the most vivid means of exhibiting the power of free men."

Part of the Problem or Part of the Solution

When it comes to the wise use of power, you are either part of the problem or part of the solution. There is no in between. If power is abused and you do nothing, you are part of the problem. If you abuse power yourself, you are certainly part of the problem.

If we are to survive and prosper as leaders of the twenty-first century, we must decide whether to be a passive part of our national and global problems or take an active role in the solutions. The power of free men and women will be greatly affected by the examples leaders set in solving the complex issues we face.

Truly great leaders of our century will posses a strategic sense, an inherent understanding of how the framework of their thinking and the tides of time fit together. They will understand how their power is applied to achieve a larger purpose.

Your Action Plan Questions for Quality 7
POWER

1. Why do I want the power that leadership brings?

2. When I have it, what will I do with it?

3. How can I wield my power so well that my followers will feel it only when needed?

CHAPTER EIGHT

Humility Matters

INSPIRING AUTHENTICITY

*Humility is like a tree whose root, when it sets deepest
in the earth, rises higher, spreads further,
and stands surer and lasts longer.*
—JEREMY TAYLOR, *Lord Bishop of Down, 1651*

HUMILITY, LIKE LEADERSHIP itself, must be earned, not claimed. The most humble and effective leaders don't even think about taking steps to be humble. They just "are." Humility is a state of "being."

Of all the leadership qualities, humility is the one least able to be taught through steps and action plans. The best way to teach humility is by telling stories and showing examples. As a result, this chapter is different from the others. You will meet some wonderful leaders and hear from others I spoke with personally. As in the other chapters, you will have the opportunity to examine meaningful questions about the challenge of humility versus arrogance.

A New Approach

In 1998, the *Washington Post* invited me to address its annual School Principals Leadership Awards program. The purpose of the event was to acknowledge educational leadership by thirty award-winning school principals from the tristate area, Washington, D.C., Virginia, and Maryland.

I felt quite honored to be on the program with Katharine Graham, publisher of the *Post*, and First Lady Hillary Clinton. They both spoke passionately about their topics for forty-five minutes without a single note, and were delightful in their naturalness and authenticity. At the end of Ms. Clinton's address, she returned to the White House. Ms. Graham stayed for the luncheon, and I was excited to be seated next to her. She was a no-nonsense woman of great personal integrity. One of the most powerful women in America, she was known for her courageous role in the *Post*'s disclosures during the Watergate scandal, which eventually resulted in President Nixon's resignation.

In 1997, she published her Pulitzer Prize–winning memoir, *Personal History*. The book was lauded for its honest portrayal of her husband's mental illness and subsequent suicide, as well as her struggle and success in taking over the newspaper.

During lunch, I said to her, "Ms. Graham, you've known every great leader for the last half of the twentieth century. What do you think is the most important leadership quality?" Without a second's hesitation, she replied, "The absence of arrogance."

I was taken aback by the simplicity and brilliance of her remark. I'd just written *Making a Difference: 12 Qualities That Make You a Leader*, and had said much about power and the value of humility.

However, I hadn't been able to express with such clarity the bare-bones essence of what leadership and power are all about. When she said "the absence of arrogance," it was an epiphany.

As I listened to her talk with others at the table, I realized she was the perfect illustration of her own definition. Even from her lofty position of power, her humility gave her total authenticity.

That eloquent phrase changed my view of leadership. Since then, as I have traveled the world, working with leaders of every kind, I watch, listen, and ask myself, "Does this person have an absence of arrogance?" not just, "Do they have humility?"

> Humility: The absence of arrogance!

I have always found it helpful to know what something *is not*, as well as what it *is*. The difference can be slight, but important. It's fine to think of humility in terms of modesty, an unassuming nature, inconspicuousness, and a lack of pretension. However, when you turn it around and measure it from the viewpoint of *a lack of arrogance*, the picture changes quite a bit. Having both definitions in hand gives you more clarity about your potential role models and who you want to become, or not become, as a leader.

Examples to Inspire

Our best leaders make a difference in the world. They create a legacy. And they use their fame and accomplishment with humility to serve something greater than themselves. The Reverend Billy Graham, the most powerful evangelist of modern times, is a true shepherd to his flock and a humble man. Warren Buffett, the third richest man in the world, is unassuming, although he certainly has much about which he could brag. Actors Angelina Jolie and Brad Pitt have turned their fame into leadership to help those in need; Brad is working to help restore New Orleans after Hurricane Katrina, and Angelina spends much of her time in humanitarian efforts abroad. Caroline Kennedy, daughter of slain President John F. Kennedy, is a quiet, modest person who lives by her father's call to action, "Ask not what your country can do for you, but what you can do for your country." U2's Bono understands the power of his fame and how to use his global appeal with humility to champion many causes.

You met Former Oklahoma Governor Frank Keating earlier in Chapter Five, "Values Matter." Here, in "Humility Matters," and especially when discussing examples of leaders who inspire us, it is important to know that Frank was sworn into office in January 1995, and the Oklahoma City bombing occurred just three months later, on April 19, 1995.

A little bit of background about his career path will give you a better perspective of how his humility helped him handle the bombing tragedy.

Frank began his career as an FBI agent. He was a United States attorney, confirmed under Ronald Reagan, in both the Treasury and Justice departments. He supervised the U.S. Customs Service, the U.S. Secret Service, the Bureau of Alcohol, Tobacco and Firearms, the U.S. marshals, prisons, Interpol, all the U.S. attorneys, and all the criminal prosecutors in the United States, and served as the General Council and as Deputy Secretary of the U.S. Department of Housing and Urban Development. His many years of experience served him well as he led us all through the tragedy. He has a depth of human understanding that shone through during this extraordinarily difficult time.

I asked Governor Keating what he thought were the most important leadership skills that he had to implement when the Federal Building in Oklahoma City was bombed. He began by telling me a moving story.

My first job was to present to the public a face of modesty, competence, and humility. I remember the morning after the bombing I was standing on the street corner; it was cold, windy, and rainy. A firefighter from another jurisdiction—I could tell he was not from Oklahoma City—was walking up the street; he looked really haggard and exhausted. I stepped out into the street and said, "Thank you for being here." He asked, "Who are you?" I said, "I'm the governor of Oklahoma." I thought he would say, "Nice to meet you. I am so and so," but he didn't. He took his finger and stuck it in my chest and said, "Well, then you find out who did this. The only thing I got out of that building was a child's finger and an American flag." And [then] he walked on up the street. It was like an apparition, a specter in the night. I knew he was frazzled, exhausted, and distraught. If his reaction was that, then the public's reaction would be that as well.

My job was to provide accurate information with humility and forthrightness, directness and kindness. I needed to show a sense of outrage along with a sense of competency. I never saw any of the TV or the radio or newspapers because I was too busy. However, I remember saying this is an attack on the American family, our communities, your family, your neighbors, your friends. We will not tolerate this. We're going to get to the bottom of this. We will find out how this happened and who did it. Whoever did this, we cannot permit these people to get away with it. All will be well, as sad and as agonizing as this period is.

You cannot prepare for that kind of tragedy. You have to have a sense of humility, a sense of modesty, a sense of a moral compass to know how you respond to things that are unexpected, frightening, disconcerting, and obviously disorienting to people. You must have a very defined, very built-up set of moral values and standards so the public can see that you are sincere, that you, too, are outraged. . . . That is the appropriate response.

Corporate Humility

INDRA NOOYI, CEO, PEPSICO

A vital part of humility is being yourself, knowing that you're okay and don't have to be someone else to be successful. Indra Nooyi, CEO of PepsiCo, often tells a humorous story about a painful but enlightening learning experience that led her to trust in who she is.

> **Authenticity**
>
> *Be yourself, and act upon it.*
> —Congresswoman NANCY PELOSI,
>   first female Speaker of the U.S.
>   House of Representatives

When she was a graduate student at Yale University with little money to live on, Indra went in search of a job. Apparently, though, she hadn't read any of the dress-for-success books. She went to a local budget store and bought a $50 business suit. Nothing wrong with that if that is all she could afford, but the suit didn't fit well. Yet that's not the worst of it. When she arrived at the job site, the interviewers gave a collective gasp of horror. Beneath her ill-fitting suit, she was wearing garish, orange snow boots, making her look every inch a country bumpkin.

When she tearfully consulted with her career development counselor about her "sartorial blunder," she was advised to wear a sari for her next interview. Further, she was told, "If they can't accept you in a sari, it's their loss, not yours." She not only wore a sari for her next interview with a very prestigious management consulting firm and clinched the job, but she continued to wear saris to work all summer and "did just fine." She insists, "Never hide who you are."

BILL WEISE, FORMER VICE CHAIRMAN OF MOTOROLA

As I mentioned in Chapter One, I had the privilege and honor to have Bill Weise as my corporate mentor for many years. I learned so much from his strength of character and by the power of his humility. It wasn't that I learned so much by his words—although he had plenty to say—but rather I learned by his actions.

For instance, I had flown into Chicago to meet with a client, and Bill invited me to join him for lunch. After my morning meeting, I took a cab out to Schaumburg, Illinois, the world headquarters of Motorola. Having visited and lunched with other CEOs, I anticipated a limo ride to a private club or lunch in the executive dining room atop a tall building, with white-gloved servers and a hushed atmosphere. I wore my best banker's gray suit, with plain gold earrings to match my wedding band and wristwatch. My briefcase and shoes were polished, and I carefully did a light job of putting on my makeup. I was *ready*.

I arrived at the building and was shown into Bill's penthouse office by his personal assistant. It was a nice office, but not opulent. The only sign of his position and power were a few tastefully framed photographs of world leaders on one wall. From his windows he had a lovely view of the Motorola campus. We sat in the "conversation area" of the office and his secretary served tea. We chatted for a few moments, then he said, "Well, Sheila, are you hungry?" I said I was, and we stood. He walked over to the door to his private restroom and opened it. He took off his jacket and hung it on a hanger, putting it in the hook on the door. He turned and asked me if I would like to take off my jacket, too. I was so unprepared for that question, all I could think of was, "When in Rome, do as the Romans do." So I took off my jacket, and he hung it next to his.

We headed out the door, and I started to pick up my briefcase, but he said, "Oh, it's okay, just leave it there." As we entered the elevator, I expected him to push the button to the "executive dinning room." Instead, we headed down. As the door opened and he paused for me to exit first, I was astonished that we were in the employee cafeteria.

Stunned, I simply followed him as he got in line and we filled our trays. He spoke to everyone and knew them all. We sat at a table right in the middle of the room. As we ate, employee after employee passed by and stopped to speak with him. He was on close terms with them all. He would ask about the health of someone's grandmother, or ask, "How is that new puppy working out?" They would tell him things about their jobs, and he would ask open-ended questions, and then listen carefully. I knew I was watching humility and wisdom in action.

When we finished and went back to his office, I told him I'd never seen someone in such a high position mingle so freely with his employees. His only answer was, "Sheila, if I don't go to where they are, how will I ever know what's really happening in this company? I learn so much from them."

BILL GEORGE, AUTHENTIC LEADER

Bill George, former Medtronic CEO and Harvard Business School professor, has a new book I highly recommend: *True North: Discover Your Authentic Leadership*. It includes many wise and valuable experiences and concepts to help you be a better leader. Let me give you three that resonated most with me as I was writing this chapter:

1. "Fundamental change of an organization takes five years. Yet the expectations of Wall Street are becoming even shorter." We discussed this in Chapter One, "Competence Matters." How can a new executive have the time to establish good and corrective policies and measures in an organization if pressure from "The Street" is so intense, manipulative, and unreasonable? When does she or he have time to become grounded in the fundamentals of the new organization and to take the time to grow and learn?

2. Self-awareness is a major trait in good leaders. But, George said, it's so easy for an executive to become isolated from those who do the day-to-day work, the "real people." He added, "A lot of leaders surround themselves with sycophants. Their feet never hit the ground because they're on a red carpet all the time."

3. The age of the celebrity CEO is on its way out. George wrote, "If you want to be a celebrity, go into the movies."

Humility does not mean being someone who's introverted or shies away from the limelight. Many extroverts with dynamic personalities and grand visions and dreams lack arrogance. They're often the *Enlighteners* in our leadership pyramid. You'll find that these people have a strong sense of who they are and have a basic but deep self-confidence, not a lack of it. They're able to move far beyond filling their internal needs through money, power, or fame; instead, they focus on making a difference.

What Is Humility?

Try not to become a person of success, but
rather to become a person of value.
—ALBERT EINSTEIN

A national epidemic of hubris has created a culture of indulgence. An entitlement mentality has slipped into our national character. We seem to be in an age of "it's all about me." However, leadership is not about "me," it is about "them": your followers, your customers, your suppliers, your stockholders, the people in the communities in which you operate.

There's a telling contrast between a leader with personal substance and one who's unable to connect with followers. When a leader is humble, it is usually because he or she scores high on emotional intelligence. Such leaders are comfortable with themselves, without a need to constantly talk about themselves or brag about what they have or what they do or who they know.

Humility comes from deep within you. It's how you feel about yourself, how you value others. It's an attitude, a philosophy, and a belief system that says, "The way for me to be the best leader is to be the best servant to my followers."

Twenty-first-century leaders need to change the thinking behind the systems and policies that support arrogance and all of its negative consequences. All of us must seek the answer for ourselves and then try as hard as possible to correct or rid ourselves of the culprits in our personality that lead to arrogance.

> Humility is knowing who and what you are. Arrogance is being afraid of who you are and what you are not.

How do you keep hubris in check? How do you determine who you really are and who you want to be? How do you become a person of value? The big questions to ask yourself are:

- What kind of person do I want to be?

- What kind of life do I want to live?

- What example do I want to set for my followers (and for my children)?

- How do I want to be remembered?

- What kind of legacy do I want to leave?

These questions will help you stay on the humility track. They will keep your mind and heart open so you don't become closed-minded or interested in having your own way, but in finding the best way. As a humble leader, you will have room in your heart and ego to consider the other person's point of view.

If you go through life with a closed ideology about how things are and how they should be, you block opportunities to broaden your leadership. Awareness, new perceptions, and sensitivities give you immeasurable resources for the future and you'll be acutely aware of them. An arrogant leader cannot see this.

Arrogance is about fear: fear of personal inadequacies, fear that people will find out the "truth." Arrogant leaders have low self-esteem or a poor self-image and a deep need to prove how smart they are. Then it's not enough to prove they are right; they must also prove the other person is wrong. Even highly competent leaders, if they're arrogant, eventually destroy themselves or their organizations. If fame and fortune corrupt a humble leader, their leadership dies. True humility wins in the end, and arrogance loses.

> Humility versus arrogance. Don't misinterpret the two. Humility is not weakness and arrogance is not strength.

So, we must have the courage to question what we do and how we operate.

It will not always be easy. T. S. Eliot wrote, "Humility is the most difficult of all virtues to achieve."

This Is a Test

Last winter Bill and I were watching television when the program was interrupted by a sharp, whining electronic sound. At first, we thought the set was broken or our cable company was having problems. In about thirty seconds, a voice said, "This is a test of the weather alert system," and went on to explain what to do if the severe rainstorms we were experiencing caused local creeks and rivers to go over their banks.

I was in the middle of writing this chapter, and it occurred to me as I listened that when leadership crises crowd in on us, it's usually life saying, "This is a test." When you're insecure and afraid, you may be tempted to take the low road of haughty, rude, egotistical dominance, in which case you've "gone over the banks." However, if you have the courage and self-assurance to call upon your better angel and act unpretentiously, graciously, and decently, you can survive the "storm" and add greatly to your legitimacy. If you understand the long-term consequences to both your own leadership authenticity and the self-esteem and growth of your followers, you can say, "I have passed the test."

Sometimes the only thing that can sustain you as you climb the ladder of success is an ego that protects you from the slings and arrows of competition. Such strength of ego doesn't automatically mean you're either arrogant or humble. In fact, personality isn't always a good indicator of the type of leader you are. The difference is in *how you treat others*. It's a character issue. There's a thin line between ego and arrogance. With the increased pressures of the world we live in, leaders will have to work very hard at not crossing that line.

Robert Greenleaf was the father of modern servant leadership. When he was in his late eighties, I had the honor to speak with him by telephone about the importance of humility. He said that to be a humble leader is not always easy; in fact, it can be risky, because it's often mistaken for weakness. However, he added, "the benefits far outweigh the risks."

A Sense of Humor

Poet and philosopher Wilfred Peterson has long been a favorite of mine. When I need inspiration or a dose of perspective and balance, I find it in his book, *The Art of Living Treasure Chest*. One of his best pieces is entitled "The Art of Leadership." Two of the thoughts go right to the heart of humility:

- The leader has a sense of humor. They have a humble spirit and can laugh at themselves.

- The leader can be led. They are not interested in having their own way, but in finding the best way. They have an open mind.

One of humility's most endearing parts is the ability to laugh at yourself and have a sense of humor about who and what you are, and what your mission consists of. To see your own foibles or mistakes makes you an approachable leader. Someone said to Abraham Lincoln, "You're two-faced." Lincoln replied, "If I had two faces, do you think I would use this one?" Humor is an important part of humble, authentic leadership.

Before we go on to how humility relates to the other seven qualities, here is a personal survey to judge arrogance.

CREATE YOUR OWN PERSONAL ARROGANCE SURVEY

Learning to differentiate a good ego from arrogance can be enlightening. Here's how you can conduct your personal arrogance survey. Whenever you're around a leader—whether it's a community leader, a CEO, or the head of a small team—be sure to watch and listen, then rank him or her: *High* (an obviously arrogant attitude), *Medium* (some signs of arrogance), or *Low* (modesty and openness) based on your answers about these questions:

- Can others give their opinions free of intimidation? Or must the leader always be right?

- Does the leader condescendingly dismiss others?

- Is she (or he) impatient?

- Does she segregate society into two groups: "people like us" and "people not like us"?

- Are power and control a major factor in her personality?

- What's her initial response when faced with a problem: Accept it and go to work finding a solution, or blame someone else?

- What kind of "toys" does she have? Is she seeking status from things like driving a Hummer? Or building, say, a 10,000-square-foot house for two people?

- Does she show sensitivity to her followers' differences? Or does she criticize those differences?

- How does she treat the waitstaff in restaurants, golf course workers, or flight attendants?

- How's her cell phone etiquette? Must you listen to very loud discussions with her stockbrokers or how she's going to fire someone? Can you have a meeting or eat a meal without constant cell phone or PDA (personal data assistant) intrusion?

- Is the dropping of names and the prices of what she buys important to her?

- Does she take two parking spaces to protect her vehicles from damage?

- What's her body language—welcoming and open, or closed and secretive?

Go ahead! Be creative. I'm sure you have a few questions of your own to add.

The Humility Puzzle Piece

Let's look at each of the eight qualities that matter most in a twenty-first-century leader. What lesson and wisdom about the power of humility can you cull from the stories and examples? Then how can you blend them into your philosophy to shape your thoughts and actions?

1. Competence Matters . . . *Building Purpose*

To build trust, a leader must exemplify competence, connection and character.

—JOHN C. MAXWELL, author

We commonly give the limelight to people whose success results from self-promotion or wealth more than any special leadership competence. However, here are two very different people, both deeply authentic leaders, who have what I term "the power twins"—competence *and* humility.

JOE MONTANA, SAN FRANCISCO 49ERS

Joe Montana is a living legend. He and his family live near us, and I often see him on the street shopping or eating out with him wife and children. As I pass him I always say, "Hey Joe!" and he always replies, "Hey, nice to see you." Even though his son and my grandson go to school together, we've never met and he doesn't know me. But he's so personable and down to earth he understands that we're all proud of him and thrilled when we see him. It's a warm community, and he's a part of our daily lives.

At the top of Joe's list of leadership qualities is humility. Known for his almost mystical calmness in the midst of chaos and nearly supernatural football instincts, he was the unflappable "Cool Joe." The legend goes that when he was a kid, his dad hung an automobile tire from a tree and young Joe practiced for untold hours throwing the football through the tire perfecting his dead-eye aim.

In 1979, late in the third-round draft, new 49ers coach Bill Walsh ignored the negative scouting reports on this rookie signal-caller ("average" arm strength, no touch), and envisioned Montana as the orchestrator of his complex ball-control passing attack. Walsh said, "Joe's . . . an excellent spontaneous thinker, a keen-witted athlete with a unique field of vision. And he will not choke. Or rather, if he ever does, you'll know that everyone else has come apart first." Walsh's system depended on a nimble quarterback with an accurate arm who could adjust quickly to each defensive sequence as it unfolded.

And adjust quickly Joe did. He had such a broad perspective of the game and of what was happening on the field it was as if he saw everything in slow motion. He took his time to throw the ball where it would be best received. He didn't have what coaches call a "bazooka arm," but his aim was deadly. At six-feet-two and rather fragile (his career was twice halted by major surgery), Montana was never physically imposing.

But what he had was "magic." Watching a young Montana practice in the early 1980s, Walsh commented, "There was something hypnotic about him. That look when he was dropping back;

he was poetic in his movements, almost sensuous, everything so fluid, so much under control." He never appeared to be brash and demonstrative, and by his own account, he struggled to articulate how he seemed to perform miracles so effortlessly. Joe Montana simply had the ability to impose a quiet order on a raw and disorderly game.

Few football fans need to have "The Catch" explained to them. In fact, it's so famous it has its own Wikipedia entry that came from the *Washington Post* blog of Joel Achenbach:

> The San Francisco 49ers, led by Montana, were fighting for the NFC Championship against the Dallas Cowboys. In the closing minute of the game, with his team trailing 27–21, Montana went back to pass and was flushed from the pocket. He drifted to his right, almost the sideline, as two defensive linemen bore down on him. After a pump-fake, Montana finally lofted a high, floating pass toward the very back of the end zone. It was up for grabs. Seemingly, out of nowhere, Dwight Clark, wide receiver, appeared in the frame and with his body fully extended, he miraculously snagged the football with his fingertips and brought it into his body as he made the touchdown.

Joe is still viewed as the Ultimate Winner, no boasting, bragging, or self-adulation. Just quiet smiles and recognition of his teammates' contribution to the team's successes, particularly the brilliant and sometimes supernatural pass-catching ability of Jerry Rice and Dwight Clark. Joe has often said that if Clark had not been such a gifted receiver, "The Catch" would not have occurred.

ADELE O'SULLIVAN, DOCTOR, NUN, ANGEL OF MERCY

When I first learned about fifty-five-year-old Adele O'Sullivan, an image of the late Mother Teresa flashed through my mind. The two have much in common. Besides their Catholic faith, each has an activist role in community medicine, a healing touch denied to no one, a love of all people, a deep sensitivity to the plight of the homeless, and the trust earned from outcasts who aren't usually welcomed by traditional medicine.

Sister Adele O'Sullivan became Dr. O'Sullivan in 1984. Her sister nuns at St. Joseph of Carondelet worked hard to put her through medical school at the University of Arizona in Tucson.

She plays a dual role as director for Maricopa County's Health Care for the Homeless Program and angel of mercy for those who receive her gentle care. Maricopa County (Arizona) is the fourth most populated county in the nation, with about 13,000 homeless. Dr. O'Sullivan uses her medical competence and deep humility as a family physician to treat 3,000 people every year at her clinic—and countless others she ministers to in the country-side from her green van. It is not uncommon for her to travel to soup kitchens with bandages, antibiotics, cough medicine, inhalers, and other medical essentials to treat her street patients.

She's an inspirational leader to thousands of young and aspiring physician, nurses, and health care professionals. The American Academy of Family Physicians named her the 2006 Family Physician of the Year. And the *Reader's Digest* wrote that she practices "street medicine and makes house calls where there are no walls."

When you're a humble leader with a high degree of competence, you earn much respect from your followers. When you perform with excellence in your role—whether you're throwing a football or treating illness—you are admired. When that excellence is accompanied by humility, you are respected and serve as an example to others so that they, too, can strive to perform at their top level. When instead of focusing on your own accomplishments, you recognize and value the efforts of your followers, you will inspire them to reach new heights. Humility is one of the most influential examples any leader can exhibit.

2. Accountability
Matters . . . *Fostering Trust*

Everyone, sooner or later sits down to a banquet of consequences.

—ROBERT LEWIS STEVENSON

Most of the business executives I've met aren't driven by arrogant, narcissistic personalities. However, those who are get into trouble of such magnitude that it boggles the mind. They do the most damage to our collective reputation.

Why do I bring up business scandals several times in this book? You may say, "Sheila, this is old news." My response is: Stay tuned. It's not old news; similar situations will keep popping up. The lack of accountability and forthrightness that has infected our society is staggering.

History proves that when huge amounts of money and power are involved, people have a very short memory. Remember the junk bonds financial scandals of the 1980s or the Keating Five saving and loans scandal of the 1990s? Well, if you don't remember or if they're just vaguely familiar, you can be sure a completely new batch of young executives don't remember either. A whole generation of young people coming into the marketplace have seen only the wealth and fame, not the lack of accountability, corruption, arrogance, and thievery that diminishes each of us by association. I'm not convinced this new generation has yet learned the lessons.

The robber barons of the late 1990s and early 2000s broke all the rules of true leadership. They were amoral and believed they were above the law. They were unaccountable, lacked openness, and equated humility with weakness. Did institutions and their leaders learn their lessons? No, as the subprime mortgage-loan disaster shows, the financial meltdown we are dealing with is a global economic problem stemming from greed and arrogance.

The lesson: No one lives in a vacuum. When you're totally unaccountable and hurt, insult, debase, and devalue people as some business leaders do, you will eventually have to pay the consequences. No secrets exist in the age of technology. Eventually, the facts come out.

When history looks back at Corporate America of the last few decades and adds up the financial, emotional, and physical harm done to millions of employees, suppliers, pensioners, and investors, one word will come to represent the cause: arrogance.

> Each time history repeats itself, the price goes up.
> —RONALD WRIGHT,
> *A Short History of Progress*

Were the culprits clearly good old-fashioned thieves? Yes. Were they highly educated? Yes. Did they know exactly what they were doing? Of course. Did they think they were somehow entitled to live like fifteenth-century kings and queens while their employees—their "peasants and serfs"—eked out a living? Yes, they did. Did they care about the damage they caused? No. They cheated, stole, and lied. They were the worst of the worst. A robber with a gun is more honest than they were. If someone robs a local store, we can see what's happening, and we know the consequences. The corporate robber barons' most obvious qualities are arrogance and secrecy. They felt they weren't accountable like the rest of us and were above the law.

In other chapters we've mentioned the destruction wreaked by the Enron triplets—Lay, Skilling, and Fastow. However, let's be fair and compile a short list of the other business stars who contributed to the whole era of corporate debacles:

Bernard Ebbers, CEO, WorldCom

- Guilty: nine counts of conspiracy, security fraud, and false reports to regulators.

- Sentenced: 25 years in prison.

Dennis Kozlowski, CEO, Tyco International

- Guilty: twenty-two counts of grand larceny, conspiracy, security fraud, and falsifying business records.

- Sentenced: 8–25 years in prison.

Mark Schwartz, CFO, Tyco, International

- Guilty: looting $600 million from the manufacturing conglomerate to fund lavish lifestyles, opulent parties, and the now-infamous $6,000 shower curtain his wife purchased.

- Sentenced: 25 years in prison.

John Rigas, Chair, Adelphia

- Guilty: 18 counts of conspiracy securities and bank fraud.

- Sentenced: 15 years in prison.

Martha Stewart, Founder, Martha Stewart Living

- Guilty: conspiracy, obstructing justice, and making false statements.

- Sentenced: 5 months in prison.

One of the saddest results of such episodes is the cynicism created about what it means to be a business leader. Rather than inspire armies of young people to lead firms that provide good products and services to make a better world, these leaders gave examples of corrupt leadership that's all about taking rather than giving, entitlement rather than earning.

History will also record another recent scandal fueled by hubris. The Jack Abramoff–Congressional lobbyist's imbroglio was from its very inception one of arrogance and mocking of the nation's rules and ethics. As columnist Cynthia Tucker wrote, "The Abramoff scandal is hall-of-fame stuff—the sort of outsized arrogance and disregard for law and decency that make it a benchmark against which other scandals will be measured for decades to come." The scandal involved work performed by Abramoff and other lobbyists on behalf of Indian gambling casinos for an estimated $85 million in fees. Abramoff was accused of grossly overbilling clients, secretly splitting multimillion-dollar profits. Abramoff was

> After two years in Washington, I often long for the realism and sincerity in Hollywood.
> —Former Congressman and Republican presidential candidate FRED THOMPSON

also accused of illegally giving gifts and making campaign contributions to legislators in return for votes. Several Congressmen were directly implicated and found guilty of conspiracy.

As of December 2007, Jack Abramoff was convicted of fraud in Florida regarding a casino and is serving 70 months in jail. He also pleaded guilty and is awaiting sentencing in a Washington, D.C., court for fraud, tax evasion, and conspiracy to bribe public officials.

The government lobbyist crisis could be fixed so easily with some courage on both sides of the aisle.

The same holds true with the issue of excessive corporate pay, which amounts to welfare at the top of the financial spectrum. We've known for years about those at the bottom of our economic scale who abuse the welfare system. Now we must grapple with the corporate welfare programs that are even more abusive, such as "golden parachute" retirement packages, signing bonuses, backdated stock options, and hidden benefit packages that aren't reported as part of executive compensation. Both "entitlement" attitudes disenfranchise people and cause grave cynicism about our free enterprise system.

But, of course, many leaders do show true authenticity and humility. Joseph L. Badaracco Jr., a Harvard Business School professor, has written two books on the subject: *The Quiet Leader—and How to Be One*, and *Leading Quietly: An Unorthodox Guide to Doing the Right Thing*. He points out that with brash, successful business leaders like Jack Welch, Steve Jobs, and Larry Ellison, it seems paradoxical to urge someone to be a quiet leader. However, Badaracco says that real leaders solve tough problems in all kinds of ways other than with arrogance. Such leaders are much more common than we think, and they apply what Badaracco calls the three virtues of quiet leadership: modesty, restraint, and tenacity. Here's an example:

JAMES SINEGAL, CEO, COSTCO

Costco is rated as one of the best of the best. It is a well-oiled organization that routinely increases profits, and there's another factor that set it apart: Jim Sinegal.

In 1983, Sinegal cofounded Costco with one warehouse in Seattle. Today there are more than 450 stores worldwide, with a value close to $28 billion.

What makes him special? It's his humility and connection with his employees. For instance:

- He spends about 200 days a year visiting and inspecting Costco's warehouses.

- If he's in his office, he often answers his own phone.

- He knows he's in a cyclical business and worries about doing "the right thing," not just achieving short-term financial results.

- He's cool under fire and doesn't make drastic changes; he has a long-term view of his business and the communities and countries in which he operates.

- His famously harmonious management style generates a warm, seemingly personal response from employees and the investment community.

- Costco pays the highest wages and benefits in the warehouse industry and provides health care converge to more than 80 percent of them. You can understand why he has half the employee turnover of Walmart.

- He has no formal PR department, just his happy customers and his loyal "ambassadors," as he refers to his employees.

- Wall Street, which likes successful risk takers, notes that he took the risk of adding luxury items into the warehouse format. They give him unusually high marks. Leo Isaac, of Spartan Capital, said, "He's done a tremendous job defeating formidable competition while maintaining high quality, service, customer loyalty, and employee loyalty. He puts the company ahead of himself."

- He startled many people when he turned down a bonus. "I rejected my bonus because we had a couple of years where we hadn't performed up to our standards. We were more profitable than the year before, but we didn't hit the standards we had set for ourselves, so we didn't think we were entitled."

Charles Munger, vice chairman at Warren Buffett's Berkshire Hathaway and a Costco director, told the *New York Times* that Sinegal is "not part of a Wall Street scene in any way. He just has a moral compass. He has that old-fashioned idea that being an exemplar is important." While this impressive list about Sinegal shows a deep sense of humility and sensitivity, another item that got my attention is his employment contract. It includes a profoundly unusual clause that states he can be terminated for underperformance. He's accountable to himself, his people, and his investors. He believes in actually earning his pay!

3. Openness Matters . . . *Generating Integrity*

Our character . . . is an omen of our destiny, and the
more integrity we have and keep, the simpler
and nobler that destiny is likely to be.

—GEORGE SANTAYANA, philosopher

Andrea Jung and Joe Driscoll (both of whom you met in Chapter Three, "Openness Matters") not only are examples of open leaders but exemplify humility in their openness. They both have a strong sense of who they are, where they fit, and what their job is. I never saw in either of them the vanity or conceit that's so prevalent in arrogant leaders. I'm convinced composure and statesmanship play a major role in Andrea's ability to build and lead a global entity and in Joe's being asked several times to lead highly successful health care companies.

In 2005, Avon Inc. took a dip in growth after five years of recording-breaking success. Wall Street unmercifully criticized Andrea. It was a very hard time for her personally because she cares so much about enabling women to be self-empowered. But when the avalanche of criticism hit, her characteristic openness and humility came through.

She needed a fresh perspective and remembered some advice given to her by another CEO. It came in the form of a question: "Pretend that you have been fired and brought back. What would you do?" She says it was hard. "Could I be humble enough to destroy my own thinking of the last five years and re-create it as if I were a new hire, as if I were brand new to the job?"

That kind of thinking, questioning, and humility paid off. Her authenticity gave her the ability to reenergize the company and take her passion and message of empowerment and independence around the globe.

Joe Driscoll talked about how it is good to have an open environment so that you can point out mistakes and acknowledge them in a positive way. That it is not about ego, it's about best work. He said:

> We were in a meeting with some of the VP-level people, and one of them was presenting. Someone said, "Wait a minute," and pointed out an error. The person who was presenting said, "Good catch," and made the correction. I complimented him and I complimented the one who pointed out the error, too, and said, "This is what we're about." It wasn't "Gotcha," it was "Good catch."

When you use positive affirming language upon finding errors, you can turn a possible negative situation into a positive winning one.

DELL COMPUTER

Most of the best companies value openness and attach it to the quality of humility. *Harvard Business Review* (March 2005) featured an interview with Michael Dell, chairman, and Kevin Rollins, CEO, of Dell Computer. In case you don't know, they work in adjoining offices separated by a glass wall with a large door in the middle that is never closed. Their comments about openness give you some clues about their enormous success and how you might look at your own leadership and how their example relates to humility.

> DELL: We don't waste money building moats and walls. We tell potential component suppliers which product features are important to our customers. If the suppliers' designs include those features, they'll have a better chance of getting our business. And by the way, we hope they're successful in selling their components to as many companies as possible, because that drives costs down for everyone and we know we'll win our fair share of the market.
>
> The worst thing you can do as a leader at Dell is to be in denial—to try to convince people that a problem's not there or play charades. A manager is far better off coming forward and saying, "Hey, things aren't working, here's what we think is wrong, here's what we're going to do about it." Or even, "Hey, I need some help. Will you help me?" That manager won't have a problem. The manager who covers up and says it's really not as bad as it looks—he'll have a big problem. We also have a huge number of people inside the company with incredibly accurate and detailed information about a whole range of things. That level of transparency makes it difficult to hide a problem. We don't have a lot of layers. Extra layers, approvals, and meetings just slow things down. Our organization is flat so that information can flow freely and quickly.
>
> ROLLINS: We asked, "What's the social contract we offer at Dell?" That led us to define the Soul of Dell: Focus on the customer, be open and direct in communications, be a good global citizen, have fun in winning. These were all elements of our traditional culture.

Jim Sinegal, Andrea Jung, Joe Driscoll, Michael Dell, and Kevin Rollins could function just as well in other business sectors. Their leadership skills are transferable because their openness and humility enable them to continually grow and expand as their world does.

4. Language Matters . . . *Connecting Relationships*

Language is by its very nature a communal thing; that is, it expresses never the exact thing but a compromise— that which is common to you, me, and everybody.

—THOMAS EARNEST HULME, English critic, poet, and philosopher

The moral tone of your organization is established and communicated by you, the leader. Your team is held together by the words they hear and the actions they see. When you use language that connects—not divides—people, you reinforce the organization's goals, values, ideas, and ideals in the minds and spirit of your followers.

The highest form of communication is example. You serve your followers more by what you do than what you say.

As I researched dozens of movies to use as an example in this chapter, unfortunately I could not find one that actually told the story of leadership humility with a positive lesson you could apply to twenty-first-century leadership. So I finally gave up and went in the opposite direction. I looked for a message about the problems and pitfalls of arrogant leadership.

Wall Street

The 1987 movie *Wall Street* is categorized as the archetypal portrayal of the 1980s excesses and insider-trading scandals. But as I watched today, it seemed contemporary. Based on the current shenanigans of Wall Street titans, the film fit perfectly as the example of what not to do, *again*, in the twenty-first century!

Michael Douglas, as Gordon Gekko, stars as the quintessential cutthroat "Master of the Universe," cocksure of everything he knows and does. He represents an unrestrained free market philosophy that *Greed Is Good*, which is the most famous line from the film.

Along comes costar Charlie Sheen as Bud Fox, an ambitious young stockbroker who desperately wants to play with the "big boys." You see Bud at his office computer, amid fifty or more traders, cold-calling for leads. He walks over to his stockbroker boss, Lou Mannheim, played by the gray-haired traditional older mentor Hal Holbrook. Bud tells him that he's going to make it big and has to move fast and can't just sit there day after day "dialing for dollars." Lou, in his quiet wisdom, says, "Son, there are no shortcuts. Good things sometimes take time."

Enter Martin Sheen as Carl Fox, Bud's father, who represents the antithesis of Gekko. He's the voice of reason in the working class. Carl is the maintenance chief at a small airline, Bluestar, and he learns that it will soon be cleared of a safety concern after a previous crash, and as a result its stock will then rise.

One of the classic lines from the film comes when Bud is trying to explain his ambition to his father and says, "Someday you'll be proud of me, Dad," to which Carl replies, "It's yourself you have to be proud of."

Desperate to get access to Gekko, Bud learns his birth date and that his favorite cigars are a banned Cuban brand. He finally gets to see Gekko by taking the cigars wrapped with red ribbon and implores the secretary to let him have "just five minutes. I promise: just five minutes." She lets him wait all day and finally he has his chance. As a desperate last attempt to earn Gekko's favor, Fox gives him the stock tip he got from his father about Bluestar being cleared by the Federal Aviation Administration.

As he's talking to Gekko, you can see the impending doom all over Bud's face. He knows he's breaking the law, and he does it anyway with a haunting awareness of what the consequences could be. Of course, the stock takes off, and Gekko and Fox make millions.

Bud is now an insider, Gordon's pal. He acquires all the goodies—an expensive new wardrobe, a flashy new car, a grand apartment in the Big Apple—and money is no object. He's on his way to becoming a new Gekko. He's cocky, arrogant, and loves to hang out with Gekko. His dad keeps warning him about what he is falling into, but Bud tells him he's old-fashioned and doesn't understand how the world works.

Bud becomes a spy for Gekko and enlists a lawyer friend to help him take over his dad's company. They will strip it, sell off the assets, and put everyone out of work. He confronts Gekko and asks, "Why do you have to wreck this company?" Gekko's arrogance jumps off the screen. "Because it's wreckable!" he answers. "I make the rules. You're not naïve enough to think that we live in a democracy, are you?"

Bud rushes to his dad and with his newfound knowledge about how the game is played. He has found his conscience again. He works with the union, the company, and the management to stop the takeover.

He gets his revenge on Gekko by using his Wall Street contacts to boost the price of a stock that Gekko wishes to acquire. Then he encourages everyone to sell, leaving Gekko with a worthless stock.

Ultimately, both Gekko and Bud are caught by the Securities and Exchange Commission and put on trial for violating insider-trading laws. We don't see the end, but we can predict the outcome.

The defense of greed in the movie is a paraphrase of the 1986 commencement address at UC Berkeley's School of Business Administration, delivered by arbitrageur Ivan Boesky (who himself was later convicted of insider-trading charges), in which he said, "Greed is all right, by the way. I want you to know that. I think greed is healthy. You can be greedy and still feel good about yourself."

When money or power trumps all, arrogance is the result, and a picture—not a pretty one—is created. Comedian George Carlin's brother observed that "doors will be closed, cigars will be lit, brandy will be poured, and people will be hurt."

When leaders set an example of greed, arrogance, or unethical behavior, they communicate these values to followers. Example is never more important than when it comes from honesty, ethics, and open dealings. It is important to ask: What pictures do you create for your followers? What messages are you sending, and what examples are you setting by the language of your leadership?

5. Values Matter . . . *Forging Community*

It's not wrong for us to be together, it's wrong for us to put
down each other and depreciate each other's value.

—ERYKAH BADU, Grammy Award–winning singer

WALGREENS DISTRIBUTION CENTER

Charles Gibson, host of ABC's *World News Tonight*, featured a powerful story about values and a humble leadership perspective. At a Walgreens Company distribution center in Anderson, South Carolina, more than 40 percent of the 700 workers are disabled. Some have cerebral palsy; others suffer from mental retardation, autism, or are wheelchair-bound. Walgreens executive Randy Lewis, who has a nineteen-year-old son with autism, said, "Maybe we could be an example, maybe we could use our position of leadership to try to change the work environment." Lewis says the Anderson distribution center of this drugstore chain is actually more productive than others in the system. The training and technologies that help disabled workers do their jobs better help all employees. Lewis said, "People come to me and say, 'Will this work in my environment?' Yes, it will. This is not just a good thing to do, it is the right thing to do." He added, "When you walk through this building, there is a sense of purpose. Everybody knows why they're here. Everybody helps each other. This has transformed the people that work here."

We met chef Graham Kerr earlier in the book. This is what he said when I asked him about humility:

> I see life's journey as a vertical ladder. The higher we climb as leaders, the more exposed we become. I see the public "me" on the right side of the ladder and the private "me" on the left.
>
> Humility is being known for who you are, so clearly pride is being known for whom one is *not*. Often the public "self" is plucked off the rung and hung out to dry on the upper levels, leaving one's true self (who we believe we really are) often at a lower level.
>
> Humility is the powerful desire and real action that it takes to look at oneself through the rungs—eye to eye—even if that means that we must publicly climb down to meet our private self.

Graham also talked about how humility—and the authenticity it brings—enables us to embody our values and live your purpose. We all have a point of passion where the power of purpose is literally combustible. When passion becomes compassion, it can become irresistible.

> I see compassion as a fellowship of suffering with God over the ruin of His creation. His broken heart is as the sun captured in a magnifying glass of the gifting He has given others and me and His calling for us to work together to achieve a solution to the ruin. The trick is to see the point of passion with one mind, a real consensus, not a power-play manipulation.

Then all the team has to do is move their gifting back and forth in order to focus the sun's rays and get the point to burst into a flaming solution. Bringing a need into focus isn't compromise, it's shared concern fueled by compassion.

6. Perspective Matters . . .
Establishing Balance

In a management team, humility is a product of diversity. Managers must humbly accept that their own perspectives need to be broadened by others.

—OLLI-PEKKA KALLASVUO, President and CEO of Nokia, in Finland

For a twenty-first-century leader, there's no better way to get honest perspective from your clients than coming out of your office and going directly to them. When you have the humility to ask questions that  are about *them and their needs and feelings*—and if you will be quiet and listen—you'll learn some vitally important information.

JETBLUE

JetBlue's David Neeleman is again an example of how you can be a successful leader. This time we examine his attitude of humility and the authenticity it brings not only to his employees but also to his passengers. Neeleman has a habit of working right alongside his employees. Sometimes he checks in passengers and handles baggage. If you know what he looks like, don't be surprised if you see him on a flight, serving drinks and talking with passengers. He's a good listener and values the feedback as a way to improve service. He's acutely aware that the only way a leader can keep his team ahead of the competition is to go out where the action is and learn to understand the real-life, real-time experiences of the customers.

Graham Kerr talked about a childhood experience that gave him a lifetime of perspective on being a part of a team.

When I was eleven years old in public school in England, I was the fastest boy in the school at the 100-yard race. I always won it until a new boy arrived. He was tall and thin and very fast. I just knew that he was a bit faster than I was. We were in the final race, and I was placed right by his side. I got down into position. I was off and running at the gun, and I got a terrific start. I was several feet ahead of him as we started the race, but at about the three-quarter mark, I felt him coming up behind me like a steam engine. I could hear him, and I just didn't want to lose. So I tripped myself deliberately and hit the deck hard. I apparently did this so well, all my friends said, "Oh, tough. You had it in the bag. You were ahead of him." And nobody knew that I tripped myself on purpose so I didn't have to suffer losing the race.

I've always thought poorly of myself for having done that. But it wasn't until about a year ago when I really felt the questions coming into me. I asked myself, "If I hadn't thrown the race and come in second, what would have been my real loss?" All you were considering at the time was the downside of losing, but what would have been the upside? My answer to myself was, "The upside would have been this: In those particular races, the fastest boys in the school would be part of a special relay-race team, and we would have inevitably won that relay race. So, I would have run a race in the company of others. Having come in second, I would have been with that fast boy, myself, and two others. But I didn't. So I won nothing." What I came away with was this: It is better not to have to set such standards where you must win all the time. Sometimes by not winning you can participate in a team rather than being the person who gets all the attention. In other words, if life is always about winning, you may not achieve very much, except some attention for a short period of time. If you're on the team, you may achieve the satisfaction of achieving a great deal in the company of others, in a community.

Personal Perspective

Leaders must also have an accurate perspective about themselves. Self-assessment increases your awareness about yourself. It opens your eyes and often your mind. When you take the risk of sizing up your capabilities and potential, you may realize that you're not as good as you thought. On the other hand, you might discover that you are better than you thought.

These are important experiences for leaders. The better you know yourself, the wiser you become. Awareness of both your limitations and your potential enhances humility. How do you get a better perspective on your leadership capabilities, your life, and the contribution you want to make? It doesn't need to be complex. Sometimes the simplicity of a quick survey of your personal development can highlight areas you can begin to improve immediately.

For many years, I've used the following list myself and with

PERSONAL DEVELOPMENT LIST FOR MORE EFFECTIVE LEADERSHIP

Commitment to goals

Managing time

Physical energy

Physical appearance

Weight control

Sports contribution

Self-assurance

Acceptance of others

Concern about others

Empathy

Feelings of accomplishment

Listening

Sexual awareness

Creativity

Flexibility

Spiritual development

Organization

Memory

Concentration

Artistic abilities

Patience

Budgeting Money

Reading

Enjoyment

Zest for living

Ability to decide on
worthwhile goals

Worthy use of leisure time

Motivation of self and others

Feelings of self-worth

Trusting and openness with others

Assimilation knowledge from reading

Integrating personal goals with
goals of the organization

Accepting and fulfilling
responsibilities

Effectively implementing my ideas

Effectively presenting my ideas

Attitudes toward parents

Attitudes toward children

Earning the respect of family

Enjoyment of social life

Sincere expression of warmth

Attitude toward mate's individuality

Freedom from unreasonable fears
of poverty, criticism, ill health, loss
of love, loss of freedom, old age,
and death

Feeling and showing enthusiasm

Making decisions and feeling good
about them

Ability to relax easily

Getting sufficient sleep

Appreciation of friends and friendship

clients all over the world. I think you'll find it useful, too. Note: Be creative. Add to the list if you have areas that are important to you that I haven't listed.

Mark the ones you can tackle immediately with an A or a 1. Mark the next with B or 2, and on down as far as feels comfortable. Behavioral science has taught us that we cannot really focus or concentrate on more than three things at a time from a list like this. So don't create stress that's self-defeating. This is about growing over time. Remember, leadership is an ever-evolving mix of skills, talents, and abilities that grow as you do. It is not about rushing or pressuring yourself.

So choose three to work on for one month. Then the next month choose three more, and so on. You'll be gratified by your growth with this simple process.

7. Power Matters . . . *Mastering Influence*

*You don't have to put out someone else's light
to let your own shine through.*
—DANIEL BURRIS, futurist, author

Power is the prime mover of people and events and is inherent in leadership. You can't lead effectively without it. Twenty-first-century leaders who make the greatest contribution will be those who use power wisely. And when they do, the other seven qualities that matter most will have room to blossom.

I met General Colin Powell in 1998 at the *Washington Post* event I mentioned earlier. The following day I met with his chief of staff, Colonel Bill Smullen, (U.S. Army, ret.), at the headquarters of America's Promise, the Alliance with Youth, the national youth movement General Powell founded and chaired. We wanted to explore ways I could help. The long and short is that Colonel Smullen and General Powell asked me to sit on the advisory board, which I gladly accepted.

In the following four years, I became friends with Bill. When General Powell became Secretary of State in 2001, Bill went with him to the State Department, again as chief of staff.

In 2003, Bill was offered the position of director of National Security Studies at the School of Public Communications at Syracuse University. He'd earned his master's degree at Syracuse in 1974 and had dreamed for thirty years of returning to teach. So he accepted the position with great enthusiasm.

The two-week NSS program is open to senior military and civilian leaders, such as those in Homeland Security, the State Department, and the GAO (Government Accountability Office) as well as some in the corporate sector. Bill invited me to present a leadership program to the group. The prior evening, he and his wife, Mary Lou, invited several of us to their home for dinner.

MEET MARY LOU SMULLEN

I knew Mary Lou had retired from the Army as a lieutenant colonel, but what I didn't know is what a dynamo she is. Five-feet, two-inches tall, with sandy blond hair and bright, sparkling eyes, Mary Lou has a quick smile and a warm, firm handshake. I was immediately impressed by her humility and the quiet power she exudes. Even in civilian life without the uniform and title, you understand why she was the first woman in Army history to hold the position of legislative liaison officer to Congress; she is every bit the lieutenant colonel rank she worked so hard to earn. She is currently president of the Syracuse Symphony Association.

I asked Mary Lou how she became so successful in her role as legislative liaison officer to Congress.

One of the civilians at Department of the Army had been in her job for thirty years. She had seen officers come and go. She had seen the good, the bad, and the ugly come through. There are many officers who sometimes consider themselves superior to everyone else and wouldn't take advice from a civilian employee. I quickly saw that here was a woman who knew "The Hill" (Congress) better than all of us who were officers in the Legislative Liaison Office.

Her institutional knowledge about how it worked and what kind of relationship you need to build with members of Congress was incredible. She took me under her wing, and she became a wonderful mentor. She saw that I was willing to listen and learn from her vast experience. I asked questions. I didn't ever pretend to know what was going on if I didn't. I truly believe that there is no such thing as a stupid question.

If I would have had an attitude that said, "Hey, I'm an Army major here, I'm the first woman in this job, and I know what I'm doing," if I'd rejected listening to her advice, I would have had a very tough row to hoe. She was an incredible inspiration to me because she shared so much that helped me do my job.

Mary Lou held a position of real power, but she wasn't arrogant enough to believe that she could succeed on her own. She was humble enough to accept the wisdom and advice from someone who could share a vast amount of knowledge with her—and Mary Lou was more successful because of it.

> I also had a sergeant who did our trip itineraries and any number of odd jobs. He handled many details. When you have someone in an administrative position like that, he had the power to make or break you based on the level of respect and cooperation you had or did not have.
>
> When you are going to China for two weeks with ten members of Congress and their spouses, you better have your ducks in a row and you had better have every single facet of that trip down perfectly. This could only happen if we had mutual respect. I had a great deal of regard for this young man and he knew it.

Appreciating the Limits of Power

When Governor Frank Keating and I were talking about the mastering influence and how leaders can best use power in the twenty-first century, he said:

> I think the most important thing is for a generation of Americans who are not well-versed in the foundations of their country, the Constitution, the statutes, the history, and the reasons for limited government, to reread the founding documents.
>
> When I began as a young man, I was an FBI agent. I was

taught early the humility of public service, that you are not and cannot be the person who determines in your own mind how an event will be resolved, but that the law and the facts permit how the incident is to be resolved. We were taught that to make an arrest was not what you wanted or what you needed; it was what the law required. The elements of a crime had to be met before an arrest could occur. Then, when you did make an arrest, there were legal requirements of advising people of their rights. Then, if it went to court, the criminal justice system required proof beyond a reasonable doubt, which means that the defendant is innocent until proven guilty, and the overwhelming burden is on the government to prove guilt, and it requires a unanimous verdict. There is a legal process based on our Constitution.

I viewed myself as an officer of the court. I was not there to convict or to acquit. When I was a defense attorney, I existed for the purpose of getting at the truth, and the truth was always supreme. That required modesty, humility, and an appreciation of the limits of government and the limits of authority. So I think for those of us in the public sector or the private sector to appreciate [our] own mortality, to appreciate [our] own limits, to be humble in the face of conflicting ideas or different opinions is . . . essential. I think that what we've seen of prosecutions of people to make political statements or behavior of public officials or chief executives of companies that are utterly consumed with hubris, there's no servant mentality out there. Instead, it is the attitude of, "How can I get ahead? How can I push the other guy off the road?" That is just antithetical to the humility of our country.

Look at George Washington, for example. King George III said that if George Washington left the presidency and stepped from the stage, he would be the greatest man of the age. Remember, this is the king of England speaking about this rebel general. And George Washington did step from the stage. He reluctantly ran for president and after he served his first term, he said [he would] only serve a second term. He knew how important it was to go back home, to go back to your roots, to realize that we are a country of equality and humility and limits. I think that's very important in the business sector as well as the political sector.

Of all the examples we set as leaders, perhaps the wise use of humble power has the most obvious impact. If the basis of your desire for power is one of service, then your leadership acquires an aura of dignity. Your influence is increased a thousandfold.

The Endless Possibilities of Humility

The virtues that govern our lives in general, but particularly a leader, are not merely external. Competence, honesty, kindness, integrity, accountability, openness, courage, dignity, humility,

DEFINING YOUR LEADERSHIP HUMILITY

By stating in your own words what you earn as a leader through the use of humility and the authenticity it brings, you'll be able to better focus on possibilities to expand the breadth, depth, and contribution of your leadership.

Finish these sentences about the eight qualities of A New Breed Leader:

- When I practice humility in my leadership Competence, I earn _____ from my followers.

- When I practice humility in my leadership Accountability, I earn _____ from my followers.

- When I practice humility in my leadership Openness, I earn _____ from my followers.

- When I practice humility in my leadership Language, I earn _____ from my followers.

- When I practice humility in my leadership Values, I earn _____ from my followers.

- When I practice humility in my leadership Perspective, I earn _____ from my followers.

- When I practice humility in my leadership Power, I earn _____ from my followers.

sensitivity, and honor are more than just words. They're inner standards, restrictions on self-interest and self-indulgence.

Now that you have focused on earning your leadership, here are the three questions for your action plan to help you further instill one of the most critical leadership qualities for the twenty-first century: humility.

Your Action Plan Questions for Quality 8
HUMILITY

1. In what leader have I personally seen the kind of humility that inspires and encourages me to be a better leader?

2. When will I have a meeting with my leadership team to discuss the damage of arrogance and the power of humility?

3. How is humility tied to my personal authenticity as a leader?

The validity you generate when you lead others with humility, not arrogance, is immeasurable. As you face the challenges that will surely come your way, your personal authenticity will generate the credibility to unite others. It'll bring your people together with a sense of community and a set of shared goals.

The End as a Beginning

As we come to the end of the book, let's take a final look at the twenty-first-century Leadership Pyramid. Using the eight qualities that matter most, how do you now view your role as A New Breed Leader?

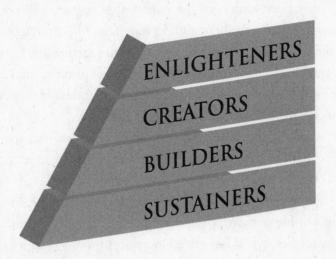

Enlighteners have a personal power that gives them the inner strength to overcome adversity that would crush most people.

Creators see opportunities others do not. They take action while others wait for a better or safer time.

Builders are the long-term, hands-on, humble leaders driven to create the best results possible.

Sustainers are team builders who follow through. They exhibit grace under fire and are the anchors for the other three categories.

Where do you fit now? And where would you like to be at the end of your leadership tenure? What do you see as the greatest possibility you have as A New Breed Leader to help people, organizations, and nations build a world community connected by a shared sense of purpose?

Truly great leaders of the twenty-first century will possess a strategic sense, an inherent understanding of how the framework of their thinking and the tides of time fit together and how their powers should be applied to achieve a larger purpose. It's time for the New Breed Leader who can emphasize and build on new networks, partnerships, and alliances.

No generation of leaders, at any level of society and across the globe, has had such an opportunity to solve our greatest problems and bring all peoples together to work and live on a safe and harmonious planet. You can stand up and be counted as one who will do his or her part, knowing that in combination with millions of other leaders, you'll leave deep footprints that form a global path to a better world for all the generations that follow.

Index

Additional Credit Information